# Web 2.0

# HOW-TO FOR EDUCATORS

## Second Edition, Revised and Expanded

Gwen Solomon | Lynne Schrum

International Society for Technology in Education
EUGENE, OREGON • WASHINGTON, DC

Web 2.0 • How-To for Educators, Second Edition
Gwen Solomon and Lynne Schrum

© 2014 International Society for Technology in Education
World rights reserved. No part of this book may be reproduced or transmitted in any form or by any means—electronic, mechanical, photocopying, recording, or by any information storage or retrieval system—without prior written permission from the publisher. Contact Permissions Editor: www.iste.org/learn/publications/permissions-and-reprints.aspx; permissions@iste.org; fax: 1.541.302.3780.

Editor: *Lynda Gansel*
Production Coordinator: *Emily Reed*
Copy Editor: *Kristin Landon*
Proofreader: *Ann Skaugset*
Indexer: *Wendy Allex*
Cover Design: *Tamra Holmes*
Book Design and Production: *Kim McGovern*

Library of Congress Cataloging-in-Publication Data

Solomon, Gwen, 1944-
Web 2.0 : how-to for educators / Gwen Solomon, Lynne Schrum. — Second edition.
    pages cm.
    Includes bibliographical references and index.
    ISBN 978-1-56484-351-7 (pbk. : alk. paper) — ISBN 978-1-56484-491-0(ebook)
    1. Internet in education—Handbooks, manuals, etc.  2. Web 2.0—Handbooks,
    manuals, etc.   I. Title.
    LB1044.87.S618 2014
    371.33'44678—dc23
                                                                          2014014407

Second Edition
ISBN: 978-1-56484-351-7 (paperback)
ISBN: 978-1-56484-491-0 (ebook)

Printed in the United States of America

ISTE® is a registered trademark of the International Society for Technology in Education.

SUSTAINABLE FORESTRY INITIATIVE
Certified Sourcing
www.sfiprogram.org
SFI-00453
SFI label applies to text stock

# About ISTE

The International Society for Technology in Education is the premier membership association for educators and education leaders committed to empowering connected learners in a connected world. Home to the ISTE Conference and Expo and the widely adopted ISTE Standards for learning, teaching, and leading in the digital age, the association represents more than 100,000 professionals worldwide.

We support our members with professional development, networking opportunities, advocacy, and ed tech resources to help advance the transformation of education. To find out more about these and other ISTE initiatives, visit iste.org.

As part of our mission, ISTE works with experienced educators to develop and publish practical resources for classroom teachers, teacher educators and technology leaders. Every manuscript we select for publication is carefully peer reviewed and professionally edited.

## Also by Gwen Solomon and Lynne Schrum

*Web 2.0 • New Tools, New Schools*

*Considerations on Technology and Teachers,* edited by Lynne Schrum

*Considerations on Educational Technology Integration,* edited by Lynne Schrum

## Related ISTE Titles

*Making Connections with Blogging*
Lisa Parisi & Brian Crosby

*Retool Your School: The Educator's Essential Guide to Google's Free Power Apps*
James Lerman & Ronique Hicks

*Student-Powered Podcasting*
Chris Shamburg

*Teaching Literacy in the Digital Age*
edited by Mark Gura

*Teaching with Digital Video*
edited by Glen Bull & Lynn Bell

*Visual Arts Units for All Levels*
Mark Gura

To see all ISTE titles, please visit iste.org/books.

# About the Authors

### Gwen Solomon

Gwen Solomon creates, manages, and edits custom websites; writes books, ebooks, and advertorials; directs webinars; and advises ed tech companies. She has been the director of the websites Tech&Learning.com, Digital Learning Environments, 21st Century Connections, and The Well Connected Educator. Gwen's books include *Web 2.0: New Tools, New Schools* and *Connect Online: Web Learning Adventures.* Her recent ebooks include *Preparing for the Future: What Common Core Standards Mean for College and Career Readiness; Quick Guide to Mobile Device Management: How to Get a Handle on all the Laptops, Smartphones, Tablets, and More;* and *Keeping Students Safe Online.* She is the author of advertorials such as *Fundamentals of K–12 Technology Programs* and *The Handheld Educator.* Prior to this work, Gwen was senior analyst in the U.S. Department of Education's Office of Educational Technology. Gwen also served New York City Public Schools as coordinator of instructional technology planning and as founding director of New York City's School of the Future. Before that, Gwen was a technology coordinator and teacher.

### Lynne Schrum

Lynne Schrum is the dean of the College of Education and Human Services, West Virginia University. Prior to that she was a professor and coordinator of elementary education in the College of Education and Human Development at George Mason University. Her research and teaching focus on teacher preparation, appropriate uses of information technology, and preparation of leaders for 21st-century schools. She has written ten books and numerous articles on these subjects. Lynne is a past-president of ISTE and served as the editor of the *Journal of Research on Technology in Education* (JRTE) [2002–2012].

# Acknowledgments

Writing the second edition of a book has been an interesting challenge. We learned a lot in the process, especially from educators who are on the front lines of innovation, and we want to thank them.

First, we thank all of the educators who filled out our survey of Web 2.0 use. We have cited many of them as examples of classroom integration. There are too many to thank individually, but we have cited them in context and so you will find their names mentioned throughout the chapters.

Second, we thank the people who responded to our call for detailed models of Web 2.0 use. Their work comprises Chapter 11, "Tools that Make a Difference." We thank (in alphabetical order) Steven Anderson, Andrew Bieronski, Serge Danielson-Francois, Vicki Davis, Chad Evans, Miguel Guhlin, Linda Gutierrez, Mike Hasley, Kevin Jarrett, Elizabeth Kahn, David Kapuler, Amy Migliore, Samantha Morra, Renee Owens, Janel Schafer, Christine Southard, Bob Sprankle, and Jeff Utecht for their valuable contributions.

Third, the people who helped us produce this book deserve our gratitude as well. We thank our editor Lynda Gansel and the ISTE Books staff. We also thank William Little, an exceptional doctoral candidate at West Virginia University, for assisting us in gathering information, checking for permissions, and providing other support. We could not have revised this book without his attention to detail and consistent help.

Finally, we thank our families for their understanding and encouragement and the many others whose work provided inspiration and support.

# Contents

## 12   200 Tools to Get Started

# Introduction

Look at the faces in your classroom and marvel that this generation of students is the first to have grown up with digital tools at their fingertips. They're always "on": texting friends, meeting on social networks, and interacting with the world in nonlinear fashion. They can get information when they want it, follow an idea in ways that have meaning to them, and jump from one thing to the next as the inspiration hits them. When they graduate, employment will be in an environment where reliance on technology is a given and the skills they need most are the ability to adapt, learn new skills, and work in ever-changing teams depending on purpose.

Using the tools that students find appealing can make a difference in their learning now and help them prepare for the future. Students can interact with information, analyze what they find, create knowledge, and then communicate the results to a real audience. The tools, like the students, are always on, accessible anywhere there is internet access. We bring Web 2.0 tools into the classroom where their importance lies in the potential to change the way we operate and maximize students' potential.

Since we wrote the first edition of this book, several important things have changed. Powerful classroom strategies such as 1:1 and anytime learning have become more entrenched. New concepts such as classroom flipping and Bring Your Own Device (BYOD)—and with them the use of powerful mobile devices—are growing. All of these practices drive an increased use of online tools and applications.

Thus, we have expanded our discussions of Web 2.0 to include new classroom examples and powerful new tools and apps. For example, the Productivity chapter (Chapter 4) is centered on the Google suite of tools, and we have added a new chapter on Mobile Apps (Chapter 9). Other new features include new how-to's and a greatly expanded list of Web 2.0 tools. Although many examples of classroom uses of tools from the earlier edition continue to be successful, this edition of the book contains new examples of still-popular tools and examples with new tools and mobile apps.

In addition, since we published the first edition, technology's role in education has become more prominent—and essential to learning. The Common Core State Standards mandate technology use for both learning and for assessment. And in June 2013, President Obama signed ConnectED, an initiative to enhance digital learning in the United States (White House, 2013). The White House press release sketched the framework for this program: "Preparing America's students with the skills they need to get good jobs and compete with countries around the world will rely increasingly on interactive, individualized learning experiences driven by new technology." The press release quoted the president:

> We are living in a digital age, and to help our students get ahead, we must make sure they have access to cutting-edge technology. [said President Obama] So today, I'm issuing a new challenge for America—one that families, businesses, school districts and the federal government can rally around together—to connect virtually every student in America's classrooms to high-speed broadband internet within five years, and equip them with the tools to make the most of it. (White House, 2013)

# Defining Web 2.0 Tools

We'll start with what a Web 2.0 tool is. A definition of any widely used term can be tricky. A Google search for "Web 2.0 definition" returns more than 13 million hits; thus, our goal is to frame just how this term is used. Webopedia (2013) defines Web 2.0 as follows:

> Web 2.0 is the term given to describe a second generation of the World Wide Web that is focused on the ability for people to collaborate and share information online. Web 2.0 basically refers to the transition from static HTML web pages to a more dynamic web that is more organized and is based on serving web applications to users. Other improved functionality of Web 2.0 includes open communication with an emphasis on web-based communities of users, and more open sharing

of information. Over time Web 2.0 has been used more as a marketing term than a computer-science-based term. Blogs, wikis, and web services are all seen as components of Web 2.0.

Some educators have added other qualifications as conditions for being considered Web 2.0 tools. Among these requirements are that the tools must be free, open source, and used online rather than downloadable. Others believe that almost any free or low-cost tool currently available online can be classified as Web 2.0.

In general, our plan is to provide readers with information about the tools that educators believe to be Web 2.0 because they use these applications in classrooms in interesting ways to promote the types of digital-age literacies that students need—applications that spark creativity, engage curiosity, and improve learning outcomes. We hope to introduce educators to a wide range of tools and the ways teachers use them, both in classrooms and professionally.

We should be able to harness these Web 2.0 tools to change education. The web is serendipitous: look up one thing and find another somewhat-related idea, and you're off on a learning adventure that can lead to a synthesis of ideas and new thinking on a topic. In schools today, students rarely see learning as an adventure even though we know that they enjoy playing with new tools and using them to communicate with others. In the past few years, many teachers have taken advantage of new tools to get their students started on the learning adventures we want them to take.

We hear that students are ahead of their teachers in web use. They spend hours texting their friends, meeting up on social networks, and displaying antics on video-sharing sites. But using tools and learning with them are two different things. Teachers have to figure out which tools to use, and when and how to use them; how to pull the tools together into a coherent strategy; and how to integrate that strategy as the teachers direct the learning experience. Teachers need easy-to-use applications that are clear about how they contribute to student learning and achievement. Students need teachers' guidance to do more than play with these tools.

Students and teachers are using mobile apps because of 1:1 computing and the move to less expensive mobile devices and BYOD programs. The impetus is to use cost-effective tools that work for anytime, anywhere learning on multiple devices. Apps are natural extensions of Web 2.0 tools, and the distinction between online tools and apps is blurring. In some cases, both Web 2.0 and app versions of the same tools are available.

The distinction is that Web 2.0 tools are online (cloud-based) and mobile device apps are small programs that you download from sites such as iTunes or Google Play. These apps run on the device even if you access data in the cloud. With Web 2.0 tools, you don't have a program that resides on your personal computer. You just go to the website where it lives.

## Challenges for Schools

Technology is driving much change in the world—and education along with it. Thus there are new challenges for students that schools have to address. Thomas L. Friedman of the *New York Times* says:

> In today's hyperconnected world, we all have to learn much more about investing in ourselves in order to succeed.
>
> The combination of the tools of connectivity and creativity has created a global education, commercial, communication and innovation platform on which more people can start stuff, collaborate on stuff, learn stuff, make stuff (and destroy stuff) with more other people than ever before.
>
> What's exciting is that this platform empowers individuals to access learning, retrain, engage in commerce, seek or advertise a job, invent, invest and crowd source—all online. But this huge expansion in an individual's ability to do all these things comes with one big difference: *more now rests on you.* (Friedman, 2013, p. A25)

Can schools address the need to prepare students to become lifelong learners who understand how and when to reinvent themselves for careers in the future? The *NMC Horizon Report: 2013 K–12 Edition* identified six challenges that need addressing (Johnson et al., 2013).

1. Ongoing professional development needs to be valued and integrated into the culture of the schools.

2. Too often it is education's own processes and practices that limit broader uptake of new technologies.

3. New models of education are bringing unprecedented competition to the traditional models of education.

4. K–12 must address the increased blending of formal and informal learning.

5. The demand for personalized learning is not adequately supported by current technology or practices.

6. We are not using digital media for formative assessment the way we could and should.

## Education Technology Trends

Fortunately, technology is improving and schools are starting to move in the right direction. The **Horizon Report** identifies cloud computing and mobile learning as technologies that should be in place in one year (Johnson et al., 2013).

Further, it identifies five trends:

1. Education paradigms are shifting to include online learning, hybrid learning, and collaborative models.

2. Social media is changing the way people interact, present ideas and information, and communicate.

3. Openness—concepts like open content, open data, and open resources, along with notions of transparency and easy access to data and information—is becoming a value.

4. As the cost of technology drops and school districts revise and open up their access policies, it is becoming more common for students to bring their own mobile devices.

5. The abundance of resources and relationships made easily accessible via the internet is challenging us to revisit our roles as educators. (Johnson et al., 2013)

# School Tool Use

The percentage of districts employing digital strategies is growing. The 2013 *Digital School Districts Survey* by the Center for Digital Education (CDE) and the National School Boards Association (NSBA) examined school boards and districts' use of technology.

Their findings showed an increase in the use of social networks. In the districts surveyed, 94% indicated that they allow educators to use Web 2.0 tools, up 12% in the past two years. And 69% use microblogs such as Twitter, up 38% in the past two years. Finally, 76% maintain a presence on one or more social networking sites, up 44% in the past two years (Center for Digital Education [CDE], 2013).

They also show an increased use of digital content; 71% of responding districts have a digital content (curriculum) strategy containing elements such as using e-textbooks, Web 2.0 tools, instructional games and simulations, video, and audio. This is an increase of 6% over last year (CDE, 2013).

Although advocates have promoted integrating technology tools into classrooms for years, traditionally change is difficult and progress often slow in schools. Yet we see from the data just shown that schools are undergoing transformations in how they manage classrooms.

In addition, *From Chalkboards to Tablets: The Digital Conversion of the K–12 Classroom,* the annual Project Tomorrow Speak Up report (Project Tomorrow, 2013a), looks at the "transformative factors that are driving this new digital conversion momentum and the new capacities to build toward to support the process." Key findings from the 2013 report include the following:

> Today's teachers, administrators and parents are increasingly mobile-using, texting, tweeting social media devotees whose personal and professional lives are dependent upon internet connectivity and online collaborative learning environments.

A majority of teachers (52 percent), parents (57 percent) and district administrators (52 percent) are now regularly updating a social networking site, and many are using a personal mobile device such as a smartphone to do that.

Four out of ten district leaders (41 percent) in 2012 pinpointed achievement measured by test scores and closing the achievement gap as top concern points for their district, a growth of 21 percent over 2011 responses.

Teachers are increasingly interested in leveraging technology for activities with students and many are modifying their instructional plans to incorporate more digital experiences. Nearly a majority of classroom teachers (45 percent) noted in 2012 that they were creating more interactive lessons because of having access to technology, an increase of 25 percent in just the past two years.

A continuation of the multi-year stagnation in funding for new education technology investments is finally forcing school and district leaders to scrap the plans they have on hold, and to test new ways to leverage technology to increase revenue or decrease costs even though some of these approaches challenge conventional wisdom and long held policy positions. In 2012, we see proof of this digital conversion happening right in the principal's office. Today, over a third of principals (36 percent) say that a new Bring Your Own Device (BYOD) to school policy for students is likely this school year.

Social media and digital tools and resources have transcended the classroom and are emerging strongly as key components of 21st century school to home communications. 37 percent of parents wish that their child's teacher or school would communicate with them via text messaging, less than one-quarter of teachers (23 percent) say that texting between parents and teachers is a common practice today. (Project Tomorrow, 2013b)

Among the drivers of change is the Common Core State Standards movement, which seeks to ensure that technology is integrated into the standards as tools for learning and assessments. According to its mission statement,

> The Common Core State Standards focus on core conceptual understandings and procedures starting in the early grades. They provide a consistent, clear understanding of what students are expected to learn, so teachers and parents know what they need to do to help them. The standards are designed to be robust and relevant to the real world, reflecting the knowledge and skills that our young people need for success in college and careers. (Common Core State Standards, 2013a)

In addition to academics, technology is key in helping students acquire intangible skills. The U.S. Department of Education issued *Promoting Grit, Tenacity, and Perseverance—Critical Factors for Success in the 21st Century*, a report that "takes a close look at a core set of non-cognitive factors—grit, tenacity, and perseverance—that are essential to an individual's capacity to strive for and succeed at important goals, and to persist in the face of an array of challenges encountered throughout schooling and life" (Shechtman, DeBarger, Dornsife, Rosier, & Yarnell, 2013, p. v).

The report states:

> If students are to achieve their full potential, they must have opportunities to engage and develop a much richer set of skills… While there is still a need for more empirical evidence that these factors can be taught as transferable competencies across situations, there are a wide range of promising programs and approaches. (Shechtman et al., 2013, p. iv)

Among the key factors is "Digital learning environments, online resources, and tools for teachers" (Shechtman et al., 2013, p. xi).

# Is Everyone Ready?

Are we ready for the change? Every year, Project Tomorrow analyzes some of the Speak Up survey's responses. Students are ready. Among the report's findings were the following:

- 29% of students have used an online video to help them with their homework.

- 30% of students say that being able to text their teacher during class (and getting a personalized response) would help them be more successful in science.

- 34% of high school students are Twitter users.

- 38% of students say that they regularly use Facebook to collaborate with classmates on school projects.

- Students' personal access to mobile devices has reached several significant tipping points: 80% of students in Grades 9–12, 65% of students in Grades 6–8, and 45% of students in Grades 3–5 are smartphone users now; middle school student tablet access doubled from 2011 to 2012 with 52% of those students now tablet enabled. (Project Tomorrow, 2013a)

Are administrators on board? The Project Tomorrow (2013a) report indicated:

Administrators are more tech-enabled than ever with laptops (96%), smartphones (87%), and digital readers, too (26%). And 44% of district administrators are now using a district provided tablet.

What are they doing with the tools? Administrators text colleagues (79%), watch online videos for professional growth (69%) and use tablets for classroom observations (32%). 51% of principals are on Skype, 48% on Facebook, and 22% on Twitter.

Technology worries are keeping them up at night, 55% of school principals and district administrators report they do not have adequate technology for students to use at school and 59% say there are not enough computers. 56% worry about the costs to implement the tests and the need to train teachers and students (54%). 69% of districts are concerned about the impact of implementing more digital content on their current network capacity.

The process of change, especially when it includes adoption of new tools and methods, isn't simple and brings with it new challenges: having devices for everyone, sufficient bandwidth, the right tools, and educators who know how to integrate them. Leslie Wilson, CEO of the One-to-One Institute, poses the issue and the questions we will encounter:

> The shift must come through effective pedagogy that creates student-centered environments where each learner is known—skills, needs, interests, talents, pace, and ambitions. Technology greatly enhances our abilities to produce within this individualized environment while ensuring a habitat for collaborative and team experiences as well.

> What we create in our minds is a vision of what this ecosystem will be and how we can best serve those who engage it. What will teachers, students, and principals need to make sure the environment is robust, dynamic, and best serves learner outcomes? What kind of curricula/experiences do we need to evolve in order to meet those needs? When each student and educator [has] multiple devices powering up learning and teaching, what will be the next level of expertise and achievement we will desire? And how can we help reach those aspirations? (Wilson, L., 2013, n.p.)

To be sure, teachers must get professional development so that they are comfortable with the tools and know how to pay closer attention to learning styles, personalization, and formative assessments. Most important, integrating Web 2.0, apps, and the next generation of tools has to be a thoughtful process that relies on best practice, research, and strong pedagogy.

The goal of this book is to offer examples of how educators are using new tools to best advantage and to take a look at which technology investments have long-term value. As tools proliferate, educators have to decide which ones work well to teach a concept, whether using a particular tool is the best way to learn a topic, and in what way the tool is essential to the process. Let's take a look at what we want tools and apps to do.

# Skills and Opportunities

Web-based tools offer new potential for learning. We see a convergence of tools as student devices become more mobile and teachers provide more cloud-based applications and apps for contextualized, personalized learning. Web 2.0 tools excel at helping students with needed skills and new opportunities. Some examples follow.

## Communication

Students have traditionally written papers and reports and submitted them for a grade. Computer applications altered the experience to the extent that students could edit their work and revise drafts until perfect. Although the web provides access to information and experts, Web 2.0 tools go a step beyond to offer ways of creating, collaborating, and distributing the final product and then interacting with an audience. Students now can post and share their work and get comments from readers globally. The potential of a real audience means that students work harder to perfect what they want to communicate. These tools include blogs, microblogs, and podcasts.

## Collaboration

Student collaboration is a complex process, but online tools can be used to transform both the process of working with others and the product that results. Students can post ideas and get feedback from others with whom they are working. They can brainstorm to narrow or expand concepts. They can discuss their ideas, share research, and collaborate on a project. And peer editing takes on new meaning when they can discuss improvements in real time. Tools such as wikis and Web 2.0 productivity suites such as Google Drive allow teachers to track changes and watch the progress of individual students in the process.

## Connectedness

Digital learners understand the connected nature of people and ideas. Almost anything is within reach. Even adults subscribe to the Six Degrees of Separation theory, which according to Wikipedia is "also referred to as the 'Human Web.'"

> [It] refers to the idea that everyone is at most six steps away from any other person on Earth, so that a chain of "a friend of a friend" statements can be made to connect any two people in six steps or less. (Wikipedia, 2010)

Young people see that everything is connected; anything worth learning happens interactively, and other people are both their sources of information and their audience in a networked world.

What this means for educators is that using students' a priori knowledge is a powerful way to present new content. Linking new information to what students already know to connect past, present, and future concepts gives them a sense that everything and everybody are connected somehow. Using familiar technology tools—with their webs of people and information— makes it just that much easier to reach students, using how they learn to affect what they learn.

## Communities of Learners

Although young people use social networks to interact on a personal level, schools can tap into the phenomenon for student learning and professional development. Learning communities are spaces that serve as electronic communities of practice where groups of people who have a common topic or theme for learning deepen their knowledge and expertise by interacting on an ongoing basis. Schools can create communities of learners in which groups of students or teachers communicate with personal learning networks near and far using microblogs and backchannels.

## Convergence

Of the many definitions of **convergence** on Wiktionary, the one that offers the best insight into the future of tools is "The merging of distinct technologies, industries, or devices into a unified whole" (http://en.wiktionary.org/wiki/convergence).

Clearly, the future will lead to a convergence of skills for students and teachers. For students, the distinctions between basic and higher-order thinking skills will merge into digital-age skills in which the ability to analyze and synthesize information, for example, includes the ability to read and comprehend complex ideas or perform mathematical computations as needed. Everyone will need to become a lifelong learner and acquire skills on demand.

## Contextualization

Traditionally, much of school learning has been in discrete segments—for example, history is kept separate from literature. Thus students do not put discrete elements of information together to make sense of the world. They can memorize and take tests, and they can perform tasks. However, the mark of educated people is that they can understand new knowledge in the context of what they already know and apply it in new situations. The web, with its ability to link objects and ideas, has the potential—perhaps using tagging and metadata—to allow students to gain context for and perspective on what they learn. Thus, for example, they could see history and literature linked by timeline, topic, theme, or other area for study.

## Cloud Computing

The advancement in complexity of computing services and the increase in the need for storage have led businesses, government agencies, and even school districts to outsource services such as data management and remote storage for greater efficiency. The servers that house the data are all online rather than on site. It is not a great leap from back-office outsourcing to using online applications for classroom use.

Whatever the device—laptop, tablet, smartphone, netbook, etc.—there are free and low-cost tools for student learning at students' fingertips. Online, students can use these applications, store documents, and find video tutorials and other students.

## Cost-Free (or Almost Free)

Teachers and students often expect Web 2.0 tools and apps to be free. In some cases, the tools replace the high cost of licensing software and having access to the latest updates. In other cases, new tools that let students learn in new ways are available that don't exist in any other format. Some teachers ask if anything is really free—isn't there always a cost somewhere, to someone? It can be argued that using open source software for operating systems means requiring staff to train, upgrade, maintain, and troubleshoot. Yet the alternative comes with a cost as well. And many of the tools need no more support than any other software.

There are new models as well. Web 2.0 tools and apps are sometimes free; sometimes there's a fee, and sometimes there's a freemium model, in which some features are free and others have a cost if you want or need them. Others are offered under a licensing model. So the question arises: With so many free tools available, why would anyone choose to pay? Chad Evans, eighth grade social studies teacher and learning facilitator in the Quakertown Community School District, says:

> The challenge for teachers is that often the free tool becomes a pay tool eventually. I'm finding that once something becomes "pay for," I can usually find something similar that is free. At the same time, paid versions typically support mass upload of accounts, integration with Google apps, and other things that save teachers time. My hope would be that districts would spend less on textbooks and more on the digital tools for all students and allow teachers a stipend to experiment with tools that aren't free. (C. Evans, personal communication, May 15, 2013)

# Things to Watch Out For

Clearly, today's students live in a world of interactivity and connectedness. They use tools to interact with information and others and to connect the dots of multiple ideas until relationships are clear. So schools must provide the same opportunities as students have outside to engage them and to individualize learning or risk apathy. Anyone used to interacting with objects and others to get information on a daily basis cannot learn by sitting still and listening to someone at the front of the room spout facts.

However, there are challenges. With the proliferation of Web 2.0 tools, the bandwagon effect—in which people flock to the latest and coolest new application and the message to use it spreads virally—can happen before there's a need for the tool, especially in classrooms. The applications are fun to use, the phenomenon of being an early adopter who finds and recommends a tool is exciting, and the novelty of being able to share with the community quickly can delay deeper thinking about a tool's significance for learning.

Students can take content from online sources, rearrange the material, and display and disseminate it as their own. Students can adopt a mixtape approach, adapting content from other sources, rearranging the material, and displaying and disseminating it as their own. Similarly, collaboration means combining the peer-reviewed best work of all team members, not allowing the strongest to do the most work.

Among the challenges for teachers is creating lessons on intellectual property rights, copyright, and plagiarism to help students understand the ethics of creating digital works. In addition, teachers should focus on teaching media literacy so that students understand such issues as fact versus opinion, multiple sources, accuracy and reliability of information, and narrowcasting.

Educators have to address other questions, too. For example, although recent surveys show that students are still ahead of teachers in using the tools, what happens if some students relish using the tools and displaying their work publicly and others don't? Similarly, what happens when students tire of using the tools, and technology no longer serves as motivation or a way to engage reluctant learners?

# Professional Development

There's a distinction between the ways in which students and teachers are comfortable with new technologies. Students seem to be born with multiple devices in their hands, whereas educators, even those who use technology for their own purposes, often aren't clear about how to integrate the various tools for learning.

There are tremendous benefits for educators who begin by using the tools for professional development. They will find a community of other educators online. They can join or create a network of their peers to share with and learn from and can build a personal learning network to turn to regularly. Online, they have access to best practices and the leader/practitioners and models that can show what strategies make a difference, what tools are effective, and they can learn where and when to use them.

The Common Core standards require use of technologies. As more districts acquire more learning technologies and apply new strategies to comply, teachers are required to integrate new tools into their classrooms for learning and assessments. What do they need to know?

Brian Byrne, curriculum associate for elementary math in the Stamford Public Schools, Connecticut, devised a Teacher Technology Bucket List (see Web 2.0 Wisdom box). He says, "This is what I consider should be the bare minimum a 21st-century teacher should be knowledgeable about and utilize during instruction time with students. The list is in no particular order" (Byrne, 2013a).

New Web 2.0 tools emerge all the time, and those educators at the cutting edge will find them, test them out, and spread the word about the useful ones to colleagues, who will further refine the list of what works for their students and under what circumstances. At some point, use of these tools will reach critical mass as they become easy to use, transparent, and an essential component of schoolwork. Educators will use sound pedagogical judgment to determine which tools—web-based and traditional—are best to use for student learning and when and how to use them.

# Teacher Technology Bucket List

Brian Byrne

A 21st-century teacher should be able to:

1. Create a Twitter account to communicate with all classroom stakeholders

2. Understand how to search for, download, use, and remove apps

3. Scan a document and save it as a PDF

4. Attach a file to an email, post, etc.

5. Create a blog and update it frequently with relevant information

6. Provide a place for students to create digital portfolios

7. Use the basic functions of Excel

8. Put together a quality PowerPoint or Prezi presentation

9. Understand how to operate and use their interactive whiteboard to enhance lessons

10. Provide ground rules and expectations for students regarding digital citizenship

11. Upload pictures from a camera and then use them within various platforms

12. Support students in being creative and presenting their information in various ways

13. Upload a video to YouTube

14. Skype or videoconference

15. Use Delicious.com and Pinterest to find teaching resources for the classroom

16. Collaborate with students via Google Drive

17. Use a community forum like Edmodo

18. Speak their language; know, understand, and speak with kid-friendly language

19. Experiment with comfort; accept that students may know more than you occasionally

20. Build a network by participating, sharing, and learning constantly

# Purpose of this Book

Our first book, *Web 2.0: New Tools, New Schools*, presented an introduction to the Web 2.0 concepts and explored why it is important to use web-based tools. In the few years since the book was published, the world and the web have changed. The first edition of this book explained how to use the most educationally sound tools we had available and discussed where we were going with using web capabilities for learning. It also provided explanations, tutorials, and activities to help you get started and ideas about what you and your students may be able to do in the future. This edition continues this exploration into technology and learning and adds new tools and mobile apps that teachers are using today.

Using web-based tools is not second nature to many educators. Some were trained to be teachers before the web existed. Others can use web tools for personal tasks but haven't learned how to incorporate them into teaching. Other reasons why online tools aren't in wider use exist as well. If these tools will make a significant difference in student learning, and if we are to achieve the mandates of the Common Core standards, their use must be widespread. Thus, one purpose of this book is to provide a practical guide to integrating Web 2.0 tools and apps into the classroom. Another purpose is to showcase teachers who are using Web 2.0 tools. In the chapters on the major tools,

Chapters 1–9, we cite examples from the web and from a 2013 survey we posted online to collect information for this book. (Those examples are cited in the text as electronic communications.) In addition, we invited educators to write analyses of the tools they use. The result is a new collection of tools for specific tasks.

## Tried and True Tools

In Chapters 1–9 we explore the top tools as they exist today. These are blogs, microblogs (Twitter), podcasting (and vodcasting), productivity applications (Google tools), social networks, visual learning tools, virtual worlds (Second Life environments), wikis, and mobile apps. In some cases, tools overlap categories because people use them in whatever ways work for them. Others prefer to adapt one tool to different activities rather than learn too many different tools. So the chapters are not hard and fast categories but, rather, ways of explaining the most common tools and their uses.

## Tools for Specific Tasks

Some of the tools we know as Web 2.0 applications are more limited in scope, yet they provide capabilities that really make a difference in classrooms. In our online survey of educators, some of these tools were mentioned often enough to warrant discussion about how to use them and how educators are employing them to enhance student learning. Chapter 11 deals with these interesting applications that readers say make a difference to their teaching and to their students' learning. They include Edmodo, Animoto, BoomWriter, and Manga High. Chapter 12 provides information on an extensive assortment of Web 2.0 tools for instructional practices and professional development.

# Framework for Chapters

Each chapter shares a common framework, one designed to make our explanations of using the tools clear and consistent. Borrowing from traditional journalistic terms, we focus on what, why, when, who, how, and where. We begin with *what*, the definition of each tool, and explain *why* it is useful. We discuss *when* teachers use the tool, whether for classroom integration or professional development, or both, and then provide examples of *who* is using the tools and in what way. Most of these examples are taken from our online survey of educators who wanted to contribute to this book. Because readers of this book may be teachers or technology coordinators and others responsible for helping teachers to use the tools, we include short tutorials, *how* to use the tools, to help you get started. Finally, we list resources so that you will know *where* to go for more information. Chapter headings are structured as follows:

*What* is a … ?

*Why* is … a useful tool?

*When* do teachers use … ?

    Classroom integration

    Professional development

*Who* is using … for teaching and learning?

How do you get started with … ?

*Where* can you find more information about … ?

## Where to Next?

Predicting the future is always risky, especially in print; but in Chapter 10 we offer you our vision of the direction the technology is moving and the implications of those changes for teaching and learning.

The point is that in the future, teachers and students will be able to find and use the kinds of tools that fit students' personal learning styles, rather than education trying to repurpose general technology to fit educational needs. If students learn best using games, they will use math and science games that teach the topics and skills. If they like to drill to remember information for an exam, they will have opportunities to create programs that help them, and even study with someone across the country or around the world. If they want to demonstrate how to do something, they have a choice of writing a blog, preparing a slideshow with photos, or creating a video or infographic. Or they might choose to use a combination of all the possibilities or be able to do things we cannot yet imagine. The most important aspect is that the tools will be available 24/7, when, where and how they're needed.

Future tools and apps will provide almost limitless features and functions that are available whenever a person wants. They may be integrated into items such as clothing, watches, or glasses and be used by students throughout the day. The web for schools will be personal and individualized but also allow for collaboration and communication. Web tools, apps, gadgets, and widgets will be transparent. Computing will be ubiquitous and portable and have metadata as its underlying organizing principle so that links among objects and ideas are clear.

There will be a great deal more about the future in Chapter 10. First, let's see what Web 2.0 tools and apps are working now, where and how they are working, and how to get started.

Before we begin, we want to stress that tools are just ways of accomplishing what needs to be done. They may contain the elements that motivate students and keep them engaged in work, but, ultimately, they have to pass the sniff test regarding how they impact learning. And although we talk about tools a lot in this book, the point is how they contribute to increased student achievement in learning both basic and advanced skills, and how dedicated and professional educators embed tool use into educational experiences and environments.

Classrooms are many things, and although a 21st-century classroom relies on technology, Linda Gutierrez, sixth grade math teacher at Heights Middle School in Farmington, New Mexico, describes her technology-rich classroom in instructional terms (Gutierrez, 2013b) in the following Web 2.0 Wisdom box.

Classrooms are changing. Since we wrote the first edition of this book, more classrooms have become technology-infused, more teaching and learning happens on smaller devices, and more information is acquired and demonstrated online. With the Common Core standards as a driver, the goals and methods are clearer. Now let's take a look at the tools teachers and students use to achieve them.

# Student Centered in a 21st-Century Classroom

Linda Gutierrez

**It is a differentiated classroom.** Although all students are working on the same basic concept, there can be big differences in what they are learning. For some students, it is all they can handle to grasp the basics of what we are talking about, yet others can dive deep into the concepts and see where those concepts are headed in their future in mathematics and how they connect to the real world.

**It is an exploratory classroom.** Rather than relying on a lot of direct instruction from me, my students use their computers to research things on their own, and I assign a variety of videos to reinforce concepts. I talk to them about the videos and encourage them to recommend resources to one another via our classroom management website as well.

**It is an academic discourse classroom.** I ask lots of questions and expect lots of answers. The students learn to do the same. I rarely give them the answer; rather, I try to lead them on a quest of finding the answers for themselves. We try to be as precise as we can with the language of mathematics.

**It is a conceptual classroom.** I try to incorporate hands-on learning as much as I can. Mostly this happens in a whole group experience, but sometimes it is within a small group. We use both physical items and virtual manipulatives quite often.

**It is a mathematically challenging classroom.** Besides concept building and skill practice, there are many opportunities for students to stretch their understanding with meaty mathematical problems. I use released test items as well as a few involved tasks. These problems are typically very frustrating for students, but also very eye-opening in regards to the challenges that math can present.

**It is a tutorial classroom.** Students who need extra support can easily get it. Some days I sit with a small group and help just a handful of students who continually struggle with a concept. Sometimes I use my data to pull groups based on a skill deficiency. Other times I just walk around and do a "touch and go" type of help, giving hints to any kid who might ask for it. Some days I just sit back, observe, and try to figure out where to take them next.

**It is a project-based classroom.** Each unit has at least one in-depth project that requires the students to be more creative and apply some of the basic concepts we are learning. It is not as integrated as I would prefer, but it is what I can do within the confines of our school structure.

**It is a technology-infused classroom.** We have a 1:1 laptop initiative, meaning that all students have laptops that they get to take home. The majority of the kids have access to Wi-Fi at home; however, a few do not. It is a rare day those computers are not used.

**It is a flipped classroom.** Although I don't record my own videos for students to watch at home, I have "flipped" most of the teaching to the kids and the technology, and I'm there to help facilitate it. Instead of a lot of direct instruction from me, the students watch videos from BrainPOP, Discovery, TeacherTube, Khan Academy, and other places first. This is usually done in the classroom, but some students will watch more at home as well. After they have self-taught, we have a group discussion about what they've learned, and I fill in the blanks a little with direct instruction. I spend about a quarter of the time I used to spend teaching. Now they have much more time for practice.

**It is a somewhat noisy, loosely structured classroom.** The students generally get to sit where they want with whom they choose. There are days, however, when desks will be moved into small groups or even facing forward for a shared experience. Discipline generally takes care of itself, because the students know the expectations up front and are usually happy with their choices and privileges.

**It is a fun classroom.** We laugh a lot. We have special "hook" activities for each unit to make them more memorable for the kids. There is a lot of banter and friendly kidding. We learn to laugh at our mistakes and stay in a learning mode. It is a comfortable environment.

**It is a gaming classroom.** Our quiz practice site, MangaHigh.com, allows the students to earn medals and compete against other schools while they learn.

They love this aspect of the class and are engaging with homework at higher rates than I've ever seen. Sometimes they even create their own competitions and motivate other students to do more homework as well. Each week I try to announce which class and which individuals are leading in points, and that can set off some serious effort to outdo one another.

**It is a mastery-based classroom.** Students have as many chances as they need to work toward the understanding that is required. All of the classwork is for practice and only counts as a small part of their grade. The bulk of their grades come from tests or other demonstrations of their learning. They soon realize that to learn something deeply takes a lot of effort, so they often choose to do extra work at home to ensure they are keeping up and understand what is going on in class. Any quiz can be reset at any time, so they know they can continue to work on them toward mastery. The nice thing about doing this is that their grades are completely up to the students. If they want a better grade, they simply have to work harder. It has nothing to do with me judging them.

**Those are the major components of my classroom.** Technology has allowed me to make my classroom much more student-centered than teacher-centered. I'm not sure what this type of classroom is called, but I do know that it is a much better environment for students to learn and grow in than it used to be. The exciting part is that the students would tell you the same thing. They love learning this way.

*Original blog entry posted August 26, 2013, at www.guide2digitallearning.com/ teaching_learning/student_centered_21st_century_classroom*

# 1

# Blogs

## *What* is a Blog?

Blog is a hybrid of the words *web* and *log*. It is a type of website that an individual develops and maintains with easy-to-use online software or a hosting platform with space for writing. Blogs feature instant publishing online and invite audiences to read and provide feedback as comments.

A blogger updates the page regularly with ideas, advice, suggestions, and other types of commentary. Entries appear in reverse chronological order, so the most recent entry appears at the top.

Blogs are primarily text, but they can include features such as photos, videos, charts, graphs, and music and other audio enhancements, such as podcasts. They contain links to other online locations and there are often discussions of topics found at these links. Readers can write comments and engage in discussion with the blogger about the topic posted.

In the real world, blogs are extremely popular because they give a voice, platform, and audience to anyone who has an idea and wants to express it. Blogs have gained both respect and notoriety for such things as opinions, breaking news, insights into contemporary events and ideas, and political writing.

Educator-written blogs are often thoughtful, well-reasoned discussions of ideas. Because blogs are public, teachers who write them can gain reputations as thought leaders and develop a following of other educators who read, think about, and comment on their posts.

Although many educators maintain individual blogs, educational websites such as Tech&Learning.com (www.techlearning.com) and Digital Learning Environments (www.guide2digitallearning.com) feature the voices of a diverse group of leading educators who post practical ideas, policy discussions, and other thoughtful opinions, impressions, and reports.

Blogs offer considerable educational benefits for students as well. Because they are predominantly a written medium and are on public display, students have to learn to write carefully, think about their ideas, and communicate effectively.

Steven Anderson, in the Digital Learning Environments blog post "So ... You Wanna Use Blogs in the Classroom," says:

> Think about when you were in school. You wrote an essay. Who read it? Most likely the teacher and that is where it ended. You poured hours and hours into reflections on Shakespeare, the economic and political effects of wars on society or how plants have evolved over time, yet the only person who read your thoughts was the teacher. Maybe you shared with a close

friend or even the class. But generally the world was unaware of your thoughts and feelings.

Blogging changes that for kids. Now the audience is global and anyone can read, and in some cases respond and comment. Kids can post their writing, projects, thoughts, and reflections. Teachers can provide prompts or starters and kids can pick up and run with it. (Anderson, 2013a)

Many teachers use Edublogs (www.edublogs.org) because it is simple for students to set up and for teachers to create for the class. A getting started guide with detailed instructions is there to help (http://help.edublogs.org/getting-started-with-edublogs). Class blogs allow students to collaborate and have ongoing discussions. Students write and share their blog posts and determine who can read and respond. Teachers manage student blogs and give students control over what they can do on a class or individual blog.

Other popular blog sites are Kidblog (www.kidblog.org), Bloglines (www.bloglines.com), CoverItLive (www.coveritlive.com), LiveJournal (www.livejournal.com), TypePad (www.typepad.com), and WordPress (www.wordpress.com).

Although having students communicate globally is beneficial, some risks are involved. Thus districts use content management systems with internal blogging capability such as Blackboard (www.blackboard.com) or use blogs designed specifically for education such as 21Classes (www.21classes.com) or Class Blogmeister (www.classblogmeister.com) or use blogs that are part of a suite of tools such as Google's Blogger (www.blogger.com), ePals (www.epals.com), and Gaggle (www.gaggle.net).

There are also some interesting alternatives to traditional blogs; these tools are similar in that they encourage writing but have somewhat different features.

For example, Tumblr (www.tumblr.com) is useful for shorter blog posts; one option allows students to incorporate someone else's blog or "tumble" it to call attention to what was said and elaborate on the point. With Tumblr, students can post text, photos, quotes, links, music, and videos from a browser, phone, desktop, or email and customize everything.

Storify (www.storify.com) is a platform for combining original writing with stories from the web or a social media aggregation tool. Students search for a topic and drag the content they want into the story pane. They add their thoughts and ideas, publish the completed story on Storify, and embed it anywhere to share.

NotePub (www.notepub.com) is a great way to manage and share information. It allows students to take notes and include images, files, links, and tags. Students can make their notes public, private, or shared with a group by setting permissions for each note. They can also store files on their own computers to work on offline.

OhLife (www.ohlife.com) is an option for older students. The site requires an email address because it generates a message that prompts students to write. They reply with their thoughts, which become student journals.

CheckThis (www.checkthis.com) calls itself a community of storytellers. It is not technically a blog because the pages are not linked and each has a distinct URL, but it is an easy way to publish and share content in writing and multimedia.

## *Why* are Blogs Useful Tools?

Blogs encourage writers and responders to develop thinking, analytical, and communication skills. Some characteristics of blogs make them excellent teaching tools.

- Blogs are brief. They are usually relatively short posts of just a few paragraphs that are crafted to communicate an idea clearly and concisely. Because readers don't want to read long, rambling treatises on their monitors, students learn how to get to the point.

- Things happen fast. Publishing is instantaneous. Students click Submit to see their blog online at once and feel that they've accomplished something. They can get feedback quickly, too.

- Visual elements enhance blogs. Students can include images, video, and sound to add to the meaning and to create and sustain interest.

Blogs can link to other websites (and have them open in a new window) to provide more information, a related idea, or even a starting point for the writer's ideas.

- Students become responsive to one another. Students think about their peers' ideas and ways of expressing them and then comment. Teachers can direct students to focus on the ideas or on the writing, or both. Thus, readers develop analytical skills, and writers learn to be better writers and communicators.

- The evidence exists forever. Blogs are stored online and remain as a portfolio of a student's ability to write, think, and communicate. Because they appear in reverse chronological order, the latest example is first. They are searchable, so refinements in student thinking can be identified.

Michelle Lynn Ross, an art teacher at Illinois' Downers Grove South High School, whose students use Tumblr to blog about photography and post their photos, outlines the advantages of blogging in general and photoblogging specifically.

---

**Web 2.0 Wisdom**

## The Benefits of Blogging

Michelle Lynn Ross

- Participating in a photo blog gives students a forum to showcase their photography, and it also helps them build critical thinking, writing, and literacy skills.

- Photo and any other type of blogging provides an opportunity for students to exhibit and write for an authentic audience. The quality and understanding of their artwork improves because they put their best efforts forth—they are aware that their audience goes far beyond the classroom.

- Students follow people who have interest and expertise in photography, which opens up a world of interesting imagery from the past and present.

- Students tag photos with descriptive words that others can use for searching. For example, students can tag their work as "surreal." When anyone clicks on a "surreal" tag, that student's work will come up as an example of surrealism.

- Commenting and reflecting on their artwork, the work of others, tutorials, and techniques promotes metacognition and visual literacy.

- Posting comments on their photo blogs gives students the opportunity to reflect about their artwork and what they have learned.

- By blogging, the students take ownership of their assignments, which gives them a sense of pride in their work.

- Blogging encourages higher levels of thinking because students are given a venue to analyze and evaluate their own work and the work of others.

- Students gain easy access to information related to digital photography.

- Photo blogging in the classroom fosters social interaction among peers as well as people of common interests.

- Using blogs contributes to growth in students' reflective, critical thinking, and metacognitive skills.

- Students learn about themselves and I learn about my students.

- While working on the photo blogs, students can gain easy access to the web, a source of more up-to-date content than a photography textbook has to offer. The world of digital imaging is continually changing, and the web is the best place to support learning basic and advanced techniques.

- Students find tutorials and use the techniques on their images. They post the results of before and after. They can see transformations and make adjustments, which increases their level of creativity and technical skills.

- Verbalizing learning is a powerful metacognitive tool. Having learners explain thoughts about what they understand or don't understand has a positive impact on learning and growing.

- Blogs create a log of learning, document development over time, and allow for feedback and connecting of ideas.

- Photo blogging takes the focus off of the instructor and makes the students more responsible for their learning.

- Students comment on each other's blogs as well as write in their own posts. This might appear to only increase the amount of grading left to the teacher, but in practice it provides students with the opportunity to have a different kind of audience—an audience of their peers. It also encourages conversation, which is at the root of the blogging experience.

(*Electronic communications, May, 2013*)

## What Are Some Rules Teachers Can Employ?

Although blogging is a positive activity that reinforces traditional skills, teachers find it useful to state and reinforce good behavior for students to follow when online. In addition to using good vocabulary and syntax, students should keep in mind the topic they have chosen, their audience, and their purpose in writing. Teachers can set parameters that include how often students should update their blogs and the number of people authorized to comment. See the later discussion of rules about commenting and how to assess student blogs.

Teachers can allow students to use trackbacks, which let bloggers automatically link from another person's blog to theirs when there is a cross-reference. Links to these trackbacks are visible, which allows readers to follow conversations on a topic across several blogs. This is one way to start a community around ideas or concepts.

# *When* Do Teachers Use Blogs?

## Classroom Integration

Classroom integration and writing instruction are natural uses for blogs. In the classroom, blogs are similar in concept to personal journal writing because they are often short, informal pieces of writing that can deal with personal topics and ideas. Even when they focus on serious topics, they are personal expressions of thoughts and ideas and contain opinion as well as facts. Although writing is most often the purview of English and language arts teachers, all subjects can involve written explanations of ideas and strategies. Blogging motivates students to tackle writing across the curriculum. The result can be that they think more clearly and organize their ideas more easily.

The difference between blogs and journals or essays lies in the public nature of blogging. With handwritten or typed journals, students write on personal topics and show selected entries to the teacher. With blogs, students write on topics—personal or assigned—with the understanding that a potential audience of at least classmates and parents, and possibly people from anywhere, can read it.

Their knowledge of an authentic audience means that students will work on their writing more than when the teacher is the only reader. In addition, using the comments box, their audience can engage with, and challenge, the blogger about the ideas presented. Therefore, those ideas must be well reasoned. Teachers can use blogs for students to develop an ongoing conversation about a topic, theme, or concept.

The goal of writing teachers has always been to engender good writing habits in students. The writing process has been the traditional means to that end, and process writing involves engaging students in creating thoughtful expressions of ideas. The traditional steps include brainstorming, prewriting, organizing, writing, editing, and revising.

Brainstorming allows students to generate ideas around the topic and narrow the field to the most appropriate. Prewriting is guided discovery; students begin to focus on a concept and assemble ideas. Organizing involves formulating a central focus for writing and developing the details most likely to express that focus effectively. Writing is the main part of the process in that it means students explain the topic using the organization they developed and adding the details that make it clear and easy to understand. This part of the process also involves revising until a first draft is reached. Editing and peer editing refine that process even more; students learn to say what they mean by presenting it and getting feedback. The final step is to revise based on recommendations.

The limitations of traditional tools have made the process complex, slow, and less than elegant. The nature of blogging changes the process; the tool's capabilities make it possible for students who engage in blogging to develop writing and thinking skills they couldn't achieve easily before.

### Creativity

Freed of the constraints of solitary writing with the teacher as the sole judge of worth, students use blogging to post ideas that will be refined with the help of their peers over time because of the feedback loop possible with the comments feature. They can be creative when they know they can get feedback for their ideas and ways of communicating. They can use multimedia elements to enhance how creative the blog appears, with images, video clips, sound, and links.

### Collaboration

One of the new skills students need is the ability to collaborate—to work with peers to produce work that has shared authorship. Using the comment feature of blogging for peer review can help students develop the trust and ability to provide and accept constructive criticism in their learning community.

### Communication

Blogging over time provides students with the ability to communicate effectively and to reinforce the experience. They share ideas and, in the process, must learn how to express them in exactly the words that their readers will understand. If they do not, peers will pose questions that serve to help students learn how and where to improve and refine their communication skills.

### Connections

The public nature of blogs provides students with a wider readership than just the teacher. Their audience can include people in the community and beyond, and peers can be students around the world. Understanding that their words can have a global impact encourages students to hone the craft of writing.

### Critical Thinking

Writing for an audience means thinking about the ideas first, and then expressing the ideas so that others understand what you mean. To accomplish this, students need to develop a logical set of facts, ideas, and persuasive arguments. As always, putting ideas into words refines the writer's ability to think. Thus, writing is thinking critically.

### Reading

Being part of a learning community in which students read one another's blogs adds the skill of information literacy: discerning fact from opinion, following the logic of others, commenting effectively, and being able to engage in well-reasoned discussions with others.

### Digital Portfolios

Because blogs are archived, the audience—students, teachers, parents, and other readers—can review the change in thinking, analytical ability, writing style, and other intellectual development over time. Blogs can serve as digital portfolios of student work to demonstrate growth in skills of communication, collaboration, and critical thinking—all through a student's writing.

## Professional Development

When educators write about their work or the ideas in education, they are performing reflective practice and developing their thinking about their craft. The audience becomes a personal learning community or network with whom they can share and learn and grow as practitioners.

According to Steven Anderson (2013a) in his blog post "So … You Wanna Use Blogs In The Classroom," "Blogging is an important part of who I am as a professional. I can use this space to share resources with you, reflect on my own practice and try to figure out how to be a better educator. It is my public reflection on technology, leadership and learning."

When Los Angeles educator Linda Yollis taught her students how to blog, she made sure to help them develop literacy skills. She says, "When I first started blogging, I thought the posts would be the primary focus of the blog. I quickly realized that the comment section was where the blog came to life" (Mrs. Yollis' Classroom Blog, 2012a).

Yollis's students became so proficient that they shared their expertise with other students and teachers on their blog and in a video. Other teachers consult the blog and video to learn how to help their students to blog.

**Web 2.0 Wisdom**

## Learning How to Comment

Linda Yollis

Content is key!

In our class, we evaluate our blog comments.

A one-point comment is a general comment that doesn't add very much to the post. Example: *I like your blog. Please visit mine!*

A two-point comment adds something to the comment conversation. A commenter might compliment the writer in a specific way or add new information. Another idea is to make a connection. Maybe the post reminds you of an experience that you've had. Share that connection! Try to end your comment with a relevant question. That way, an interesting conversation can develop.

(http://yollisclassblog.blogspot.com/2011/08/learning-how-to-comment.html)

# *Who* Is Using Blogging for Teaching and Learning?

Teachers are sometimes reluctant to introduce blogging but soon see the advantages. Chad Evans, eighth grade social studies teacher and learning facilitator in the Quakertown Community School District, Pennsylvania, notes the benefits.

> Especially at the elementary level, we have seen an increase in teachers having students' blog. We have had fifth graders blogging about books they are reading in small literature circles and second graders blogging about an upcoming trip to the zoo. All of the teachers who have tried blogging with their students this year have enjoyed reading what their students wrote and seeing the increased interaction and conversations about books.
>
> My favorite story regarding student blogging was a teacher's reluctance and fear about how students would respond back to one another. Within two hours of leaving school for the day, every student had gone back onto the blog and responded to one another appropriately and positively. (C. Evans, personal communication, May 15, 2013)

Once teachers see the benefits, opportunities for teaching and learning grow.

## Sophomore English

Cathy Swan, technology integration teacher at New Canaan High School in Connecticut, describes a project called The Invisible Influence (Figure 1.1), which won an ISTE Special Interest Group award in 2012. She and librarian Michelle Luhtala and sophomore English teacher Susan Steidl developed and ran it. For the project, students study how visual media affects social norms, national pride, gender issues, and other issues. They use the blog function of Facebook to discuss. She says,

> In studying the role of advertising in establishing gender roles, students use their cell phone to snap photos of ads from 1950s *Life* magazines and send the photos to our Facebook group for

the project on our library Facebook page. Students post reflections about why they selected the ad and classmates respond with comments. We also asked seniors and alumni (mostly college freshmen) to add their comments.

What one student sees in an ad may not be the same as another. As such, students are exposed to various points of view, especially given the peer posts from older students. The final product is a research paper on one of the issues that an individual student selects. The blog on Facebook helps them to expand their thinking on their chosen issue, giving them a broader base for their research. (S. Steidl, personal communication, May 2013)

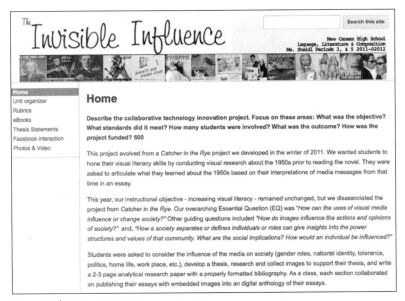

Figure 1.1 | The Invisible Influence project homepage
(http://sites.google.com/a/ncps-k12.org/istesigms12nchs)

## Photo Blogging

Michelle Lynn Ross, an art teacher at Downers Grove South High School in Illinois, uses Tumblr with students to have them blog about photography.

Her students investigate concepts, techniques, and the history of photography and post their findings on Tumblr. For example, each student adopts a famous photographer, then finds a photo, a quote, a video, and other information about the photographer and posts it on his or her blog. The other students provide comments that range from simple to elaborate descriptions, interpretations, comparisons, and judgments.

Students also post finished photographs from assignments and critique their own work and the work of others. They learn the elements and principles of design and relate them to famous photographs as well as their own. They find and practice tutorials on their own and show the results. They may explain the techniques used to create photographs or the ideas behind taking and making them. Ross says:

> I post examples of photographs related to a particular assignment and tag them so students can go to tutorials, examples, videos, and links related to a concept, technique, or assignment. I use Tumblr to model my expectations for students in any given task.
>
> For example, for an assignment to make a composite image (combination of more than one photo to make a completely new photo), I post tutorials with composite techniques such as Adobe Photoshop's "Refine Edge" and masking techniques. These include both videos and written step-by-step directions to address the students' different learning styles. I too will follow the tutorial and show my results by posting picture #1, picture #2, and composite picture #3 and write about it. (M. L. Ross, personal communication, May 2013)

## Connecting with Other Learners

Los Angeles elementary school teacher Linda Yollis runs "Mrs. Yollis' Classroom Blog," (Figure 1.2) which she says has "grown to be the centerpiece of our third-grade classroom. It has become a true global learning community that offers myriad rewards for students, parents and teachers."

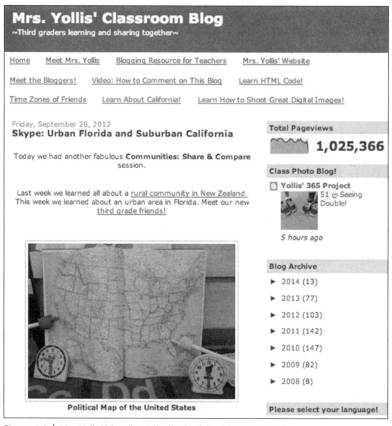

**Figure 1.2** | Mrs. Yollis' blog (http://yollisclassblog.blogspot.com)

Among her favorite global projects is "Flattening Classroom Walls with Blogging and Global Collaboration" with Kathleen Morris from Australia. She says,

> Of all the riches that blogging has brought to my class, the relationships we've built with other classrooms around the world have been the most rewarding. The collaborative projects we have joined not only support the educational standards required at my grade level but have also given my students a real understanding of other topics such as geography, time zones, cultures and friendships. (Mrs. Yollis' Classroom Blog, 2012b)

Linda and Kathleen began their online collaboration through the comment sections of their blogs that showed that the classes had a strong interest in one another. They created the Collaboration Corner to further develop student relationships and focus their learning. Topics included projects about lunch-boxes and school environment and led to others on more global topics such as The Ugandan Global Project; Our World, Our Stories; and The Tale Trail (Yollis & Morris, 2012).

## Forensic Science

Petrina Puhl, forensic science and AP biology teacher at Robert McQueen High School in Reno, Nevada, uses Glogster with her 11th and 12th grade forensic science classes. Glogster lets students create interactive posters called glogs (short for graphical blog). Students developed their glogs about the collection and preservation of arson evidence and background on explosives for the other students in class (Figure 1.3). They learned to present the information they learned from doing research in a dynamic way with photos, videos, and info-graphics that they embedded in the blogs. Puhl says,

> They loved that it was so much more than just a paper poster! Having the capability to do more inspired them to do deeper research and investigate multimedia sources to give a more complete picture of their topic. Students took notes on each other's blogs.

> Forensics: Collection and Preservation of Arson Evidence, an example of a student project is available at http://missjeanine. edu.glogster.com/forensics-collection-and-preservation-of-arson-evidence/?voucher=1d2e7332f8035f8c720d49e578fd bb1f (P. Puhl, personal communication, June 2013).

Figure 1.3 | Example of a student project created using Glogster

## Provide Evidence of Learning

Anne Mirtschin, who teaches Grades 4 through 12 at Hawkesdale P12 College in southwest Victoria, Australia, uses blogging with her students. This rural prep to Year 12 school is culturally and geographically isolated. Students are connected to the world using digital tools. She says:

> It is essential for a teacher, the class, and individual students (at a perceived responsible age) to have a blog that serves as a space for authentication and connection. I use blogging in my classroom on a regular basis because student blogs provide evidence of learning, allow reflections, and develop into digital portfolios.

> Students use blogs to log global connections and projects that they are involved in and use widgets on the sidebar—such as clustrmaps, flagcounter, a digital clock for the time zone, a Google translate widget —to reflect their global publishing.

Years 9/10 students are involved in cross-culture blogging with schools from Taiwan, Korea, USA, and Australia over a 12-week period each year. The purpose of this project is to exchange culture information and perspectives with students from other countries. There are two elements involved: posting on the blog and leaving comments on others. Shih Ting in the USA set up the topics with a global flavour.

Students were grouped in teams of 4 or 6 across schools globally. They wrote posts on a set topic—such as Introductions, Technology Used, Illegal Immigration, Favourite Local Tourist Attractions, Waste Disposal, or a topic of their choice. As the posts were written in the student's native language, they had to work out a means for translating. They learned a lot from blogging including digital literacy, netiquette, publishing for a global audience, digital citizenship, use of imagery, HTML coding, and more. (A. Mirtschin, personal communication, July 2013)

## An Audience for Student Work

Allison Hogan, a primer teacher at the Episcopal School of Dallas, Texas, created a blog (Figure 1.4) for her kindergarten and first grade students to get their ideas out to the world. She says,

I used Weebly to create the blog, Quad Blogging to connect with teachers and students, and Twitter and Facebook to ramp up excitement. My students also used iPad apps such as Sock Puppets and Pic Collage for their assignments.

During a long vowel study, the students collaborated in pairs to write a list of long vowel U words. After composing the list, they showed it to me so that I could verify their understanding. Then they worked together to create a puppet show using the Sock Puppet app. They had to decide on their setting, characters, and story line. They also had to incorporate their long vowel U words. After completing the assignment, the students had to share with me their recorded puppet shows. I took pictures of them and even posted a few of their Sock Puppet shows on Facebook.

After completing the assignment, we shared the work with their Quad Blogging Friends. This meant we had to post the video and a summary of the assignment on our blog. Together in writing workshop, we wrote a summary of the assignment. We made a collage using the Pic Collage app to include a picture of each group. After blogging, we tweeted and posted a link on Facebook to our blog.

Because my students have an audience for their work, they feel more motivated to complete their assignments. Their excitement just overflows. I saw a big shift of engagement in my classroom this year due to including Web 2.0 tools such as blogging, Twitter, Facebook, Quad Blogging, and Sock Puppets. (A. Hogan, personal communication, June 2013)

Figure 1.4 | Allison Hogan's Quad Blogging webpage
(www.primerattheepiscopalschoolofdallas.com/
1/previous/3.html)

## Global Sharing

Leesa Mangino, teacher at the Leamington School in Cambridge, New Zealand, maintains a class blog and individual student pages. She says:

> We use Blogger (blogger.com) for our class blog and Kidblog (kidblog.org) for the student pages. A great advantage with using these is that there is an iPad app for each. Each Monday I pose a question for the students to blog about and have set expectations around the quality of their blogs. We discussed having a global audience and how that is different from writing a personal diary entry. We set criteria for each blog entry for writing quality and expected content. We looked at a variety of children's blogs from around the world and took note of their strengths, weaknesses, and interesting aspects.
>
> From the start my students found it easy to post comments and photos and add links. They also liked that they could personalise their pages. It is easy to post comments on each other's blogs, and we discussed what makes a good blog comment. We have parents, friends, and family post comments, too, which gives students a real sense of audience. I believe that if learning has a "real life" aspect to it, then it happens in a more natural, self-motivated way. This is what is happening with the blogs. For safety reasons, all posts and comments have to come through me first. (L. Mangino, personal communication, July 2013)

## Catalyst Channel Blog

Sandy Wisneski teaches Grades 6 through 8 at Catalyst Charter Middle School in Ripon, Wisconsin. She says, "Family engagement is important, especially as students enter the middle school grades. Parents find it harder to feel connected with their students." She uses a blog to maintain communication with parents and engage them in their students' learning (Figure 1.5). She says:

> One tool Catalyst Charter Middle School uses to communicate with parents and the global community is a blog. Our school blog (http://catalystchannel.blogspot.com) contains information on projects we have completed. Parents can check out the latest

photos of students as they progress through a project up to the final showcase night. We share the purpose of projects as well as specifics with parents so they are better informed. If teachers get emails with questions that impact all families, teachers use the blog to share the information with a wider audience.

Our parents have questions about how blended learning looks in the classroom and how a specific online program like ALEKS is used. We write a blog entry to discuss how this approach works and offer specific examples, with links, to better inform.

We highlight field trips along with the learning activities that accompany the events. We create tags—labels that are added to posts to categorize what the main topics of the post were. Parents can use these tags to find past entries if they want to go back and look at them. It is important to stay current with the blog. Parents appreciate weekly updates on what is happening in the school, offering them an avenue for discussion with their son/daughter. (S. Wisneski, personal communication, July 2013)

**Figure 1.5** | The Catalyst Channel blog (http://catalystchannel.blogspot.com)

## Parent Collaborations

Erin Jackle and Stephanie Hopkins, early childhood special education teachers in School District U-46 in Elgin, Illinois, connect with families using a variety of platforms. They say:

> As early childhood teachers, we know that parent communication is as much a part of the curriculum as reading and math. Having a classroom blog through Blogger (or another free blogging platform) is a great way to share what's happening in the classroom. A blog is in many ways better than a class website because it is dynamic and interactive.
>
> Blogger allows us to delve deeper and make curricular connections. Parents love to see pictures of their children and examples of student work. This is a great lure to get them looking, and then we can sneak in helpful tips or ideas to use at home! For example, while doing a project on the ocean, we shared a slideshow of student work and included a YouTube video of a song sung in class, a video about types of fish that live in the ocean, and questions that parents could ask their children about what they learned.
>
> The more adults who are connected to the child's school experience, the better a child's chance for success. (E. Jackle & S. Hopkins, personal communication, June 2013)

# *How* Do You Get Started with Blogs?

Creating a blog is relatively simple. We've included the top-level steps to creating a blog using Edublogs. The detailed user guide is online (http://edublogs.org). You begin on the home page (Figure 1.6).

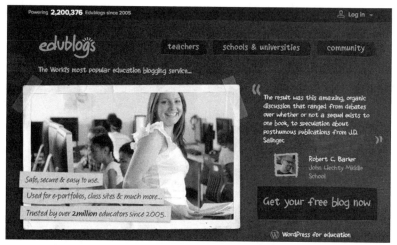

Figure 1.6 | Edublogs homepage

- Sign up and register blog

- Log into blog

- Use dashboard

- Publish first post

- Edit published post

- Learn about posts versus pages

- Publish a new page

- Edit page

- Connect with others

- Change blog title

- Change theme

## Five Rules for Blog Commenting

Commenting on someone else's blog post is simple: read the post, write your comment, type your name, and click Submit. Doing it well takes practice.

1. Read the blog post carefully.

2. Consider its strengths and weaknesses.

3. Start with the strengths.

4. If you have something nice to say, say it—and give specifics.

5. If you have criticism, say it nicely. (Constructive criticism is helpful, not vindictive.)

## Six Assessment Points for Student Blogs

1. How well did student writing address the curricular topic and/or discussion theme?

2. How well reasoned was the logic of what students wrote?

3. How well developed was the writing?

4. To what extent was their writing analytical about the topic?

5. How well did they communicate their thinking?

6. To what extent did their blog generate real discussion?

### Starting Over

If you're not happy with your blog, you can delete it and start a new one later. Be aware, however, that as with virtually everything stored on the web, a deleted blog may still actually exist in an archive.

## A Word About RSS

RSS (Really Simple Syndication or Rich Site Summary) is a way to get regularly changing web content delivered rather than going to individual sites. Bloggers, websites, and other online publishers syndicate their content as RSS feeds. Readers subscribe so that they can use an RSS reader to get the content they want updated regularly.

For example, Bloglines Reader (www.bloglines.com) is a news and feed aggregator. Students can subscribe, create, manage and share news feeds, blogs, and other web content. They can customize it to get updates from classmates and news from sites around the web.

# *Where* Can You Find More Information about Blogs and Blogging?

## Blogging and Blog-Like Tools

Blogger (Google): www.blogger.com

CheckThis: www.checkthis.com

CoverItLive: www.coveritlive.com

Glogster: www.glogster.com

LiveJournal: www.livejournal.com

NotePub: www.notepub.com

OhLife: www.ohlife.com

Storify: www.storify.com

TypePad: www.typepad.com

Tumblr: www.tumblr.com

WordPress: www.wordpress.com

## Blogging Tools for Education

21Classes: www.21classes.com

Class Blogmeister: www.classblogmeister.com

Edublogs: www.edublogs.org

ePals: www.epals.com

Gaggle: www.gaggle.net

Kidblog: www.kidblog.org

## Resources

There are so many choices and opportunities that educators often want advice from others who include blogging in their classrooms. Below are resources recommended by Steven Anderson (2013a), director of instructional technology for the Winston-Salem/Forsyth County Schools in Winston-Salem, North Carolina.

Five Steps to Starting a Class Blog in 2012: Great and personal advice on classroom blogging learned from trial and error.
http://primarytech.global2.vic.edu.au/2012/01/29/
five-steps-to-starting-a-class-blog-in-2012/

Two Critical Tips for Classroom Blog Projects: More great advice on blogging in the classroom and how to make it successful.
http://teacherleaders.typepad.com/the_tempered_radical/2008/04/
tips-for-classr.html

Collection of Blogging Resources: Resources for classroom blogs that are extensive and worth spending a lot of time with.
http://langwitches.org/blog/category/blogging/

Tips on Blogging with Students: Sue Waters (from Edublogs) has written a lot about blogging with kids. This is her collection of tips.
http://theedublogger.com/2008/02/13/
tips-on-blogging-with-students/

Student Blogging Guidelines: Some teachers will want some guidance in place when they undertake blogs with kids. Here are easy-to-follow guidelines that might make implementation go more smoothly.
http://kimcofino.com/blog/2009/09/06/student-blogging-guidelines/

# 2

# Microblogs— Twitter

## *What* is a Microblog?

Products whose names become the generic term for a category enjoy tremendous branding and promotion opportunities. In the world of microblogging, or sending short messages quickly to multiple readers on various devices, Twitter has become the generic term. It is a cross between blogging and text messaging, with a character-count limitation.

Twitter is a free microblogging service that allows its users to post comments called tweets, of up to 140 characters, and read the tweets posted by others. Its power to connect people makes it a social network, and its character limit means that people must make their ideas clear and concise. Users can write anything as long as it falls within the 140-character limit. The prompt for each message is "What are you doing?" People have generated creative shortcuts to communicate well beyond text messaging codes and employ services such as TinyURL (www.tinyurl.com) to abbreviate long links into ones that leave room in the 140-character limit to say something about them (Figure 2.1).

Figure 2.1 | ISTE's Twitter account

People "follow" others by reading one another's tweets. They can make their tweets available to anyone, limit their audience, or make messages private. They have control and can decide who should follow them. Users can log in to send and receive tweets on the Twitter website or use the communications protocol Short Message Service (SMS) on any mobile device that has web access to email, texting, or instant messaging. People with smartphones can use a Twitter app.

Twitter advocates often turn to online applications and desktop clients such as Twitterrific (http://iconfactory.com/software/twitterrific) to view tweets rather than rely on the Twitter site. Many more third-party applications and add-ons exist, including some that allow scheduling of tweets. Examples are

Twuffer (www.twuffer.com) and Socialoomph (www.socialoomph.com). Because Twitter has a flexible architecture, add-on applications can include additional features well beyond the basics of Twitter itself. For example, desktop clients shorten long URLs (digg.com, bit.ly, snurl, twurl, or is.gd); display notifications for new messages; connect to multiple Twitter, StatusNet (formerly Laconical), FriendFeed, and Seesmic accounts; cross-post updates to Jaiku, Facebook, MySpace, LinkedIn, and other social network services; and automatically find tweets mentioning you, noted by @username.

# *Why* is Twitter a Useful Tool?

Twitter has become a popular tool for educators to connect with one another to get advice or information quickly, share points of view, or just stay in touch. Although the messages are short and sweet, the power is in how Twitter connects individuals and enables educators to assemble a group of people to turn to for instant advice and leads on where to get needed information. Even the short statements that do no more than let others know what one is doing helps people get to know those in their personal learning networks.

Illinois technology coordinator Jon Orech gave the reasons he tweets in "Why I Tweet" (2009a).

> I cannot tell you how much I have learned and been able to share since joining Twitter.... If I need materials or a question answered, my PLN (Personal Learning Network) is right there.... There are stimulating discussions.... Also, whenever I have a new blog post, I can post it on Twitter, and be sure to get constructive feedback from colleagues ... I am content with using it as a means to connect with people whose opinions and ideas I value. (n.p.)

Since then, Twitter use has grown among educators. In 2013, he said, "This is still true, more so now than ever, since we are starting to see more people here in my district using it" (J. Orech, personal communication, May 2013).

Teachers can search for others who use Twitter by name, email address, or location; or they can choose from the extensive lists of educators arranged by interest on the Twitter4Teachers wiki (http://twitter4teachers.pbworks. com). You can add people whom others find interesting and create an online community of people who share such things as subject area to create a personal learning network. In practice, many people use Twitter to share news, link to interesting articles and ideas, point to their blog posts, inform about online events, and promote themselves as thinkers.

Although Twitter is popular with educators, many are also using other microblogging tools such as Edmodo or TodaysMeet.

Edmodo (www.edmodo.com) started as a private communication platform designed specifically for teachers and students to share notes, links, and files and has grown into a robust tool for sharing and connecting. Teachers can send alerts, events, and assignments to students and chat with individual students, groups, or the whole class. They can continue classroom discussions online, give polls to check for student understanding, and award badges to individual students based on performance or behavior, and more. See Chapter 11 for a how-to on Edmodo.

Mike Hasley, secondary social studies specialist, Henrico County Public Schools, Virginia, uses TodaysMeet (www.todaysmeet.com), a microblogging website that allows a teacher to create a chat room or backchannel where students can post messages with 140 or fewer characters. He shared:

> I began using it with teachers in a class I taught on internet tools in the classroom. I was trying to show them how they can make a basic lecture more interesting and relevant for students. When the teacher needs to lecture about a topic or do a presentation, students can use the chat room to help further their understanding of a topic. It makes the lecture more interactive because students can ask each other questions and a teacher can read the back channel later and answer the questions in the next class.
> (M. Hasley, personal communication, 2010)

Other educators have found additional uses for microblogging tools such as TodaysMeet. For example, Steven Anderson, director of instructional technology for the Winston-Salem/Forsyth County Schools in Winston-Salem, North Carolina, says:

As 1:1 and Bring Your Own Device (BYOD) are taking over our schools, it is becoming even easier to formatively assess what our students know and for our students to leave feedback as to what they need. . . . A backchannel provides a way for participants to share in conversation while participating in learning. In terms of formative assessments, questions at various points through the lesson could be posted there and kids could respond. My favorite backchannel service is TodaysMeet, which is simple to set up (all you need is a room name and to decide how long you want the room to be open). It is free as well and available anytime, anywhere. (Anderson, 2013b, n.p.)

## Hashtags

Twitter is a powerful search engine. With it, you can find the information and people you need. One of the ways to search—and help others to find you and your information—is to use the power of hashtags.

A hashtag is the pound or number symbol on your keyboard: #. In the Twitterverse, it appears ahead of the word and indicates that this is a topic or theme for others to read and share information about. According to Wikipedia, a hashtag is a word or a phrase prefixed with the symbol #. It is a form of metadata tag. Short messages on microblogging social networking services such as Twitter, Tout, identi.ca, Tumblr, Instagram, Flickr, Google+, or Facebook may be tagged by putting "#" before important words, as in: #Wikipedia is an #encyclopedia that anyone can edit.

Hashtags provide a means of grouping such messages, because you can search for the hashtag and get the set of messages that contain it. For example, Shawn Storm, a social studies teacher in Quakerstown, Pennsylvania, searches the Twitter feed for #mysteryskype (Figure 2.2) to find project partners for his classroom Mystery Skype lessons (S. Storm, personal communication, July 2013). (See Chapter 6, Visual Learning Tools, for information on Mystery Skype.)

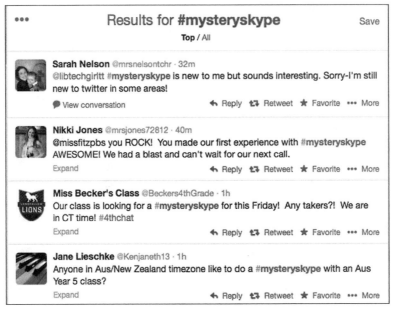

**Results for #mysteryskype**    Top / All    Save

Sarah Nelson @mrsnelsontchr · 32m
@libtechgirltt #mysteryskype is new to me but sounds interesting. Sorry-I'm still new to twitter in some areas!
View conversation    Reply  Retweet  Favorite  More

Nikki Jones @mrsjones72812 · 40m
@missfitzpbs you ROCK!  You made our first experience with #mysteryskype AWESOME! We had a blast and can't wait for our next call.
Expand    Reply  Retweet  Favorite  More

Miss Becker's Class @Beckers4thGrade · 1h
Our class is looking for a #mysteryskype for this Friday!  Any takers?!  We are in CT time! #4thchat
Expand    Reply  Retweet  Favorite  More

Jane Lieschke @Kenjaneth13 · 1h
Anyone in Aus/New Zealand timezone like to do a #mysteryskype with an Aus Year 5 class?
Expand    Reply  Retweet  Favorite  More

Figure 2.2 | #mysteryskype page from Twitter

According to Steven Anderson:

> It's a tag in your post so that you or someone else can find it later or track it as it is happening. For example, if you are watching the Super Bowl and want to know what other folks are saying about the game, you can do a search (on search. twitter.com) for the hashtag #SuperBowl and see what others are talking about. Many TV shows, events, companies, and more are creating hashtags to monitor conversations and just generally engage with other followers. (Anderson, 2013c, n.p.)

## The Power of Hashtags

Steven Anderson, director of instructional technology for the Winston-Salem/ Forsyth County Schools in Winston-Salem, North Carolina, believes it's important to establish the value of Twitter with educators before asking them to use it. He says, "What a lot of people don't realize that Twitter is a very powerful search engine. Just like Google, if you know how to use the search effectively you can find pretty much anything. And one of those effective ways is leveraging the power of hashtags."

A hashtag is a tag in your post so that you or someone else can find it later or track it as it is happening. You create one by putting a hash symbol (#) before a key word. Once you have done that, you have created it. Steven advises to "do a search on Twitter for the hashtag you want to use, just to make sure other stuff isn't posted to it already."

"Once you have it in mind, start using it. This can be great for schools/ districts or classrooms to create tags to allow other members of the community to see what's being said to follow along with events, games, etc.

"The hashtag provides a way for anyone, no matter who, to reap the rewards of the information that flows across the Twitterverse and have it delivered to you whenever you need it."

(*Comments from Anderson's article "It's All about the Hashtag," www.guide2 digitallearning.com/tools_technologies/it%E2%80%99s_all_about_hashtag*)

## @ Signs

In addition to finding information and topics, you can also search for people on Twitter by using the @ symbol before their username. For example, you can find one of this book's authors at @gwensol on Twitter.

# Nine Reasons to Twitter

Laura Walker

1. **Together we're better.** Twitter can be like a virtual staffroom where teachers can access in seconds a stream of links, ideas, opinions, and resources from a hand-picked selection of global professionals.

2. **Global or local: you choose.** With Twitter, educators can actively compare what's happening with others on different continents. GPS-enabled devices and advanced web search facility allow searches that tell you what people are tweeting within a certain distance of a location, so if the other side of the world isn't your bag, you can stick with your own patch.

3. **Self-awareness and reflective practice.** Excellent teachers reflect on what they are doing in their schools and look at what is going well in order to maintain and develop it, and what needs improvement in order to make it better. Teachers on Twitter share these reflections and both support and challenge each other.

4. **Ideas workshop and sounding board.** Twitter is a great medium for sharing ideas and getting instant feedback. You can gather a range of opinions and constructive criticism within minutes, which can help enormously, whether you are planning a learning experience, writing a policy, or putting a job application together.

5. **Newsroom and innovation showcase.** Twitter helps you stay up-to-date on news and current affairs, as well as on the latest developments in areas of interest like school leadership and technology.

6. **Professional development and critical friends.** One of the best things about training days is the break-out time between sessions, when teachers can get together to talk about what they are working on or struggling with. Twitter enables users to have that kind of powerful networking capacity with them all the time. It's just a matter of finding the right people to follow.

7. **Quality-assured searching.** Trust the people you follow. Hone and develop the list of people whose insights you value. Once your Twitter network grows past a critical mass, you can ask them detailed questions and get back higher-quality information than a Google search would generally provide.

8. **Communicate, communicate, communicate.** Expressing yourself in 140 characters is a great discipline. You can become better at saying what needs to be said in professional communications with less waffle and padding (even without txtspk).

9. **Getting with the times has never been so easy!** Twitter is anything but complicated! You simply visit Twitter.com and create your account. A little light searching using key words for your areas of interest will soon yield a list of interesting people to follow. There are plenty of websites offering advice on getting started and how to avoid a few common beginners' faux pas. Your biggest challenge is likely to be getting twitter.com unblocked on your school network if your main usage will be at school.

*Laura Walker is director of e-learning at a UK mixed secondary comprehensive.*

# *When* Do Teachers Use Twitter?

## Classroom Integration

Although most educators who are on one of the microblogging sites use them to be in touch with peers, classroom uses are gaining popularity as well. For example, the ability to feel connected can mean that students have a voice and an audience. They can reach out to others in their class, school, or community, or get answers from experts in their network. For students who are hesitant to write much, tweeting can provide an introduction to the power of communication and motivate learners to hone their writing skills. Writing fewer words to communicate a thought is harder to do than writing many words and requires thinking carefully about exactly what one wants to say.

No one wants to promote writing only short statements. However, students can start with something easy to handle—one thought in one sentence—then develop more sentences to build on that thought.

Students often think they don't really know enough to write for an audience. Using Twitter requires such short answers that students are more willing to write something, secure in the knowledge that they aren't allowed long answers. Getting their ideas down improves their confidence. Exchanging ideas with others and providing and getting feedback improves their confidence even more.

Interactivity is one way of engaging students and keeping them motivated to work. Twitter provides interactivity in that students can explain, clarify, and compare their thinking as part of a collaborative project. As they send tweets back and forth about the topic, they provide feedback to one another and are engaged in thinking analytically about the subject and explaining these thoughts effectively. Thinking and communicating promote increased understanding and remembering.

Some uses for microblogs include:

**Classroom polls.** Twitter is a great tool for getting feedback from students during and after a lesson as well as a way to collect answers to quick polls while you teach. If you're not sure that students get a point, ask a question and gauge their understanding by how they answer. Using TwtPoll (www.twtpoll.com) lets you create custom polls in advance and link to content. Your poll generates a URL that students can access. The result is data you can use. There's a minimal charge for TwtPoll.

**Research gathering.** When students find valuable resources, they can tweet the topic, site, and URL to their team or to remember and return to later. This speeds up research as they work and allows them to sift through all the possibilities later.

**Homework alerts.** You can remind students and parents about homework, trips, and long-term assignment deadlines with tweets. The advantage is that you don't need to know the phone numbers of students to get messages onto their devices: they are the ones who authorize their mobile phones from the Twitter site, and they subscribe to your Twitter feed.

**Homework checks.** It is hard to know if students understand the homework. You can create surveys on TwtPoll for students to take after they've finished the assignment. You'll be able to see what students understood and what you have to go over.

**Language learning.** Students can tweet to one another about a topic of choice in the language they are studying. They will work quickly to make their use of the language automatic—they won't be discouraged, because the interactions are limited to 140 characters each.

**Lesson backchannels.** Although this has to be explained carefully and monitored closely, students can tweet their thoughts or questions and replies during explanations and discussions in class. They can write thoughts quickly and be able to check what they were thinking later. A brave teacher can display the backchannel to go over with the class.

**Role playing.** Students can understand characters in novels they read by taking on a role and tweeting to one another in character. They can act out particularly complicated scenes and discuss the implications later. They can expand on the lives of the characters by tweeting a new ending or the characters' actions after the book's events end.

## Professional Development

Educators connect with one another using microblogging's short, quick message system to ask questions and share information. Tom Murray, director of technology and cyber education for the Quakertown Community School District in Bucks County, Pennsylvania, says in his 2013 blog post "Utilizing Twitter Chats for Professional Development" on the Digital Learning Environments website:

> Each week, educators from around the world take part in various conversations on Twitter known as "chats." These conversations have become an excellent way for educators to connect on relevant topics, share resources and best practices, all while challenging each other's thinking. The premise of a

Twitter chat is simple. Each lasts for 60 minutes, moderators pose questions on a predetermined topic, and participants use a consistent hashtag (#) to communicate. (Murray, 2013, n.p.)

For example, Tom Murray and Darin Jolly moderate #SBGchat for standards-based grading discussions on Wednesdays from 9 to 10 p.m. ET. Murray recommends several others, including #Edchat on various education topics and trends; #Edtechchat on educational technology (Figure 2.3); #PTchat on home-school partnerships; #Satchat on a variety of educational topics and trends; and #SSchat for social studies teachers from around the world. There are state-based chats as well.

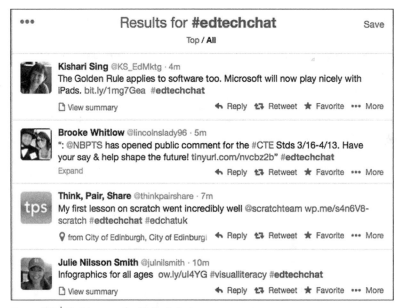

Figure 2.3 | Twitter page for #Edtechchat

Twitter chats have evolved into a real form of personal professional development. Jim Forde, a science and technology teacher at Scofield Magnet Middle School in Stamford, Connecticut, is tasked with providing a quality STEM education and focuses on STEM issues on his STEMnetwork twitter feed, @stemnetwork.

In his Digital Learning Environments blog post "Twitter and STEM: Perfect Together," he recommended other STEM feeds: STEM connector, @STEMconnector, is one-stop shopping for everything STEM; NPR Science Desk, @nprscience, is the Twitter feed with content from NPR; and the National Science Teachers Association maintains its NSTA blog, @nsta (Forde, 2012).

One concern Forde has is that gender stereotypes can affect the performance and level of engagement of women in STEM. He recommended Twitter resources for girls in his Digital Learning Environments blog post "Girls + STEM + Twitter = Awesome!" For example, Techbridge, @techbridgegirls, inspires girls to discover a passion for technology, science, and engineering; @steminist features the voices of women in science, tech, engineering, and math; and @blackgirlscode attempts to empower young women of color between the ages of 6 and 17 to enter the current tech marketplace as builders and creators.

Jessica Evans, learning support teacher at Strayer Middle School in Pennsylvania's Quaker Community School District, uses Twitter to connect with, share, and learn from educators from around the world. She says, "Participating in weekly education chats provides me with the opportunity to discuss philosophies, classroom ideas, grading, school improvement plans, and specific topics." She shares student accomplishments with her learning community, too. She adds:

> I enjoy sharing my students' work through media such as a picture collage of the class assignment and student products, videos that the students made, and videos that I compile showcasing my students' work.

> Educators in my professional learning community have expressed their appreciation that I share student work with them via Twitter. I've had educators reach out to me and ask how they could transfer my idea into their classroom. It's all about being connected and learning from each other.

> My students get excited when I post their work on Twitter. Whether it is a video the class made or a project they worked on, they enjoy the feedback from other educators, even if it is only a retweet or a "favorite."

My class has its own YouTube channel where we upload a lot of our work. Then we use the links to tweet out, or send them home to parents so they can see the hard work and effort the students put into their work.

My students benefit when I learn and share with educators through Twitter. I have been a more effective and connected classroom teacher. When I have a question or want to find a new idea for my classroom, Twitter gives me access to an endless amount of links, resources, opinions, and educators willing to offer their ideas. By modeling learning and sharing in connected ways, my students realize that learning and growing never stops. (J. Evans, personal communication, May 2013)

Michelle Guilbeau-Sheppard, first grade teacher at Hillcrest Elementary School in the Elgin School District U-46 in Illinois, has made Twitter her connection to other educators and personal learning network (PLN). She says,

I initially started out using Twitter as a social media connection. However after a few years of use and connecting, I have come to realize it is my favorite PLN. Not many people in our district were using Twitter, but our superintendent started using and promoting it, so slowly the interest and momentum has increased.

I also did a presentation on using Twitter as a PLN in our district in October 2012, and because of that presentation, I have connected with even more fellow coworkers.

My Twitter "education friends" within my district and outside my district have given me insight, knowledge, and courage to grow personally in my classroom, within my district, and the best part … within myself. What I tell people is that Twitter has helped me grow as an educator beyond *any other* professional growth activity that I have used, and the most meaningful aspect of being a part of the Twitter community is the relationships I have built in the education world.

Twitter friends have helped to keep me sane, on-track, and knowledgeable with a renewed excitement about education and being a teacher. The learning that I have gained through my PLN on Twitter has resonated into my classroom teaching, and thus my students have benefited from my involvement with Twitter. (M. Guilbeau-Sheppard, personal communication, June 2013)

**Web 2.0 Wisdom**

## Twitter Tips and Tricks

Steven Anderson

*Steven Anderson (2013c) spends a lot of time running professional development sessions. He is asked quite a lot of questions. Here are answers to the top three questions from his blog post "Top Secret Tips and Tricks for Getting the Most Out of Twitter." He says:*

I get asked these three questions all the time. There really aren't any secrets. It's just great resources that I use to leverage more out of Twitter to find what I am looking for or to keep myself organized.

### Where Do You Find All Those Links That You Post?

Almost three years ago, when I created my account, I was looking for a way to share the resources I was finding with the teachers across my district. Twitter was a great and easy way to do it. And that has continued into my current role. I get to spend lots of time looking for resources for teachers across my district. Sharing is caring, so I figure if one teacher in my district can benefit, there are probably others out there, too.

So, the long and short of it is I usually start with a Google search. And that will yield some good results … sometimes. One of my favorite resources is the wisdom of the crowd. And there is no better place for that then Diigo. With Diigo search I can look for specific tags of items that folks have shared. Most of the time I get better results there than anywhere else. And I keep my links there too for anyone to be able to find. Most every link I have ever posted ends up there, eventually. And I don't hesitate to revisit and post something I already posted a while back.

I use an RSS reader to follow lots of different blogs on lots of different subjects. And I almost always find great content there. Sometimes it's like going down the rabbit hole. I will check out a post on one of my favorite blogs, FreeTech4Teachers, from my good friend Richard. He will post something that will lead me to something else, that leads me to something else, and so on, and so on. I can get really deep looking for stuff, finding great content to share along the way.

A lot of what I post is retweets from other folks. Again, letting the wisdom of the crowds do the work for me to find great content. It goes back to following people for their quality, not following as many people as I can. And retweets extend the reach of your network. You and I might follow each other, but someone who follows me might not follow you. So the RT extends the content and grows the network. It's a win-win!

### How Do You Make Sure You Don't Miss Everything Without Staying on Twitter 24/7?

Hashtags are a great way to keep up with stuff. Lists are another. Both allow you to go back in time up to two weeks to find stuff. While hashtags are a great way to track conversations and to find people to follow, many will post resources and hashtag them so others will find them. You can then put all your favorite people in a list so that you can see their posts any time. (And if you use something like TweetDeck or HootSuite, it is easy to set up columns to follow those things any time.)

There are tons of great websites too that will find the most important stuff for you. The Tweeted Times and Paper.li are two sites that, when you connect them with your account, will analyze the resources of the people you follow and find the best ones and present them to you in a newspaper format. (These are two more ways I find great content, too.)

Know About It is a new service I have been playing with. Instead of finding the most important content, it gives you every link that comes through your stream along with the tweet and who tweeted it. You also get a daily email of the most popular content along with what they call Hidden Gems, content that might interest you based upon what comes through your stream.

The point is, you don't have to be on all the time or feel like you have to see everything that comes by. Be smart and use these tools, and let them do the work for you.

### How Do You Organize Everything You Find on Twitter?

I have lots of tools that I use to help me keep track of everything I find. One is Read It Later [now called Pocket]. This is my favorite tool. When someone posts something and I don't have time to check it out, I just add it to my Read It Later list and go over it when I do have the time. The best part, I can access my list from anywhere on any device. So if I am sitting somewhere for a few moments, I can go through my list.

Diigo, which I mentioned before for finding loads of great content, is where I put my content, too. I have always been a fan of Diigo because of the great stuff they offer educators, but really I like just being able to save my links there and give them tags so that I can find them easily.

The point to all this is that Twitter isn't work. It's not supposed to take up massive amounts of time or energy. Sure, you have to spend some personal capital keeping up and growing your network—but as you have seen, there are loads of great tools out there that you can put to work for you to find amazing and valuable resources for you and your classroom.

*Steven Anderson is the director of instructional technology for the Winston-Salem/ Forsyth County Schools in Winston-Salem, North Carolina. "Top Secret Tips and Tricks for Getting the Most Out of Twitter" is available at www.guide2digitallearning.com/ tools_technologies/top_secret_tips_and_tricks_getting_most_out_twitter.*

# *Who* Is Using Microblogging for Teaching and Learning?

Microblogging helps educators stay in touch with their personal learning networks. Using microblogs with students enhances classroom learning as well. Some examples provide good models.

## Twitter in First Grade

Karen Lirenman, a Grade 1 teacher at Woodward Hill Elementary in Surrey, British Columbia, Canada, uses Twitter with her students. She says:

> My students use Twitter in a variety of ways. As a class we have created hashtags to show and practice skills. During our study of *Little Red Riding Hood*, for example, we created the hashtag #LRRH13 and tweeted in the voice of *Little Red Riding Hood* characters.
>
> During math we tweeted geometric shape clues to #2d3dshapes. Other young children read and answered our clues and wrote clues for us to solve. A surprise benefit of this particular Twitter interaction is that many of the children from other schools around the world showed my students how they solved the problems. Some tweeted pictures of the manipulative they used, and others tweeted how they solved the problem. My students were exposed to many different ways to solve the same problem.
>
> My students have also used Twitter to communicate with an author. Twitter has allowed my students to learn with other children in the world in authentic, meaningful ways. (K. Lirenman, personal communication, July 2013)

## Twitter and Rural Students

Anne Mirtschin, who teaches Grades 4 to 12 at Hawkesdale P12 College in South West Victoria, Australia, uses Twitter with her students. The school is a rural prep to Year 12 school that is culturally and geographically isolated but whose students have connected to the world using digital tools. She says, "Twitter is a great tool to use for 'immediate learning' in the classroom. I use it in an impromptu, teachable moment basis." Here are a few examples of how she incorporates Twitter in her classroom:

> When students have a problem to be resolved, we use Twitter to find an expert who can solve it. For example, at one point, Year 9/10 students were looking for copyright-free photos. Another time, they needed a tool that would convert their .flv video files to .mpg or .wmv. They asked and got answers almost immediately from the Twittersphere.

> Year prep/one students were studying animals, so they sent out a tweet seeking the favourite animal of people across the globe. They got many responses and learned not only about the animals but also about the countries where they got responses. For example, they learned about the location of these countries and did a comparison of attitudes to certain animals. In one case a red fox was the favourite animal in Canada but it is seen as a pest on our students' farms.

> Students from Years 10–12 across Australia used Twitter as a backchannel during a recent virtual forum with federal politicians based in Canberra. This web conference took place just prior to the Australian elections. Seven schools were able to ask questions of the politicians so all students who participated either face to face or virtually had a "voice." They used Twitter and a hashtag to seek answers to youth issues, to share experiences, discuss responses and articulate their points of view. The Twitter stream proved to be a highly engaging tool for students who were involved. (A. Mirtschin, personal communication, July 2013)

## Home-School Connection

Erin Jackle and Stephanie Hopkins, early childhood special education teachers in School District U-46 in Elgin, Illinois, integrate technology into what they do every day with students and parents. They say,

In addition to all the ways Twitter helps us grow profession-ally, it is also a tool that we use to connect with families. As one teenager said, "Nobody uses Facebook anymore. Too many parents and grandparents are on it! Everyone uses Twitter." Imagine being on a lunch break and being able to see what is happening in your child's classroom in real time. Or imagine getting a direct message (DM) that fieldtrip money is due or reading about an app your child is using on a classroom iPad that you can download at home to bridge the home-school gap. Our tweets for families include things such as classroom reminders, links to articles or ideas to use at home, photos of student work, photos of what's happening in the classroom, links to the classroom blog or YouTube videos, and general conversation with parents. (E. Jackle and S. Hopkins, personal communication, June 2013)

## Social Awareness

Eric Walters, director of technology at the Marymount School in New York, runs a project that involves students in using Web 2.0 tools to solve problems. He describes the project:

According to water.org, in many countries, women are respon-sible for finding and fetching water for their families. All the water they need for drinking, washing, cooking, cleaning. They walk miles, carry heavy burdens, wait for hours and pay exorbi-tant prices. The work is back breaking and all consuming. Often the water is contaminated, even deadly. In these instances, they face an impossible choice—certain death without water or possible death from illness. Once they are old enough, girls join this effort. They spend countless hours trying to provide this basic life necessity.

In this project, students were asked the following: How can we, as a class, harness the power of social media to find a solution to this problem?

Students brainstormed solutions and developed a three-pronged approach: creating awareness through a Facebook page, spreading the word with a Twitter account, and creating a viral video. Students also wrote and produced a 15-minute newscast that addressed the issues of the social, economic, and political impact of women and water. Their project is called H2Opportunities.

This was a self-directed project. Students were given the key question, and they had a "voice and choice" in how they wished to answer it. They worked independently outside of class in small groups on their assigned task (creating the Twitter account, the Facebook page, writing the newscast, or producing the viral video) and reported back. The students learned about time and project management, strategies for communication, utilization of a communications medium familiar to them in an educational and public service arena, and collaborative work skills. Moreover, their understanding of the impact of the lack of clean, safe drinking in many places in the world—not just in Africa—was increased substantially. (E. Walters, personal communication, June 2013)

## Making Connections

Shawn Storm, sixth grade RELA/social studies teacher at R. E. Strayer Middle School in Quakertown, Pennsylvania, engages his students with debates. Twitter is the connection to other debate teams in other locations. Shawn says:

Through a connection made on Twitter, my sixth grade class had the opportunity to participate in a virtual debate. My class teamed up with another school in Pennsylvania, and argued against two schools from New Jersey. They planned and coordinated and communicated. We teachers decided on the format of the debate and how it would be scored.

The topic was if homework is beneficial and necessary for students to be successful. It wasn't a typical debate just with the students in my class. Using Twitter to find the other schools turned it into the "Great Interstate Homework Debate." (S. Storm, personal communication, July 2013)

### Six Tips for Microblogging

1. Establish goals for the project.

2. Explain the concept of microblogging.

3. Practice brevity.

4. Pick a topic that is simple enough to communicate in 140 characters.

5. Time your tweet so that there is enough time to gather answers before you need them.

6. Display the answers in a Twitter client to avoid seeing tweets on other topics.

# *How* Do You Get Started with Twitter?

Go to Twitter.com and click Join for Free. Type your full name, a username (it will check for availability), a password, and an email address. You'll have to type in the CAPTCHA code word (the strangely written word that people can decode but computers can't) and click Create My Account.

Click on Settings. Create a profile and upload a picture (optional). Also optional: check the Protect My Updates box so that people won't be able to read your tweets unless you authorize them.

Send people to your Twitter page: twitter.com/username. Send a tweet by typing in the Compose new Tweet box at the top. You can use up to 140 characters. Your latest post will appear at the top of your page.

Add people: Log into your account, go to a person's Twitter page, and click Follow. (Use the search box on your page to find people.) Read the tweets of people you've added on your page. See who others are following by moving your mouse pointer over the pictures in the sidebar on their pages. You can click on the pictures to go to their pages and add them to your list. (They will be notified.)

# *Where* Can You Find More Information about Microblogging?

Sue Waters's wiki with information about using Twitter:
http://suewaters.wikispaces.com/twitter

Are You Twittering? Here's How I Use Twitter, by Sue Waters:
http://theedublogger.edublogs.org/2008/04/02/
are-you-twittering-heres-how-i-use-twitter

Twitter4Teachers: http://twitter4teachers.pbworks.com
22 Ways to Use Twitter in the Classroom (Choose the Twitter box
from the selection of presentations organized alphabetically.):
www.ideastoinspire.co.uk

Twitter Handbook for Teachers, by Tomaz Lasic:
www.scribd.com/doc/14062777/Twitter-Handbook-for-Teachers

# 3

# Podcasts and Vodcasts

## *What* are Podcasts and Vodcasts?

Have you watched an episode of your favorite television show on your iPod? Have you longed for the opportunity to revisit a favorite television program from the 1980s? Want to listen to a weekly travel show with Rick Steves? Planning a trip to China and want to listen to an expert historian talk about the country's history? Or perhaps you are looking for gardening tips. With a few simple clicks, you can download an audio file (a podcast) or an audio-video file (a video podcast or vodcast) that meets your interests or needs at the very time you want it. There are many directories of what is available: iTunes (www.itunes.com), TeacherTube (www.teachertube.com), Schooltube (www.schooltube.com), PodcastDirectory.com (www.podcastdirectory.com), and Podcast Alley (www.podcastalley.com).

### Definitions

A *podcast* is an audio or video netcast (streamed or nonstreamed). A *vodcast* is a video podcast.

Wikipedia's definition clearly indicates the audio and video capabilities of a podcast: "A podcast (or netcast) is a series of digital media files (either audio or video) that are released episodically and often downloaded through web syndication. The mode of delivery differentiates podcasting from other means of accessing media files over the internet, such as direct download, or streamed webcasting. A list of all the audio or video files currently associated with a given series is maintained centrally on the distributor's server as a web feed, and the listener or viewer employs special client application software known as a podcatcher that can access this web feed, check it for updates, and download any new files in the series. This process can be automated so that new files are downloaded automatically."

Although the technology has been available for as long as the internet has been around, it really began to catch on in popularity in the early 2000s. The most common audio file format used is MP3 or MP4. For a simple explanation, watch CommonCraft's video "Podcasting in Plain English" (http://commoncraft.com/podcasting). One podcast site (Podcast Alley) reports statistics (as of June 2013) regarding the numbers of podcasts as 91,783 types of podcasts, a little more than a quarter of a million comments about podcasts, and more than 6 million unique podcast episodes. This site also has users vote and then highlights the top 10 podcasts each day, as well as the five newest ones as they are posted. Interestingly, the word *podcast* was named the New Oxford American Dictionary's Word of the Year in 2005! By the way, you can receive a Merriam-Webster's Word of the Day by podcast (www.learnoutloud.com/Podcast-Directory/Languages/Vocabulary-Building/MerriamWebsters-Word-of-the-Day-Podcast/19450).

Podcasts can be differentiated from regular MP3 files by virtue of their ability to be syndicated. This is referred to as Really Simple Syndication (RSS). This involves special client software the user installs, often called a podcatcher (for example, Apple's iTunes; however, Wikipedia now lists a number of podcatchers currently available for smartphones and other platforms [http://en.wikipedia.org/wiki/List_of_podcatchers]), that automatically searches for and downloads the new files you have specified. Once these files are on your computer, or other device, you can access them offline when you are ready to use them. You also can retain them for as long as you choose.

A vodcast is a video podcast; in essence, it is an on-demand production that contains video and audio information. It can be downloaded as a file, or received as streaming video, delivered live as it is being produced. Another term for vodcasts is "screencasting"; both of these support the flipped classroom. A flipped classroom is one in which the video and other materials are delivered as a vodcast, so that the traditional "lecture" is seen at home and the interaction and learning activities take place during the face-to-face time with the teacher and other students.

# *Why* is a Podcast a Useful Tool?

Your class may be participating in an Antarctica adventure in which scientists post podcasts as events occur. Your students may be following the scientists as they track animals and gather flora and fauna from the frozen environment. You can set your podcatcher to check for new postings routinely, and then it will alert you after each new adventure has become available. This of course saves considerable time and effort; you no longer have to check each day for new and appropriate materials.

The possibilities are truly endless in society these days; many people, including ourselves, pursue their interests and entertainment through podcasts on a daily basis. Interestingly, educators have discovered endless uses for education, too, and podcasting has become one of the most frequently used Web 2.0 tools.

# *When* Do Teachers Use Podcasts?

Although the use of podcasts has been very popular for purposes of entertainment, educators soon began to see value for teachers and their students as well (Kay, 2012). Podcasts are now being used at all levels of education, from preschool through higher education (Harris & Park, 2008). The best news is that podcasts really are simple to create or use. They provide teachers and students with a tool that is user friendly, flexible, and convenient. Students are able to create podcasts to demonstrate their understanding of material, present research, and express their points of view.

## Classroom Integration

In recent research, interviews with teachers resulted in teachers reporting the creation of podcasts for introducing a unit topic and main ideas, or inclusion of vodcasts to stimulate students' interest in creative topics such as broadcasting, robots, or digital media (Schrum & Levin, 2012). Educators are using podcasts and vodcasts in exciting ways. First, they take advantage of the huge number of prepared and freely available "casts," on a wide variety of subjects, for professional development and curriculum integration. Second, many teachers are now moving to the next step and are finding ways to have students at all levels demonstrate their knowledge, understanding, and questions by creating their own podcasts and vodcasts. Many schools that in the past may have had student-developed, -created, and -produced news shows have moved those shows into the digital age by creating them as pod- or vodcasts. Family members can stay up-to-date and involved by means of these tools. Three distinct teaching approaches are evident in the current literature and include receptive viewing [passive], problem solving [active], and [student] created video podcasts (Kay, 2012, p. 822).

Of course, students have been producing audio programs for generations, typically using tape recorders or reel-to-reel machines. Podcasts, of course, are easier to edit than splicing a tape because they are recorded digitally on a computer. However, educators say that the biggest difference is that podcasts are available to a worldwide audience. Anyone anywhere can subscribe to them and have them automatically downloaded to their computers when a new installment is posted.

In general, Harris and Park (2008) identify four characteristics of podcasting based on their usages. "Teaching-driven" podcasting allows educators "not only to provide a repeat or summary of a lecture given but also to provide timely academic material, such as law-related-news" (p. 549). "Service-driven" podcasting offers the opportunity to provide detailed information to families and others by offering podcasts on policies, events, or student academic activities. "Marketing-driven" podcasts can be useful to promote the school or district to potential students, or for parents to take a virtual tour of the facilities and community. "Technology-driven" podcasts are used to support the teaching method and offer the opportunity to share teaching practices. More information and links to current educators can be found at Flipped Learning (http://flippedclassroom.org).

Students investigating, designing, creating, and teaching: what could be more educational or valuable to them? Three unique ways of using podcasts in the classroom have emerged. First, many prepared lessons and support for lessons exist for students of all ages and in all content areas. Teachers of very young children can find podcasts of stories, dramatic events, musical instruments, art, and information on science experiments. All are readily available.

An enormous number of choices can be found at a variety of locations. The BBC has a large number of learning podcasts (www.bbc.co.uk/podcasts/genre/childrens), Harper Collins offers children's favorite authors doing podcasts (www.harpercollinschildrens.com/kids/gamesandcontests/features/podcast/), and Learn Out Loud has dozens of podcasts about many topics (www.learnoutloud.com/Podcast-Directory/Literature/European-Classics/Childrens-Fun-Storytime-Podcast/23099). Or children can listen to National Geographic's introductions to the orangutans of Borneo or the penguins of Antarctica (www.nationalgeographic.com/podcasts) or a 60-second science tidbit from Scientific American (www.sciam.com).

The Science Show for Kids provides five-minute audio podcasts on burning science questions through iTunes.com. Bookwink (www.bookwink.com) provides video booktalks (three minutes each) about new books for Grades 3 through 8. And Storynory (www.storynory.com) offers podcasts of familiar stories (*Jack and the Beanstalk* or *Little Red Riding Hood*) as well as less familiar ones. Happily, these stories come with full English text so that beginning readers or English language learners (ELL) can see the words as they are spoken. The Inkless Tales Podcast for Kids (http://inklesstales.wordpress.com) provides retelling of familiar and ethnically diverse stories. For example, in the well-known story *Princess and the Pea*, the princess is rather passive. In the new version on this website, she is filled with spirit and is active. For truly exciting renditions of favorite books read by famous actors, try Storyline Online (www.storylineonline.net).

Other examples abound. Podcast tours are available for museums, battlegrounds, and other important locations. The Blazing Guns and Rugged Hearts podcast, created by the Kansas Historical Society (www.kshs.org/audiotours/blazingguns/tours.htm), prepares those students lucky enough to visit this location and provides information to those who are unable to take a tour. Or perhaps your students would like to take a real tour of Gettysburg National Military Park (www.nps.gov/gett/historyculture/gettysburg-podcast-tours.htm) or the Smithsonian Museums online (www.si.edu/Museums). The Smithsonian's History Explorer website (http://historyexplorer.si.edu) allows your students to learn interactively about history through exposure to more than three million important artifacts held within Smithsonian's collection. You can learn about how to utilize this informative resource by visiting http://historyexplorer.si.edu/howtouse.

Poetcasts bring poetry to anyone who wishes to learn how to enjoy this literary form (www.learnoutloud.com/Podcast-Directory/Literature/Poetry), and Learn Out Loud writing (www.learnoutloud.com/Podcast-Directory/Education-and-Professional/Writing) helps writers in a wide variety of activities. Classical music podcasts are available to introduce music in a fun and engaging manner; these could easily be used as signals to transition from one activity to another (www.npr.org/rss/podcast/podcast_detail.php?siteId=14946301). Are you looking for math or science or geography? Podcasts on these content areas, and more, are all easily found from national content organizations.

Students are now becoming the creators of their own learning through their own design and development of podcasts. Podcasts have changed the ways in which educators conceptualize their content and pedagogical strategies. For example, Julie Willcott, a high school science teacher at Foxcroft Academy in Dover-Foxcroft, Maine, uses iTunes U to develop her curriculum. She teaches chemistry for 10th graders and physics for 11th graders, and she posts her lectures to iTunes U and adds supplemental information throughout the semester. As a result, Julie reports noticing that her students appear to be empowered to be in charge of their own learning because they can move ahead or review at their own pace (J. Willcott, personal communication, June 2013).

Why would a teacher want to use podcasting as a teaching tool? Research has shown that active writing, with an authentic audience, makes learners more committed to their activity, more engaged, and more willing to revise their work (Dalton & Proctor, 2008; Magnifico, 2010). With a podcast, writing can include images, spoken words, and written texts. It can also include moving images if the creation is a vodcast. Learners are then able to share what they have created and demonstrate their understanding of the content. Podcasting also requires that the students plan, organize, rehearse, and then produce their podcast using effective oral presentation skills. The Very Spatial geography site (http://veryspatial.com) also offers podcasts to make geographical events (for example, natural disasters) useful to non-geographers. Another web page, Podcasts for Educators, Schools, and Colleges (http://recap.ltd.uk/podcasting/subjects.php), offers curricular podcasts already categorized by subject area.

When you let students create their own podcasts, you do want to make sure that they are safe. One site, Kid-cast.com, calls itself a kid-safe place. It prides itself on safety, on allowing children to create their own podcasts, and on giving them a voice of their own. Each upload is rated: E for everyone; E10+ for those 10 and older; T for teens; and T16+ for those over 16. Each podcast sent to the site is reviewed to make sure the content and the rating are appropriate. To learn more about how to use podcasts in and out of the classroom, check out Teaching Ideas: Podcasting, a neat and informative resource (www.teachingideas.co.uk/ict/podcasting.htm).

Vodcasts are also growing in use. This is an exciting turn in education, whether the goal is to flip the classroom or simply to use vodcasts in the traditional class. One interesting team, Brad and Barb Newitt of Sioux Falls, South Dakota, created physics homework tutorial vodcasts to assist their students (www.physicsvodcasts.com). They take typical homework problems, recording a solution as they go through the steps using an interactive whiteboard. They stated, "Many students tell us that when they are stuck on a homework problem, they will look for a similar homework tutorial vodcast." This innovative team says:

> The time investment to make the videos was significant, but we feel that it has been well worth it. The videos have significantly improved the quality of instruction we have been able to deliver to our students. Almost all of our teaching colleagues have been reluctant to invest the time to make their own videos, which is very understandable, but they are very appreciative of the videos we have made. (B. Newitt & B. Newitt, personal communication, June 2013)

While teachers at the same school in Colorado, Jonathan Bergmann and Aaron Sams, authors of *Flip Your Classroom* (ISTE, 2012), spent time one summer creating vodcasts to enhance and flip their chemistry classes. They found that students were more engaged, but also said it turned out "to be an effective way for absent students to catch up, for struggling students to review a lesson, and for us instructors to have high-quality lessons available in our absence. Now podcasting has helped us reconfigure our chemistry courses so that students still receive direct instruction, but class time is not used to deliver it" (Bergmann & Sams, 2008–09, p. 22). They found that the way class time was spent changed dramatically (Figure 3.1). Bermann and Sams have since gone on to promote this flipped learning model.

| Before Vodcasting | | With Vodcasting | |
|---|---|---|---|
| Activity | Time | Activity | Time |
| Warm-up activity | 5 min. | Warm-up activity | 5 min. |
| Go over previous night's homework | 20 min. | Q&A time on video | 10 min. |
| Lecture new content | 30–45 min. | Lecture new content | 0 min. |
| Guided and independent practice and/or lab activity | 20–35 min. | Guided and independent practice and/or lab activity | 75 min. |

Figure 3.1 | Comparison of class time before and after vodcasting (Source: Bergmann & Sams, [2008–09], p. 25)

Emilia Carrillo, Spanish teacher and co-head of department at International School of Uganda and Pamoja Education, teaches Spanish as a foreign language for Grades 11 and 12. She now uses a TED-Ed tool to create videos of engaging, authentic Spanish-language listening activities for her students to use as supplements to in-class activities. An example of these videos can be found here: http://ed.ted.com/on/OekMnVHT. Carrillo has also recently designed the project "A Talk for TED" which she uses as a platform for her higher-level students to develop their own "TED-Talk videos" about a particular issue or event. She then asks her students to use the tool to create comprehension questions for their classroom peers (E. Carrillo, personal communication, June 2013).

Creating podcasts is not limited to learners of a certain age. At the Point England School in New Zealand, students have been creating podcasts since 2005. Their first program was called Korero Point (Pt.) England, or KPE; they went on to win the ComputerWorld Excellence Award in 2006. Most of their creators are between 9 and 11 years of age, and they use their podcasts to let people throughout the world know about books written by New Zealand authors (http://tamaki.net.nz/index.php?family=6,41,1456,1471,2936,3021).

The potential for students to make their own podcasts has recently created new interest in using cell phones in the classroom, rather than just automatically banning them. Using students' cell phones, podcasts can be created and uploaded, certainly with oversight from the teachers. Andrew Trotter (2009) reports in Education Week that some classes are allowing the use of cell phones so that students can use their personal cell phones to make podcasts, as well as to take notes and maintain a school schedule. This is one possible way to reach a true 1:1 access for all learners. As an example, Tim Johnson, the Technology Leadership Coordinator at Medicine Hat School District No. 76 in Medicine Hat, Alberta, Canada, now uses Socrative (www.socrative.com) to survey his junior high students. Students complete surveys using their cell phones in the classroom (T. Johnson, personal communication, June 2013).

Finally, podcasts are being used to expand and extend the notion of school. One school, Empire High School in Vail, Arizona, pushes learning beyond the classroom through providing students with computers, subsequently enabling them to access online lessons, do their homework, and listen to podcasts of their teachers' lectures from anywhere. At Cienega High School, also in Vail, students who have their own computers are able to take digital sections of traditional required classes, such as English, history, or science.

Misha Leybovich, the founder and CEO of the new program Meograph, reports that thousands of schools around the world are now using this new and exciting tool (www.meograph.com/education). He states that Meograph "is the easiest way to create multimedia stories for educators and students." Meograph makes it easy to combine video/audio/pics/text/links/maps/time-lines into contextualized, interactive presentations (M. Leybovich, personal communication, June 2013).

## Professional Development

Thousands of educational opportunities exist for professional development, and it is best to consider them in two different ways. First, educators tend to be lifelong learners. They value learning and continually add to their under-standing of current events, in global issues, and in just learning about the world in which we live. They are also responsible for staying current in their content areas. Thus, on a personal level, podcasts offer an opportunity to improve their knowledge about a wide range of topics.

Educators, like others, are using podcasts to learn languages, history, music, and more. Some find them on places that are not specific to education such as Digital Podcast (www.digitalpodcast.com) or iTunes (www.apple.com/itunes), where they find topics of interest to themselves. In addition, educators are finding podcasts to be a source of incredible opportunities to improve their professional practice, no matter where they happen to live. Professional devel-opment on demand is an extremely popular resource for busy teachers!

For example, NPR collects a wide variety of education podcasts for educa-tors who may have missed them, or just want to hear them again (www.npr.org/sections/education). Learning Matters (http://learningmatters.tv/blog/category/podcasts) features interviews about current events in education and is hosted by John Merrow. Another well-known source is Teachers Network—Podcasts on Education (http://teachersnetwork.wordpress.com) where one can find a wide variety of topics of interest to educators.

Edutopia, sponsored by the George Lucas Educational Network, offers a variety of videos on teaching and learning (www.edutopia.org/videos). New Teacher

Hotline (www.newteacherhotline.com) offers podcasts for new teachers, where teacher candidates will find wise educators to help model the use of pod- and vodcasts to prepare them to teach their future students. Anita Jetnikoff, at the University of Technology Victoria Park, in Australia, is using vodcasting to enhance teaching of Shakespeare to preservice English teachers (A. Jetnikoff, personal communication, June 2013).

Another organization, Russell Educational Consultancy and Productions (Recap), has set its goal to collect, verify, and make publicly available a wide variety of professional podcasts (http://recap.ltd.uk/podcasting). Recap offers links to a number of university podcasts (http://recap.ltd.uk/podcasting/colleges) including The Imperial College of London, which provides information on solving world hunger, Nobel lectures, updates on China, and much more; and the Bowdoin College Music Department, where you can listen to famous music programs and interviews with conductors and performers, or revisit old masterworks. Recap also has a blog for those who want to talk about their use of, and recommendations for, podcasts (http://recap.ltd.uk/podcasting/weblog/blog.html).

Edudemic (www.edudemic.com) has a website that constantly updates new pod- and vodcasts, as well as other educational links (Figure 3.2).

Figure 3.2  |  The Edudemic homepage

Siobhan Curious's blog (http://siobhancurious.com/2009/01/11/listening-and-learning-mark-smilowitzs-classroom-teaching-podcasts) heaps high praise on one type of professional development podcast. The blog states:

> The Classroom Teaching podcast is the work of Mark Smilowitz, a Judaic Studies middle school teacher, originally American, now working in Israel. Each podcast explores a nugget of educational theory, replete with concrete, everyday examples drawn from Smilowitz's and others' classroom experience. Smilowitz's clear, friendly, and no-nonsense tone makes you want to be a teacher like him before he's said more than a few sentences. And although he's talking about teaching students younger than mine, in an educational context very different from mine, I'm finding his mini-essays on classroom management, student questions, and, especially, the role of the teacher very inspiring and reassuring. (S. Curious, blog post, January 11, 2009)

Other educators have developed sites that support new efforts to support teachers and their challenges. One is the Center for Teaching Quality (www.teachingquality.org). On this site you can find blogs, podcasts, and vodcasts that can inform and challenge you. One such vodcast is a look at Teaching 2030 (www.youtube.com/watch?v=vk-aulXHymQ). Another is Blow the Doors off your Classroom (www.youtube.com/watch?v=VGaPLHVmv8U); these will bring new ideas to consider and discuss with others.

WETA, a PBS station, produces Reading Rocket, a popular show that teaches students to love reading and helps them learn. To support teachers learning how to teach reading, they post pod- and vodcasts online in which teachers can watch experts (www.readingrockets.org/podcasts/classroom) provide strategies, examples, and experiences. These can be used with preservice teachers, as a professional development activity for a school, or for a teacher to review alone. Titles include The ABCs of Teaching Reading, Classroom Strategies, and more. The ESL Teacher Talk podcasts assist teachers of students who are learning English by offering interviews and strategies from experienced teachers, and it is available through iTunes or www.ESLteachertalk.com.

In addition to learning from podcasts, educators at all levels are using podcasts for communicating with various audiences. Podcasting thus offers school districts the potential of expanding knowledge in the areas of instruction, curriculum, parental engagement, and distance driven instruction. For example, one podcast is Eric Langhorst's "Speaking of History" podcast (http://speakingofhistory.blogspot.com). This eighth grade American history teacher from Missouri routinely creates episodes about history and social studies. The goal is not only to extend his students' learning beyond the classroom, but also to reach out to parents and families. Even more exciting, the students are the ones who author and produce these podcasts that their families can then enjoy.

Teachers are not the only educators using podcasts for professional development; they are also tools for school leaders. Michael Waiksnis, principal at Sullivan Middle School in South Carolina, writes a blog about his uses of technology in his capacity as a school leader (http://edleaderweb.net/blog).

He states:

> Podcasting—This is another way to communicate with your school stakeholders. I have a principal's podcast. The audience is still growing and I plan on continuing it this year. To gauge the amount of interaction, I always include a trivia question for a small prize. We always get parents calling in, so I know someone is listening. There are many direct uses of podcasts in the classrooms as well. I have seen them used as a culminating activity on a research project. I have seen them used in conjunction with photo story. There are many other uses as well! (M. Waiksnis, blog post, August 10, 2009)

There are other ways school leaders can stay connected and continue their learning. The National Association of Secondary School Principals maintains a site with School Leaders' Podcasts (www.principals.org/knowledge-center/school-leaders-review-podcasts). Oakland University in Rochester, Michigan, offers Podcasts for Leaderful Schools (www.oakland.edu/podcasts4collaborativeleadership/). TED is a nonprofit organization devoted to "Ideas Worth Spreading." It started out (in 1984) as a conference bringing together people from three worlds: technology, entertainment, and design. Since then, its scope has become ever broader and includes the award-winning TED Talks video site, which tags some of its videos specifically for education (www.ted.com/talks/tags/education). You can of course also find them through iTunes (http://itunes.apple.com/us/podcast/tedtalks-education/id470623037). These podcasts discuss a range of current issues and exciting developments that continue to unfold in the ever changing world of education in 21st century.

It is also worth mentioning the newest development, MOOCs. MOOC stands for massive open online course. Although free online courses have been available on the internet for years, their quality and quantity has increased. Access to free courses has allowed students and educators to obtain a level of education that many only could dream of in the past. Thus, as a teacher you can participate in a large course about teaching and learning, or perhaps start your own!

# *Who* Is Using Casts for Teaching and Learning?

Debbie Prunty and Jean Nelson, teachers in the Oconomowoc Area School District of Oconomowoc, Wisconsin, have their students create a vodcast on a current event in the news. They report that 80% of the lesson is really the research and writing; the other 20% is the creation of the vodcast by recording, adding graphics, and then publishing it in the correct MP3 format. Their students develop their story as a news report and must include the background, data from a survey or interview if appropriate, and their own opinion on the topic.

A wide variety of podcasts are available on the Beyond Penguins and Polar Bears site developed by The Ohio State University College of Education and Human Ecology (http://beyondpenguins.ehe.osu.edu/podcasts). These science education podcasts are entertaining as well as educational. Teachers will also find stories, magazines, and webinars available to all.

Brett Moller has developed a fantastic way to integrate technology and teaching in the digital age (http://brettmoller.net). On his website, visitors can learn about his work integrating education and technology and can find informative text entries and podcasts about his experience with that process.

The Math Dude (Algebra I) is great podcast operated by the Montgomery County Public Schools. This resource provides students with a helpful chance to hone their math skills while they progress in the classroom (http://itunes.apple.com/us/podcast/the-math-dude-algebra-1/id306250988).

Many schools are now having their students create podcasts and vodcasts to maintain contact with the educational community, to promote creativity, and to celebrate success. The Philadelphia School District lists many on its podcast website (http://podcast.phila.k12.pa.us). Gadsden City Schools, Alabama, makes their podcasts available (www1.gcs.k12.al.us/~podcast), and the Smithsonian Education site offers help to podcasting with your students (www.smithsonianeducation.org/educators/lesson_plans/podcast) Also, Matt Montagne, director of educational technology at Sacred Heart Cathedral Preparatory in San Francisco, developed a fascinating blog that presents interesting podcasts, including some by students. His site, Digital Down Low (http://middleschoolblog.blogspot.com), is worth reviewing, or you might choose to go straight to the links to the podcasts (http://middleschoolblog. blogspot.com/search/label/podcasts).

## *How* Do You Get Started with Casts?

We recommend getting started creating your own podcasts and then bringing in the students to create curricular activities that include them. One place to start is About.com's "How to create your own Podcast" (http://radio.about. com/od/podcastin1/a/aa030805a.htm). It will walk you through the steps regardless of the type of computer or software you are using.

You will want to learn the following steps:

1.   How to record your audio and save it to an .mp3 file

2.   How to create an RSS file that holds the "directions" for sending your file when a user's program, such as iPodder, requests it

3.   How to write the "directions" that are inside the RSS file

4.   How to upload the RSS "feed" and your .mp3 file

5.   How to validate that the file is written correctly and will send the file correctly

Specific directions are available at About.com: Radio (http://radio.about.com/ od/podcastin1/a/blpodcast1hub.htm).

An innovative school in New Zealand has been involved in one podcasting project for some time. Dorothy Burt, e-learning facilitator, Manaiakalani, Auckland, has created a graphical representation (Figure 3.3) for thinking about the creation of podcasts, for you as the instructor or for your learners. KPE stands for Korero Pt. England, mentioned earlier in the chapter.

**Figure 3.3** | Creating podcasts (Korero Pt. England)

You may find the "Five Easy Steps for Creating Podcasts" Web 2.0 Wisdom box helpful. You and your students may want to add to this list after you create your first set of podcasts.

One school district in Texas has a novel approach to teaching how to create podcasts. They asked teacher participants to bring 10 pictures representing themselves: their hobby, pet, places they like to go, food they like, favorite things, and so forth. They then asked teachers to make podcasts about themselves to post on their web pages. The technology specialist, J. J. Pool, said, "This is how we taught them the process so they could use it in the classroom. We did it this summer in a one-day workshop for which they received a comp day during the year."

## Five Easy Steps for Creating Podcasts

Allisyn Levy

1.  Have students write a script for their podcasts. This could be a rough outline or a multi-draft, finished paper, but it must show that the student(s) have thoughtfully planned out and practiced their podcast.

2.  After approving their script, I teach students how to use a USB microphone and iMovie to record their podcast. I like iMovie because I can use it for an audio-only podcast or for video as well, and I'm able to hand over the editing to the students because of its ease of use. In iMovie, simply click on the Audio tab and use the record/pause button. Be sure your settings reflect an external microphone as your input if you are using one.

3.  Have students take turns being the "audio engineer" and record themselves. This is a great way for them to hear their own mistakes or the quality of their voice, fluency, etc., and be self-motivated to improve. Once they have a recording they are happy with, save the file. We are ready to make any quick edits.

4.  To edit a podcast, I teach students to focus on the beginning and ending of the podcast. They should pad both ends of the recording with at least five seconds of silence. This applies to video recording as well. We can edit this down later, but it ensures that none of their words will be missed. It's also a nice place to add a bit of intro/outro music. iMovie makes it extremely easy to import music from a CD or from iTunes in that same Audio tab. Be creative!

5.  Finally, once the students are happy with their podcasts, you can Export (now under the Share menu) your podcast and play it for the class, burn a CD, or post it online.

*Allisyn Levy is the director of BrainPOP Educators.*

# *Where* Can You Find More Information about Casts?

An excellent resource for learning about podcasts is PoducateMe. This easy-to-use website provides clear information about finding and using podcasts. It also has detailed instructions about how to create and share a podcast, including a discussion on the types of hardware and software you might need.

www.poducateme.com/guide

For a beginner tutorial on using GarageBand, check out this video:

www.youtube.com/watch?v=B0AqMkTmlvM

Tech Tutorials & Resources:

www.evalamar.com/tut_Podcasting.htm

Learn how to plan a podcast or vodcast for your classroom:

www.ehow.com/how_2029095_plan-podcast-class-lecture.html

Or, watch this slideshow on Podcasting in Education: The Use of Technology to Better Students' Learning:

www.slideshare.net/guest57333da/using-podcasts-in-education

And find a wealth of casting information at:

http://sites.google.com/site/myweb20adventures/Home/podcastingvodcasting

# 4

# Google Tools and Productivity Applications

## *What* Are Productivity Applications?

If we asked you to name some of the things that computers help you do every day, you might talk about the types of things you could not do without their assistance. Asked what software you use the most, you might say word processing, spreadsheets, databases, presentation tools, and collaborative calendars. A large proportion of organizations and individuals choose to purchase these items as a suite of products created by the same company so that the software works well together in an integrated fashion. These products are of course available for both Mac and Windows platforms.

This chapter is devoted to introducing you to the same types of tools, and more, that are considered Web 2.0. In general, these tools mirror the typical productivity tools you have on your own computer, except that they are available for free, stored on the company's servers, and reachable by the computer owner or, for those with access, from any computer connected to the web. These tools have added advantages over the software on your computer in that they are stored securely online and only those invited to participate in a particular conversation or collaboration may do so. They are available from anywhere with an internet connection, and multiple people can edit at the same time. Although all of these are completely accessible from any browser, sometimes you also want to keep them on your own computer. Happily, you can also download your files to your own computer to keep, if you so choose. You and others can create something collaboratively and then publish these documents.

If you asked 100 individuals what their favorite productivity applications online are, it is probable that there would be 100 different answers based entirely on what each person uses and likes the most. These tools typically include word processing, spreadsheets, project management, form generators, sketch tools, and presentations. It would also include other tools, such as a calendar system, task management, project management, and to-do lists. These tools have been termed the Get Things Done (GTD) tools!

Productivity tools from Google, specifically those under the name "Google Apps," represent a collection of products that allow you to do many things. The most commonly used is Google Docs, which is a fairly sophisticated word processor; these apps are tied to a Google account that is linked to a specific email address. In addition, Google offers Google Drive, which is a virtual "hard drive" that allows the user to store products developed using any of the Google Tools. Thus, when you or your students sign up for a Google account, you have access to the "tools" or "apps" and you store your work in the Google Drive. Google Docs has a wide variety of templates to get you started on many of the most common activities (http://drive.google.com/templates?category=7&sort=hottest&pli=1#). You can join more than 3 million viewers in watching

**Figure 4.1** | Google Docs in Plain English: "Say goodbye to messy email attachments"

a Common Craft video called Google Docs in Plain English at www.youtube.com/watch?v=eRqUE6IHTEA (Figure 4.1).

# *Why* Are Productivity Applications Useful Tools?

The answer to this question is relatively simple: imagine if we took away, for a month, the traditional productivity tools that reside on your computer. You would have difficulty doing your job, conducting your personal and professional activities, and perhaps even staying connected with your support system. Let's consider one set of these tools, Google Apps for Education, because it offers the largest suite of tools currently available.

In addition to word processing, a spreadsheet and a presentation tool are built into the Google Apps system. But Google Apps does not stop there. You can also create a calendar (http://calendar.google.com). You can draw, create 3D models, and more, with SketchUp (http://sketchup.com; formerly owned by Google, but still available). You can conduct polls and create forms easily and for free with Google Forms (http://docs.google.com/forms). Finally, Google Sites (http://sites.google.com) allows even beginners to create and publish websites. And again, you have access to a virtual hard drive to store all files and even share them in Google Drive.

However, some schools have an entry point or software platform that goes beyond Google Tools and Apps. Daniel Townsend, District Media and Technology Supervisor for the Godfrey-Lee School District in Wyoming, Michigan, explained the benefit of the product his district uses, Stoneware (www.stone-ware.com). This serves as a software platform that allows you to create a "unified cloud" for your organization. A unified cloud delivers private cloud, public cloud, and local device resources through a common webDesktop with a single password. His district's mascot is the Rebel, and thus, RebelNet (see Figure 4.2) allows for one logon for all administrative, curriculum, and other activities. He said:

> This [product] does not have productivity tools itself, but teachers, students, parents and administrators have an infinite campus. The Google tools sit within this system, so they can look at grades, attendance, network files, maintain a home directory, store files shared or not, easily get to Google docs, spreadsheets, desktop image, calendar, district level activities, and even athletics. (D. Townsend, personal communication, 2013)

Figure 4.2  |  Example of RebelNet entry point

Of course, the use of Google Tools does not stop with the things that we might first think about. The tools allow forms or tests to be developed on the fly, as a formative assessment tool. Parents can see homework activities in the shared spaces. A single calendar organizes routine and other meetings. Overall, this has made the communications within the school seamless, as well as encouraging broad community interaction.

## Some More Useful Productivity Tools

Here are some examples of other programs that will help you grasp the wide variety of possible tools:

**Coggle** (http://coggle.it). Coggle is a free, easy to use mind-mapping tool. Users can sign in with their Google account. Once you create your map, you can share it with others and have them collaborate, or save it as a PDF or PNG.

**eFax** (www.efax.com). Perhaps this is most helpful when you find yourself with email but no fax machine or you wish to make something available to others. This program allows you to receive the fax through a temporarily assigned phone number. You can receive for free, but there is a small price for sending.

**Gliffy** (www.gliffy.com). Gliffy is a collaborative tool for creating graphical representations online and in teams. The products, charts, graphics, or diagrams can be published online.

**Instapaper** (www.instapaper.com). Instapaper is handy when you want to read something but are unable to do it at the time you come across the material (a web page or other document). Once you have registered, you will just click a "read later" button to be able to access it from your computer, a phone, or offline.

**iRows** (www.irows.com). This is another option for spreadsheets that can be stored online and collaboratively constructed. This tool does allow the creation of charts and saves in a variety of formats.

**JotNot Scanner** (http://itunes.apple.com/us/app/jotnot-scanner/id310789464?mt=8). JotNot Scanner is a free downloadable app from iTunes. This app allows you to turn your smartphone camera into a portable scanner. Imagine being at a library when you want to capture detailed information or a graphic.

**SlideShare** (www.slideshare.net). This service has two distinct benefits. First, you can go to the site and search for presentations that others have created on a topic of interest. It is an excellent way to get started learning about themes or content; once you join, you are also able to download some of the presentations. Second, you can post your presentations and then access them from any computer that is online. This makes it easy to create presentations as well as share and receive feedback.

**Smartsheet** (www.smartsheet.com). Smartsheet allows individuals or groups to work to plan a project, assign tasks, collaborate with others, coordinate activities, manage workflow, set reminders, and to collect, organize and track data. This site is not free. However, users are treated to a 30-day free trial, and the program is highly respected in both business and education.

**ThinkFree Office** (www.thinkfree.com). ThinkFree Office is a versatile Java-based tool that allows you to create documents, spreadsheets, and presentations. Your creations can be shared with others online, making collaboration easy.

**30 Boxes** (www.30boxes.com). Simple, with a quick learning curve and sharing that is easily arranged, 30 Boxes might be the calendar of choice for your students. With this one, you can also include an RSS subscription to monitor items of interest or items you wish your students to hear or read.

## More Reasons Why Teachers and Students Use These Tools

Imagine this situation: You and your colleagues create a paper, presentation, or report. You pass the file around, each adding the date or your initials, or both. After several iterations, you are not really sure which is the latest version, whose tracking or changes have been accepted and incorporated, or who has made the final decisions on the document. But assuming you end with the correct version, you show up with your thumb drive only to discover that the best version is not the one you have with you. The correct one is really on your home computer or on the thumb drive in your other coat pocket!

If this has happened to you, or to someone you know, you might begin to understand the lure of Google Apps. One of the authors was in this situation and, instead of the scenario just described, used the Web 2.0 tools effectively. Four people who had never met created a slideshow for presentation to an audience in the U.S. Senate building. Each person added her slides, made comments on them, checked for redundancy and adequate coverage, and then when the time for the presentation arrived, it was readily available online, in its final form. To be sure, each of us had downloaded the presentation and had it on a thumb drive, *just in case!* Had we been delivering the presentation online, we might have chosen to narrate the show; or if we had been delivering it live, the audience might have been able to simultaneously participate in an online chat. The potential is enormous.

Another reason for the enthusiastic embrace of these online productivity tools may be fiscal reality. Schools often spend a significant portion of their technology budget on software and upgrades. Beyond the cost of the software itself, technical and professional development dollars must be expended with each software upgrade. With Web 2.0 tools such as Google Apps, these expenses are no longer necessary. The upgrades are automatic, and the end user is typically not even aware as minor changes are made. Everyone involved is using the same system at the same time.

Most of these tools also include protections and a high level of privacy. The creator of a document allows or invites others into the collaborative process as necessary. The control ensures that no one sees a document until its authors are ready; conversely, drafts can be made public for comment and discussion across a wide group, if desired.

Educators have found some imperfections in these tools. For example, some formatting is not as easy as in the commercial products. Also, as the teacher, identifying individual contributions to collaborative projects requires preplanning. Students may be assigned colors or taught to add their names so that their contributions can be identified. Although these are relatively minor issues, it is important that an educator preview the tools before planning a student project with them. One advantage is that there is a history of revisions so that teachers can see the changes over time since the file was created.

# *When* Do Teachers Use Productivity Tools?

## Classroom Integration

Teachers and other educators have begun using these tools for a variety of activities. As the tools become more familiar, teachers see other ways for students to benefit from them. In general, the goal has been to make public the types of development, creativity, and other activities that their students typically do individually. These tools have also afforded educators a way to promote and encourage collaboration authentically in the development of projects and papers.

On the Classroom 2.0 Ning (www.classroom20.com/forum/topics/wiki-or-google-docs) this appeared:

> My school has been using Google Apps for almost a year now, and we are really liking it. Docs are great for creating content with group members and getting feedback—the draft/brainstorm stages, while Sites have been great for "publishing" or displaying content and creating a showcase of learning. (Allison, blog comment, April 13, 2009)

Melissa Gill, a sixth grade language arts teacher in the Godfrey-Lee School District in Michigan, explains her use of Google Apps:

> I use Google Sites for my class website in conjunction with Google Docs and Google Calendar to keep my students and their families informed with easy access to what we are doing in class. Having my class web based allows my students to access what we are working on anytime, anywhere, on any device. This helps eliminate excuses other than "I don't have internet," which is eliminated by always giving ample time to complete electronic assignments in class and having students stay after school to use the devices and internet to complete assignments.

> Device usage is not limited to the netbooks that are provided by the school. I allow students to use any device they own and

feel comfortable with. I make sure the students are aware that I am only responsible for troubleshooting/fixing the devices that I provide, and otherwise they are on their own. Students enjoy the fact they can use their own devices to complete work from as simple as looking up a definition on the internet to creating a unit final project. Because of this, students become more involved in their work and take more ownership. I receive some creatively unique projects that never cease to amaze me!
(M. Gill, personal communication, July 2013)

Jill Malpass (http://jmalpass.blogspot.com/2009/03/using-google-docs-in-classroom.html) writes in her blog about the ways she has used Google Docs and says her school has accomplished many educational goals by getting started with productivity tools. She describes how her school received funds for a Web on Wheels (WOW) cart with 28 laptops designed to use Web 2.0 tools with learners. She got started in an interesting fashion:

> Ms. Pritchard created a form that she posted on her website for band parents to complete. It was a questionnaire regarding email addresses and other contact information. I clicked on the link to the form, completed my information and submitted. I got a message that my information had been added to her spreadsheet. Instead of spending hours compiling a contact list from handwritten information, the band director created one form, added it to her website, and notified band parents to access the link. In essence the band parents collaboratively completed her contact list for her. This was amazing to me! I was instantly interested in finding out more about Google Docs.
> (J. Malpass, blog post, March 30, 2009)

She went on to explain that her use of the tools has increased. For example, she stated that for her, it "means that teachers can create short quizzes by using a form and posting a link to their website. Students can take the quiz by clicking on the link and signing into their Google account. When their answers are submitted, the teacher's spreadsheet will show the date, time, and username of each submission."

Ana Balboa-Guenthner (www.classroom20.com/main/search/
search?q=Zoho+Writer) asked teacher Kevin how he integrates science and
technology with his middle school science students.

> This year I did a collaborative writing assignment with my
> middle school science class on Zoho Writer. Everyone contrib-
> uted to an ongoing story about how to remember pi (3.14. . . ). I
> taught them the Peg system to remember numbers by changing
> them to letters and words. This way, the students contributed to
> the story from home as an assignment.
>
> I also use WizIQ to tutor some of my students from home. I also
> tutor my MathCounts students on WizIQ as it has an interac-
> tive whiteboard. I will be teaching a class on WizIQ next month
> on how teachers can use the Peg system in class. (Kevin, blog
> comment, May 26, 2008)

His goal of encouraging participation outside of the classroom is one that is
shared by other educators who have come to depend on these tools.

One teacher, Graham Balch (http://sites.google.com/site/grahambalch/
biology) described his use of Google Pages (now Google Sites):

> I have used it as an online syllabus and as you can see all my
> lessons are online as well as my homework assignments. I also
> put my tests and quizzes on there (password protected) so that
> other teachers who use my website as a resource can also get
> the tests and quizzes once I give them the password. (G. Balch,
> blog comment, May 24, 2009)

## Professional Development

Teachers are learning to use these tools in authentic ways. Susan Stein, Johns
Hopkins University School of Education, reports using Google Docs in their
graduate program in administration and supervision. She communicated with
the authors (August 2009) that "cohorts process information and post onto a
common document for submittal to the instructor" routinely.

Nia Ujamaa, technology coordinator, middle school tech, and eighth grade global studies teacher at Mirman School in Los Angeles, California, uses Google Docs to "share research papers with all members of the class to prep for a Jeopardy game about world religions. Each student researched a different belief system, so this allowed them to learn about many in a fun way" (N. Ujamaa, personal communication, June 2013).

Ken Messersmith, University of Nebraska at Kearney, uses Google Docs with his teacher education students who are studying about classroom diversity. He described how he divides students into cooperative learning groups and has each group read a different book on the topic of diversity. Then, using Google Docs, they discuss their book for three weeks, and finally they create a document to share with other students. He said:

> The collaborative nature of Google Docs allows the discussion to take on a chat-like character when two or more students are discussing at the same time but also allows asynchronous discussion to meet the varying schedules of students.
> (K. Messersmith, personal communication, August 2009)

Bruce White, Thames Valley District School Board, London, Ontario, Canada, provides professional development to teachers in his district. He uses Google Docs to prepare the workshop outlines and content and to modify the resources as the course is taught. Participants have access to the document and add to it as they use the resources. Teachers then use Google Docs in their classrooms with their students. He also described a laptop project for which the resources, lesson plans, support, and training material are all posted to Google Docs. He reports that the teachers are enthusiastic about their access and the ability to add to all professional resources.

Jennifer Weible, from the Punxsutawney High School, in Punxsutawney, Pennsylvania, uses Google Docs for creating group documents or projects, writing position papers on authentic learning problems, working with other teachers to plan inservice programs, creating strategic plans for the district, and working together on group projects for online classes.

Cheryl Lyman, from William Tennent High School in Warminster, Pennsylvania, describes her school's use of Google Forms and states that everyone "*loved* them!" They use the forms for feedback on professional development, questionnaires, and anything for which they need information that can be easily tabulated. She added, "One teacher is trying to get Google Forms unblocked for students to take quizzes from her Wikispace this way." Her story brought up an important consideration. In many districts the tools are automatically blocked from students; thus, their potential may not be realized. Lyman explained:

> I am trying to educate administration to realize that Google Docs is a wonderful way for students who have computers but may not have Microsoft Office products to still use word processing and spreadsheet capabilities. I would like to see our elementary students use Google Docs in the classroom, and then we begin teaching the Microsoft Office suite in middle/high schools. Google Docs is a little less intimidating and they can use it at home if they have an internet connection.
> (C. Lyman, personal communication, August, 2009)

As an example of working with adult learners, Michael Wesch from Kansas State University describes his efforts to produce a three-minute video. He calls his project a video ethnography. The goal was to present information about how students learn and what they need to learn, as well as their goals, hopes, dreams, and what kinds of changes they will experience in their lifetimes. He used Google Docs for the students to write a survey for other students, and within a week they had 367 contributions to the document. The process would not have been possible without this type of shared brainstorming and editing. Ultimately, the entire class put together a video of the results of their survey: www.youtube.com/watch?v=tYcS_VpoWJk&list=PL8305209F433E1CA B&feature=c4-overview-vl.

Anthony Carter, the lead teacher for special education in the Quakertown Community School District, Pennsylvania, shared that he has used several Web 2.0 tools in the classroom. But for him, the most effective and influential one has been Google Docs:

> I have used Google Docs for formative assessment as well as classroom culture surveys. Google Docs has[sic] assisted me in collecting readiness information from my students on curriculum skills as well as executive functioning skills. I have used Google Docs to collect present levels of performance data from

teachers. I have also been able to survey students and parents on transition information that directly contributed to IEP development and true team collaboration in the IEP process. I have used the Google Docs to track students' homework and learning target evidence completion through the students self-monitoring and parent and teacher monitoring. After collecting the data I have met with students and parents to compare the data and develop remediation plans or provide celebrations. (A. Carter, personal communication, June 2013)

Petrina Puhl, who teaches AP Biology for Grades 11 and 12 at Robert McQueen High School in Reno, Nevada, uses Google Draw and Google Docs in her classes.

I use flipped learning to help my students gain the knowledge that they need for the AP exam. At the end of each unit they must defend the work they have done on their own. They use Google Draw to map their activities and explain the importance of what they have learned and how it connects to the other learning and activities in the unit. (P. Puhl, personal communication, June 2013)

# *Who* Is Using Productivity Tools for Teaching and Learning?

Productivity tools offer classroom teachers the potential for effective strategies. For example, global activities, which promote project-based learning and international perspectives, become easier when tools facilitate the conversations, collaborations, and interactions. Students are able to develop their own authentic questions based on their interest in other cultures. There is also evidence that students become engaged when they share their work with other students who serve as a real audience. A wide variety of ideas for educational experiences are available at 4Teachers.org's Project Based Learning site. To learn more about the 4Teachers.org project, check out their homepage (www.4teachers.org). Clearly, finding the educational goals and purposes for which these tools can be used will be the first step.

Michele Whaley, a teacher in the Anchorage, Alaska, School District, reports on her use of productivity tools with her students:

**Methodology Training Google Docs.** Last year, a Russian teacher in Alaska and another in California encouraged their students to become acquainted over Google Docs. Both teachers wanted students to practice using the vocabulary to truly communicate with students who didn't know them. This year, a new project began. Students in three schools (an additional one in Moscow, and possibly two more in Siberia) are sharing pictures of their schools and comments about what is important to them at school. Again, the purpose is for students to truly use the vocabulary to communicate.

**Skyping.** Teachers in the Anchorage area are gathering to learn a new methodology once monthly. Because we are so far from the experts, the experts are calling in on Skype. Being able to see the faces and hear questions on both ends makes a huge difference in the amount that we are able to learn.

**Google Docs.** Students honed their short passages about themselves so as to post them on Google Docs. By reading about the other students and directing questions to them, they were able to truly use the language for communication with others who didn't know them and who were interested in people from another area. The teacher has to present the vocabulary and help students to word-process their information. The teachers must also collaborate on the method, the rubric, and a schedule of connections so that students experience communication. (M. Whaley, personal communication, August 2009)

Beth Richards, Division of Accountability and Achievement Resources in New York, reports that students in her district are doing many activities using these tools:

Using [Web] 2.0 tools, students can collaborate on projects. For example, students working in collaborative groups can prepare for a presentation. The students are more interested in the assignment. They don't have to find a home to work in, they can work at any time that is convenient, they can share ideas, peer edit work, reach out to other peers for assistance, and submit to the teacher for review and comment. Students are more inclined to do the project because they are constructing their own knowledge, researching and developing ideas for a broader audience. Their work is done in an environment they are very comfortable in. (B. Richards, personal communication, August 2009)

Peg Weimer, from Paul VI Catholic High School in Fairfax, Virginia, said that in her school "Google Docs is used as both a collaborative tool and electronic storage. Students across the curriculum are producing digital photo stories to summarize information, construct meaning, teach a process, and create infomercials" (P. Weimer, personal communication, August 2009).

Karline Clark, from Douglas High School, in Box Elder, South Dakota, described how she uses Google Docs with her high school students:

> I set students into groups of three. Each group picked a topic of interest to research and present. Students set up a Google Docs and Presentation for their group; they collaborated to put their research, links, pictures, and URLs together. They then used Google Presentation to put their research into a presentation for the class. The best example was when a student who was home sick for the day collaborated with his group via the internet to complete the project on schedule. It continues to grow and evolve every time I use it! (K. Clark, personal communication, August 2009)

Cheryl Lyman, from William Tennent High School in Warminster, Pennsylvania, has her students respond to articles and requires them to summarize and provide their opinion. Only students in the class can respond, and they may respond to each other's discussion. This opens the way for collaboration, and they are sharing these technology tidbits, something she says she does not have time to do in class each week. She summarizes:

> While it has taken me a little bit of time to get this project moving, it has been very easy and I am beginning to see myself as more of a facilitator to my students' learning while they are

collaborators to each other and myself! It is exciting to see them engaged in their own learning—heads aren't down anymore and they are doing work outside of the school walls. (C. Lyman, personal communication, August 2009)

Elizabeth Pressler, from Lamar State College-Orange in Orange, Texas, uses Google Drive as an informal educational tool. She teaches her students how to save files for later access when they are not carrying a flash drive. This "just in time" intervention helps her "students learn about file size, different file types, cloud storage, general online literacy" (E. Pressler, personal communication, June 2013). Pressler works with students who have little experience with technology.

Renee Markley, Roger Kortes, and Mr. Beale, math teachers in the San Juan School District in Orangevale, California, routinely use Sketchup for projects. Their website (www.sanjuan.edu/webpages/pribadeneira/view.cfm?subpage=77265) states,

Students will design a house of their choice using the application Google SketchUp. Mathematics skills such as four quadrant graphing and trig functions will be used, as well as an interactive protractor and ruler. When complete, each project must be made into an animation movie to be shown to the class.

Another place to find great ideas for using Sketchup in mathematics can be found at http://mathforum.org/sketchup. But other uses for it abound. Jeff Patin, the technology teacher at the Godfrey-Lee Middle/High School in Wyoming, Michigan, for his technology applications class, also uses Sketchup to develop design features. His students began by designing and redesigning their school and finished by designing their dream house and yard.

Tara Seale, a ninth grade English teacher at Bryant High School in Bryant, Arizona, reports on a day devoted to digital citizenship, netiquette, and the school's core values for ninth graders. She stated that the students meet in advisory groups and do some small group activities, then "break into groups around the core values and the students choose the Web 2.0 tools they want to use to send a message (movie, poster, comic, etc.). Google Apps drive the whole site and allowed us to receive feedback quickly and easily" (T. Seale, personal communication, August 2009).

Using the tools is not confined to traditional classroom settings. David Gibson, from Stowe, Vermont, describes the Global Challenge Award and his efforts to create global work teams of high school students. They create four student teams (two U.S. teams and two from outside the United States) that use a variety of tools to create a solution to global warming. Teams may submit their goals as either a global business plan or technical innovation plan, or they may just work on content "Explorations." These efforts are judged, and teams may earn letters, certificates, and cash or prizes. Gibson said, "The students form their own teams using a custom Web 2.0 application, then use a wiki-style content system, electronic portfolio, and a variety of tools such as Skype, SketchUp, Google Docs, etc., to perform the activity" (D. Gibson, personal communication, August 2009).

Matt Gomez, a kindergarten teacher at Plano ISD in Plano, Texas, uses Google Docs to aid teaching science, geography, and digital citizenship. He uses collaboration on Google Docs with live games. This technology allows him to teach his young students how to become good digital citizens. Gomez shared that this technique allows his "students to experience the world outside their school bubble and learn about geography and science as we collaborate" (M. Gomez, personal communication, June 2013). You can see examples of this exciting work here: http://mattbgomez.com/playing-20-questions-live-via-google-docs.

More information on Global Challenge activities is available at: http://en.wikipedia.org/wiki/Global_Challenge_Award

# Why We Use Google Tools

## Mike Malcolm

> *We invited Mike Malcolm, the principal of Leamington Elementary School, Cambridge, New Zealand, to tell us why he made the decision to go totally to open access and Google tools, apps, and other easily available software for his teachers and students. Here is his answer:*

It is important to step back and consider the bigger question that we asked, which was why we had to make any decision in the first place! The key driver for effective ICT implementation, I believe, is to have a clear picture of what pedagogy lies around effective learning for children in a future focused education system. Our core beliefs around what will make learning effective for children is to provide an education that will be relevant both now and for their future lives around what we call our 5 C's: Communication, Collaboration, Creativity, Connections, and Consumers (about to become our 6 C's as we are looking at adding another "C"—Curiosity).

When a clear picture of how we want our children to engage in their learning is formed, then the technology in many ways becomes invisible as we are able to focus primarily on "How can we most effectively allow this to happen?" which means that the second question, "What tools best facilitate this?" in many ways answers itself. Drawing an analogy to a toolbox, it is easy to find a suitable tool when you have a clear understanding of the task at hand. A hammer is a great tool (and one of my favourites!) but is completely ineffective when the task at hand is to hang a picture on a concrete wall, which requires a screw to be drilled into the wall. Knowing what the task requires allows the many distractions in the toolbox to be quickly laid aside.

With this backdrop, the decisions we made/make can occur fluently as we sift through various options (free and paid apps, Google tools, etc.) to see what will best allow us to develop our "C"s. It is also important to note that no one person made these decisions for our organisation. I believe having the right people sitting in the right seats, who can see issues from a range of perspectives and collaborate together, and actually giving them the authority to make important decisions for our organisation is essential to maximise the potential that they bring. (A question I often challenge our team with is, "A champion team will always beat a team of champions, but what would have happened if a team full of champions could work together as a champion team?") My role as a leader then is to keep us focused on what we are trying to achieve and measure whatever we choose against this to see if it better allows us to achieve our goals.

We are not constantly looking for better apps; rather we are constantly looking for more effective ways to engage children in learning experiences that we believe are important. Apps like Pages, which on the surface cost more than other apps (including free apps like Notes), actually allow our children to engage with a range of media (photos, graphs, tables, text, etc.) to create, communicate, and collaborate in more powerful ways than other apps we have looked at. The opportunity cost of choosing an app that may be cheaper (or free) is the lost potential for children to express their thoughts as fully as possible. Our bottom line is not the size of our bank balance, but rather the strength of the creativity that is being expressed/developed. Google Docs and other Google tools provide an opportunity for children to collaborate in real time with a range of people in a very authentic way. Whilst it does not have the smooth feel of Pages, in the context of children focusing on their work and getting and giving immediate feedback on the work engaged in, it is not an impediment. Being able to cut and paste this finished work into an app like Pages to then deliver a quality finish with other media means we maximise the potential each app brings. Choices around moving away from Dropbox to Google Drive were made as we looked for ways to more effectively share work to collaborate with others at different times and in different places—and in the same place at the same time as well. (The extra space that Google Drive offers, as opposed to Dropbox, is a bonus, but did not carry any weight in our decision making.)

It is this resolve to focus on what is really important to us that allows us to now make decisions about both hardware and software, free versus paid, online versus local, mobile versus stationary, BYOD versus supplied in an efficient and focused manner. Chromebooks is cool, but it doesn't allow us to take photos and movies and work with these instantly, which is something we value our children doing. iPad 4s are great, but the iPad 2 still allows us to do everything we want to do, meaning we can maximise our budget. This focus also means that we can evolve quickly because we are not changing our focus for our teachers. Flip-flopping from one app to another is one of the biggest deterrents for our reluctant adopters. Focus on what we are trying to do for children, and then teachers talking about, leading, and exploring the most effective ways to do this means we can gain more traction, which ultimately results in better outcomes and contexts for our children.

# *How* Do You Get Started with Productivity Tools?

We are using Google Drive and its tools as our example in getting started because it is the most popular, but also because others will be very similar in terms of what you will need to do.

To begin your adventure of using online productivity tools, start by reviewing this video on Google Drive (http://howto.cnet.com/8301-11310_39-57419559-285/how-to-get-started-with-google-drive/). Once you are ready to begin, there are a few steps to take.

First, you need to create an account for your classroom. Your students will need to have an email address. If your school provides email addresses all within the same domain name, then you can sign up as a team (www.google.com/enterprise/apps/business). However, it does cost to use this method. Otherwise, you can sign up as individuals, again making sure that all your students have an email address. Once you have the email addresses, you simply create a Google account (Figure 4.3). Students must be 13 to use Google Apps and Google Drive at school; however, Daniel Townsend stated that his Grades 3 through 12 students have accounts, so it is possible to organize that. In addition, you will want to start with your own account to gain familiarity with the tools. We encourage you and your colleagues to begin by creating documents and sharing them collaboratively with your department, team, or group.

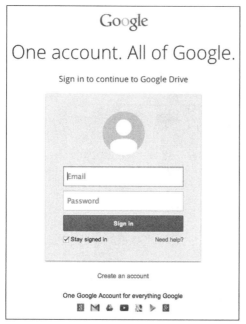

**Figure 4.3** | Getting started with a Google account

Once you have your account, you can begin with the tools, for example, Google Docs, just as you would in a word processor. From your Google Drive starting page, you can select Create, and at that point you will be able to create a document, presentation, spreadsheet, form, or drawing.

To share that document, you will click on the Share tab and enter the email addresses of the individuals with whom you wish to share. These individuals do not have to have a Gmail account to receive your information, but to access the document they do need to have a Google account tied to a specific email address. You can assign permission to others who "Can View," "Can Comment," or "Can Edit." There is a 200-person limit per document (which does seem like quite a large number!), and there is a limit to how many individuals can be editing simultaneously. For documents and presentations, that limit is 10; for the spreadsheet, 50 can edit at one time. A document on how to use Google Docs was created using (no surprise) Google Docs (http://docs.google.com/View?docid=dcdn7mjg_72nh25vq). It provides some excellent information to expand your understanding about using these tools. You may also want to listen to a podcast, Google Docs in Education (www.twenty-fortech.com/?tag=google-docs-in-education).

Figure 4.4 provides a view of the entry page once you have established a Google account. You can see all the things you can do from this screen.

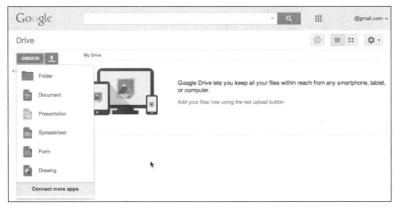

**Figure 4.4** | Interface of Google Drive

Another excellent reason to use these types of systems is that they have an interface that is similar to the one many people are familiar with. For example, similar icons to commonly used word processing programs are used, and a mouse-over produces reminders for the icons. Figure 4.5 shows the familiar layout of the document toolbar.

**Figure 4.5** | Toolbar from Google Docs

# *Where* Can You Find More Information about Productivity Tools?

Try this crib sheet for using Google Apps in education:
www.google.com/educators/learning_materials/WR_cribsheet.pdf

This site is especially for educators getting started with Google Tools:
www.google.com/edu/teachers

Watch a video on ways that teachers are using Google Sites in their professional practice (To view the video, you need to login to TeacherTube):
www.teachertube.com/viewVideo.php?video_id=255377

View this video of teachers and principals talking about Google Docs in education:
www.youtube.com/watch?v=TYPjJK6LZdM

Don't miss the Common Craft video on Google Docs:
www.commoncraft.com/
google-docs-video-over-million-views-you-tube

# 5

# Social Networks

## *What* Is Social Networking?

Educators have always had communities of practice; in the past, though, a teacher's community may have been the teachers in a particular school, or all the math educators in a district. The point of communicating with others is to learn, develop, and expand all that we know; to share ideas and information; or just to enjoy social interactions.

One definition of social networking comes from Green and Hannon (2007):

> Social networking refers to the aspect of Web 2.0 that allows users to create links between their online presence such as a webpage or a collection of photos. These links may be through joining online groups or by assigning direct links to other users through lists of "friends" or contacts. (p. 13)

It is widely accepted that learning has a strong social component, and that this learning often is situated in our relationships with others (Lave & Wenger, 1991). With the advent of electronic communications and communities, the possibilities have expanded so that people affiliate by interests, questions, or ideas rather than geographically or by happenstance.

Many examples of social networking are evident on the web. These include communities discussing medical issues, playing games, and planning a trip to the moon. Educators often engage in discussions about learning, pedagogy, curriculum, assessment, and standards. In fact, the web is filled with millions of individuals who are looking to meet others who share their interests and goals.

According to one explanatory website (www.whatissocialnetworking.com), some networking communities focus on particular interests, and others do not. The websites without a main focus are often referred to as "traditional" social networking websites and usually have open memberships. This means that anyone can become a member, no matter what their hobbies, beliefs, or views are. However, once you are inside this online community, you can begin to create your own network of friends and eliminate members that do not share common interests or goals.

Wikipedia says:

> A social networking service is a platform to build social networks or social relations among people who, for example, share interests, activities, backgrounds, or real-life connections. A social network service consists of a representation of each user (often a profile), his/her social links, and a variety of additional services. Most social network services are web-based and provide means for users to interact over the internet, such as email and instant messaging. ... Social networking sites allow

users to share ideas, pictures, posts, activities, events, and interests with people in their network.

According to Statistic Brain's social networking statistics (www.statisticbrain.com/social-networking-statistics), online social networks have emerged as the new way in which people connect socially. The leader currently is Facebook with more than 1.2 billion members. Based on poll results, 56% are on some type of social network, and 98% of those aged 18–24 say they use social media (as of November 2012). In another survey (http://socialhabit.com/downloads), over half of social networking users are between 12 and 34 years of age. Of those, they are sharing more personal information on social media sites: 91% share a photo of themselves with their profile (up from 79% in 2006), 92% use their real name on their most-used profile, and 20% include their cell phone number (Madden et al., 2012). Web-based social networking services make it possible to connect people who share interests and activities across political, economic, and geographic borders.

Some of the things that distinguish and support the way social networking works in this environment include the fact that comments or artifacts are tagged as a way to categorize content. Those tags can be created and managed collaboratively, and that adds to the collective development of knowledge. This system of classification is termed *folksonomy* (Wikipedia reports that this term comes from *folk* and *taxonomy*) and is also known by the terms *collaborative tagging, social classification, social indexing,* and *social tagging.* In addition, the possibility exists for the software to offer recommendations to individuals based on their usage, and people are able to identify so-called friends, which then allows individuals to stay current with what those friends are doing or saying.

The concept and adoption of social networking has become so important that now institutions are creating courses on social networking and Web 2.0. What's interesting is that it's not just a presentation or learning event but an actual full course. In 2010 we found one institution, the University of Arizona, that intended its students to learn about Web 2.0 products and social networking; in 2013, the number of these courses has expanded dramatically. In fact, dozens of free online classes related to social media exist (http://kommein.com/25-free-online-social-media-classes) at the post-secondary level, and many are offered at the high school level. There is an abundance of jobs in social media.

# *Why* Is Social Networking a Useful Tool?

Humans are social creatures, and educators as well as students want to communicate with others. Facebook and Twitter are usually the first social networks people think of. Millions of individuals have joined these networks from all parts of the world and all walks of life, and one can find discussions on just about any topic. The main types of social networking services are those that contain category divisions (such as former school-year or classmates), the means to connect with friends (usually with self-description pages), and a recommendation system dependent on trust. Popular methods now combine many of these, with Facebook widely used worldwide. Across the globe, other networks have emerged, too: Facebook, Twitter, and LinkedIn are the most widely used in North America; Copains d'Avant is very popular in France, Hyves is favored in the Netherlands, and Tuenti remains important in Spain, and in Germany Facebook, Google+, and Xing top the list (socialmediatoday. com). In Asia, WeChat is popular in China, KakaoTalk is popular in South Korea, and the social network Line continues to maintain a strong user base in Japan. Some believe that Asian social networks will continue to grow (WeChat, KakaoTalk, and Line) and may surpass Facebook in popularity once they reach North America and Europe (wired.com). Others you may have heard of include Tagged, XING, Badoo, Skyrock, Friendster, Multiply, Orkut, Wretch, Xiaonei, and Cyworld. Each of these has people who are passionate about their particular service, but in general they all work in similar ways.

A recent study (Project Tomorrow, 2013c) looked at access to mobile devices. It found that 59% of 6th graders, 75% of 9th graders, and 82% of 12th grade students have access to a personal smartphone. Increasingly, these students use their devices as their primary access to the Internet. Equally interesting, 71% of high school students and 63% of middle school students use text messages to communicate. According to a recent review by Edudemic (http://edudemic. com/wp-content/uploads/2013/05/socialmedia-school.png), the following information was identified:

- 69% of U.S. school districts have student website programs

- 22% are involved in creating or maintaining wikis

- 46% have students participate in online pen pal or other international programs

- 35% have student and/or instructor-run blogs

- 27% have teacher/principal online community

- 59% say at least half their staff members participate in social networking for educational purposes

Dodge, Barab, and Stuckey (2008) argue that social networks are analogous to:

> third spaces … informal public spaces such as coffee houses, affording novelty, diversity, and learning. Unfettered by school protocol or family emotions, third spaces allow groups to meet in generous numbers, and while no individual constitutes the third space, close friendships can be developed unlike those found at home or school. (p. 229)

Educators used to be reluctant to use social networking tools in the classroom, or even to encourage students to participate in them (Ferdig, 2007; Green & Hannon, 2007); that seems to be changing. Instead, the idea emerged that if individuals or groups of individuals could start their own social network, they might be able to better organize, protect, and define the goals of that "space." Thus, in 2005, Ning (www.ning.com) was started as an online platform for people to create their own social networks. The term Ning is Chinese for "peace," and the number of Nings has expanded quickly. A popular site now is The Educator's PLN (personal learning network), and this Ning offers opportunities for educators to share, collaborate, and develop joint projects (http://edupln.ning.com). Many other educational social networking sites have also appeared; in general, they all share similar characteristics and features. These are some of the advantages of educators' social networking sites:

- Small groups can collaborate on projects.

- Students can post questions and concerns.

- The site can be used to retain teacher notes, videos, podcasts, and other classroom activities.

- Students who are absent can catch up on work.

- Students can develop, collaborate, and retain their own efforts over time.

- Access can be granted to families and others to share the information.

Other educational social networking examples abound. For example, LibraryThing (www.librarything.com) is a social network of 1.7 million people who love books. Participants catalog their own books and are then connected to others who read what they do, for conversation and recommendations. They call it the world's largest book club. Perhaps Rushkoff (2005) said it best: "It's the simplest lesson of the internet . . . it's the people, stupid. We don't have computers because we want to interact with machines; we have them because they allow us to communicate more effectively with other people" (p. 74).

Tapscott and Williams (2006) summed up the nature of social networking:

> While the old web was about websites, clicks, and "eyeballs," the new web is about communities, participation, and peering. As users and computer power multiply, and easy-to-use tools proliferate, the internet is evolving into a global, living, networked computer that anyone can program. Even the simple act of participating in an online community makes a contribution to the new digital commons—whether one's building a business on Amazon or producing a video clip for YouTube, creating a community around his or her Flickr photo collection, or editing the astronomy entry on Wikipedia. (p. 19)

There are many ways that people are connected on social networking sites. Some sites use profile matching, which requires individuals to enter personal details that are either matched against the profiles of others or searchable by others. Some are personal networks that have shared contacts systems: databases of contacts and contacts of contacts. These are often geared to plain sociability (e.g., Facebook) or are for business contacts (LinkedIn).

One other type of matching is an affinity system that allows people to register their membership of groups. Thus, you may be a member of the 1989 high school graduating class from Thomas Jefferson High School, or you may be someone who worked at Apple from 1990 to 1995. Then, others who match those requirements can be found in a simple search on one criterion (Owen, Grant, Sayers, & Facer, 2006).

# *When* Do Teachers Use Social Networking?

Social networks have been focused on supporting relationships between teachers as well as between teachers and their students. Moreover, these networks are now used for learning, professional development of educators, and content sharing. A variety of sites have evolved specifically to provide the type of content that encourages and supports teacher-specific activities and needs. For example, Ning for teachers (www.ning.com), School Net Global (www.schoolnetglobal.com), Learnhub (http://learnhub.com), and other sites are being built to foster relationships via educational blogs, e-portfolios, and formal and ad hoc communities. Social networks also encourage communication through chats, discussion threads, and synchronous forums. These sites also have content-sharing and rating features.

Perhaps one of the most popular places for educators is Classroom 2.0 (www.classroom20.com). It offers a feature that allows users to select the level of privacy needed. It also includes a forums feature, a feature to personalize pages, embedded blogging, groups, chat options, and an easy way for students to embed media. This site has guides for beginners, forums to exchange information, a network for creating collaborative projects, and an easy way to start new discussions. There are also archives of podcasts, lessons, and interviews, as well as other items of particular interest to educators.

Another popular site is Edmodo (www.edmodo.com), which serves multiple functions. Its byline states, "Where learning happens. Edmodo helps connect all learners with the people and resources needed to reach their full potential." Barbara Levin, professor at University of North Carolina, Greensboro, teaches current and future teachers about curriculum, as well as about thoughtful use of technology. She says:

> Edmodo is a free, easy-to-use course management tool. Students like it because it feels like Facebook, and teachers like it because it has an excellent grade book, a seemingly unlimited library that will house numerous types of files, and ways to post group or individual messages, assignments, polls, and quizzes. Overall, it is easy to organize and create multiple classes with

multiple groups. Edmodo adds new features periodically—most recently a squiggly red line under spelling errors. One of the best features of Edmodo is the ability to connect with other educators interested in the same things you are. When you ask, someone answers your questions about content, curriculum, or technical issues almost immediately.

## Classroom Integration

Teachers are known to do whatever will help their students learn. And students these days are using social networking tools seamlessly and smoothly. The National School Boards Association (2007) reports that almost 60% of students who use social networking talk about education topics online; surprisingly, more than 50% talk specifically about schoolwork. Yet the vast majority of school districts have stringent rules against nearly all forms of social networking during the school day, even though students and parents report few problem behaviors online.

One study (Crook, 2008) suggests the relationship between Web 2.0 tools and learning:

> A second significant reason for educators to turn to Web 2.0 is that it seems to fit with certain experiences emphasised in contemporary theories of learning and modern thinking about how best to design the conditions of learning. Within the psychology of learning, there are four influential but overlapping frameworks (this term more appropriate than "theories"). These are: behaviourism, constructivism, cognitivism, and the socio-cultural perspective. (p. 30)

It is worth asking if teachers believe that students will learn better and develop better skills when being taught by traditional methods or if they believe students will learn better and develop new and unique skills when teachers create a learning environment that includes Web 2.0 social networking tools. There is some evidence that the large number of humans engaged in Web 2.0 may be the key to innovative thinking and problem solving (Surowiecki, 2004). The most straightforward reason for using Web 2.0 for teaching must be recognition that young people are already engaged by Web 2.0

applications. So, for pupils, there will be familiarity with a style of interacting and inquiry that arises from browsing within these spaces, even when the young learner has not been an active producer. In a research study, Green and Hannon (2007) found that teachers, parents, and students agree on the types of learning that come from the use of these digital tools, especially social networking, as shown in Table 5.1:

**Table 5.1 | DIGITAL SKILLS**

| Social / Personal | Cognitive / Physical | Technical |
|---|---|---|
| • Communication | • Multitasking | • Hand–eye coordination |
| • General knowledge | • Logical thinking | • Technical confidence |
| • Creativity | • Problem solving | • Web design/content creation |
| • Collaboration | • Trial-and-error learning | |
| • Self-esteem | | |
| • Parallel processing | | |
| • Persistence | | |
| • Peer-to-peer learning | | |
| • Risk taking | | |

Source: *Their Space: Education for a Digital Generation*, p. 36

In addition to the obvious goal of supporting instruction, learners' needs and interests, and the attainment of digital-age skills, educators, of course, want to improve their practice. One educator wrote about his number one reason to use technology in English language teaching:

> I have thought about this long and hard. I'm not a big proponent of using "tech for tech's sake" or just because it is there and students like it. I sympathize with the argument that we should use technology because it is such a ubiquitous part of our life/living (or that of our students'). However, I still think we need a reason, a rationale for its use. In general, technology is valuable for what it does to the continuum of space and time. Technology allows us to access knowledge like never before—the library doors are wide open and so many can enter. There

is no bottleneck and no 9 to 5 access. So I did consider the #1 reason to use tech as being "time on task" or "connectivity". Students have more access to language, the distinctions between ESL and EFL are blurring, they can have more contact with language through online immersive experiences and contacts. Still, I'm voting for differentiation when it comes to "teaching", when it comes to the typical language classroom. (http:// ddeubel.edublogs.org/author/ddeubel; ddeubel, blog comment, May 7, 2013)

## Professional Development

Teachers are very happy to share their favorite websites and their reasons for joining together through social networks and electronic learning communities. Examples of such networks abound, and the difficulty is in choosing some to feature. Your favorite may not be here, but we encourage you to check out the following, too.

### BLC/MELC Middle School Teachers in Action

The Maryland Electronic Learning Community has as part of its network a Baltimore Learning Community of Middle School Teachers in Action (www. cs.umd.edu/hcil/blc/partners.html). Their goal is to develop a library of multimedia learning resources and facilitate interaction among teachers. This began with five middle schools and 35 teachers but is being expanded to high schools as well. It includes an extensive collection of video clips, lesson plans with metadata tags, and content organized by topic that is also aligned to the Maryland learning outcomes. It even includes a feature similar to social bookmarking, in that teachers can document their favorites in a public fashion, on an individual "bookshelf," and can enter their own materials into the community digital library. It is searchable, so that you can find other teachers' recommendations and then examine other resources used by those with whom you have some affinity.

### TERC MSPnet

TERC has long been involved in teacher professional development and now has taken another step. For some time TERC has supported a Math Science Partnership in a variety of ways. The TERC MSPnet (Math Science Partnership

Network) provides the MSP program with a web-based, interactive electronic community. Its goal is to build capacity and expand each educator's level of knowledge regarding the MSP projects, but in addition, they strive to increase the development of the entire learning community. They call their network "An Electronic Community of Practice Facilitating Communication and Collaboration" (http://mspnet.mspnet.org).

## DO-IT

The National Center on Accessible Information Technology in Education offers another electronic community and a promising practice in creating a completely accessible electronic community, DO-IT (Disabilities, Opportunities, Internetworking, and Technology). It is designed to allow educators, students, and mentors an opportunity to exchange information.

The center provides computers, assistive technology, and internet connections for the homes of disabled college-bound teens who have been accepted into the DO-IT Scholars program. Participants have many different types of disabilities, including those that affect the ability to hear, see, speak, learn, and move. The community offers many ways to interact to accommodate all disabilities. To learn more about the program, check out www.washington. edu/doit.

### Kansas Future Teachers

Some faculty members at postsecondary teacher education institutions have found authentic ways to introduce preservice teachers to social networking tools and to help them begin to build a sense of the professional learning community. As part of their responsibilities, students participate in an electronic Ning with inservice teachers. In Kansas this is called Kansas Future Teachers (http://futureteachers.ning.com), and the teachers from the trenches join with students in the discussions. Cyndi Danner-Kuhn, who runs this program, states, "The Teachers from the Trenches add the real meat and guts to the discussions." She welcomes others to join her conversation and has as a goal helping new teachers (who are expected to know and use new tools easily) to understand the complexity of, and rationale for, using such tools in pedagogically strong ways.

## Additional Nings and Communities

Some Nings are for all educators to join and share—for example, Fireside Learning: Conversations about Education, which invites educators to "sit by the fireside and share your thoughts" (http://firesidelearning.ning.com). English educators hold a virtual book club through the English Companion Ning (http://englishcompanion.ning.com) and have been finding ways to support their own personal and professional growth.

Educators who have specialized responsibilities also are using the features of social networking to improve their professional activities. Teacher-librarians and other educators (http://teacherlibrarian.ning.com) have created a way to work, share, and help each other. Teachers of English as a Foreign Language have a place to learn ways to improve their practice at EFL Classroom 2.0 (http://eflclassroom.ning.com).

Some of these social networks are comprehensive, such as the ISTE network of communities for educators who wish to interact with other technology-using educators (www.iste-community.org), or the ones that national organizations run for content-specific educators: for example, the National Council of Teachers of English (http://sites.google.com/site/onlinereadingandwriting/stuff-of-interest/nationalcouncilofteachersofenglishnctening), National Council for the Social Studies (http://ncssnetwork.ning.com), or Art Educators Ning (http://arted20.ning.com).

Others are more narrowly focused:

- High school math teachers (www.classroom20.com/group/highschoolmathteachers)

- Middle School Portal 2: Math & Science Pathways Online Social Network (www.msteacher2.org)

- Secondary art teachers (http://naea-secondary-teachers.ning.com)

- Synapse for biology teachers worldwide (http://thesynapse.ning.com)

- Teaching Digital history (http://teachingdigitalhistory.ning.com)

- Smart Board Revolution, for teachers who use interactive whiteboards (http://plus.google.com/communities/114280125118878234579?hl=en&partnerid=gplp0) Note: this is a Google+ community so you will need to have a Google+ account.)

## Twitter

Administrators also use social networking sites for both communication and personal growth. Michael Waiksnis, principal of Sullivan Middle School in South Carolina, said this about his Twitter network and social media in general:

**Web 2.0 Wisdom**

### Social Media

Michael Waiksnis

Social media and social networking has completely transformed the way I carry out my job responsibilities and lead our school. It has proved to be a powerful personal professional medium for learning as well as a very effective way to communicate with my school community.

I have been very active on Twitter for several years. When I started using Twitter, I thought I would give it a try and see what everyone was talking about. I will admit I was slow to catch on several years ago. However, once I started to see the potential, I was hooked! Twitter is the probably the best professional development I have had in my career. You have total control over when and where, and you get to choose the topic! Once you get going, you develop a lot of followers and connections on Twitter. This is where the true power comes into play. I get to learn from teachers, administrators, college professors, and anyone else across the world. It is powerful. We share ideas, share links, and have great time learning from others with similar and different perspectives. Simply powerful.

Social media has also assisted in our school's quest to improve parent communication and "brand" our school. We noticed on our school report card that many parents did not feel we communicated well. In today's changing world of education, we knew we had to act. As more and more options for education become available for parents, we knew we had to tell our story. We did not want to leave it to chance with our local media or the "grapevine." We knew we had to share all of the great things going on in our school. These thoughts led us down the road we have traveled the last several years.

Our first social media tool was creating a principal's podcast. Basically, this was an audio recording of what was going on around our school that I posted to a website. While it served a purpose at the time, it quickly became too cumbersome to keep updated on a regular basis. This podcast turned into our school blog. It can be found at sullivanms.edublogs.org. The first post was posted in July of 2008. That's right, 5 years ago. This can be quickly updated and parents can count on it to keep them up to date on the great things happening on SMS. It can also be subscribed to via email so the news gets sent directly to our community. We have shared this with our local media as well. We want them to be aware of the great things as well.

As the social media landscape continued to evolve, we knew we needed to as well. In addition to our news blog, we started a school Twitter account. This can be found at twitter.com/smfalcons. This tool has become much more popular over the years and it is very easy to keep up to date. We post frequently on some of the great things going on at our school. We also have a school Facebook page. These are two very popular ways we continue to use to brand our school and tell our story. Our school Facebook page is very popular and a great way to keep parents informed. If you have middle school experience, you know notes, notices, and information often get trapped in a locker and never escape! We have found several ways to circumvent this fact of adolescent life.

We also use the service Constant Contact to keep in touch with our school community via email. This is the only paid service we use for school commu- nication and branding. However, it is well worth the small cost. We set up email groups at the beginning of the year and use them on a regular basis. Our teacher teams also use some form of electronic communication to send out team updates, homework information, etc. Our student work showcase has become a popular spot for parents to visit electronically to see student work. This is a website, and we add all types of student work samples to show off their great work! Finally, we have started using a service that allows us to send text messages to our families. We use this on a limited basis. It has come in very handy when we have had weather related closings and early dismissals. We have decided this tool would be used rarely and only for these types of messages.

Through the use of these technology tools we have been able to help shape the story of our school. Unfortunately, the general public often has a poor perception of schools. We have decided to take this into our own hands and do something about it. We know all of our schools have tremendous things happening each and every day. We just want to make sure our parents and the public get a regular glance at the "real" Sullivan Middle School.

*Michael Waiksnis, Sullivan Middle School, sms.rock-hill.k12.sc.us @smfalcons*

# *Who* Is Using Social Networking for Teaching and Learning?

It is challenging to select a few of the many examples of ways that teachers are using social networking in classrooms to improve student learning, to support inquiry and self-directed learning, and to expand students' horizons. The following examples run the gamut of what is possible and are offered for two reasons. First, it is quite a tribute to our fellow educators to see the wide range of ideas and creativity that they have come up with. Second, we hope that you will be inspired and encouraged by something that you read here and, also, recognize the similarities that bind all of these projects. You may decide to try to adapt one of the ideas you read here, or you may figure out a way to change something to fit your curriculum. Whichever works for you, we hope you will try a project that fits your and your students' style and educational goals.

Educators have created a wide variety of ways to involve their students in social networking. One teacher uploaded a song to a Ning and asked the students to interpret the lyrics. A math teacher has been using a Ning to post homework and share a "puzzle of the week." In addition, the teacher has been embedding VoiceThreads into the Ning to share test preparation tips and for student mathcasts. Through a Ning, U.S. college students are connecting with adult learners of English from a language school in Spain. This teacher said, "I like [the Ning] better than Blackboard for certain tasks. I definitely feel more connected to my students than before, which I think is essential in foreign language teaching (to reduce students' anxiety)" (P. Munday, blog comment, February 22, 2009).

**Project Peace** (http://projectpeace.ning.com) is one social community designed to teach English through students' singing, promoting peace. Their stated goal is "Project Peace is a place for educators and students to sing, learn English, and help make this world more peaceful." Teachers join the network, and then their students create videos, podcasts, and other projects to post online along with others from around the globe.

**English Companion** (http://englishcompanion.ning.com/group/teachingwith technology/forum/topics/introducing-ning-to-students) is an English education-tion Ning set up to foster the use of Nings in classroom curriculum and to help teachers begin the journey of integrating these tools into the classroom. One teacher, Susanne Nobles, Fredericksburg Academy, Fredericksburg, Virginia, said:

> I am just now finishing a Ning unit with my seniors and got some feedback from them about how it went. They loved it! They felt very comfortable with how the Ning is set up and works because of their experience with other social networking sites, so I think showing it to them, then giving them some time to play on it (get their personal pages set up, write on each other's walls, maybe do a quick first blog post) would start things off well. We are a laptop school, so I do this in my class-room, but I think for this first day in a non-laptop school, you should bring them to the lab to get started all together. I think they will understand the site pretty quickly. (S. Nobles, blog post, March 15, 2009)

One of the results of becoming known in the educational social networking community is that one activity often results in other opportunities. After Susanne Nobles posted the results of her activities, she received a message from another teacher:

> Hi Susanne. I was wondering if you and your students would be interested in participating in a nationwide SAT Vocab Video Contest @ MIT university. If not, perhaps you have some educator contacts you could direct me to. You can view contest details at BrainyFlix.com. Please let me know. Thanks. (Jack, blog comment, March 2009)

**FieldFindr** (http://fieldfindr.wikispaces.com) aims to connect global volunteers with teachers and their students. Teachers can create posts if they are looking for volunteers or people who have expert knowledge to enrich their classes' study of global topics such as immigration, peace studies, playgrounds, and the Holocaust. Teachers can also search for other collaborators through posted comments.

**Rolling on the River** (http://rollingontheriver.ning.com) is centered on the study of rivers and other bodies of water. It is "a resource for global collaboration" where users can "share information, find global partners, and learn more about rivers, lakes, and oceans through participation and collaboration." Teachers also share web resources, and videos of the projects are available on this site to inspire teachers and learners.

**Greenovation** (www.greenovationnation.com) is designed to "energize education and inspire action." Many teachers have gone to Greenovation to engage their students or the entire school in a project designed to consider the environment. The website has a counter to record the kilowatt hours saved due to their efforts, and it also has a contest to engage students: "If you could dream up the ultimate energy-efficient classroom of the future, what would it look like? Lutron Greenovation invites you to take a good look at your entire school—from the classroom to the science lab to the lunchroom and beyond—and tell us your big, bright ideas for improving energy efficiency."

**Digiteen** (http://digiteen.ning.com) is a place for teens to communicate in a Ning that focuses on what it means to be a digital teenager today. It also offers a private and safe place for teens to post their own social information because the pages are protected and only available to those the teen allows. For an example of how one teen put together what she learned, check out the SlideShare production at www.slideshare.net/Gemma58284/digital-citizenship-1589336?type=presentation.

**Flat Classrooms** (http://flatconnections.net) is designed for transforming learning through global collaboration. It was started for the purpose of "Fostering new ways of learning using Web 2.0 and global collaborative 'flat classroom' ideals and practices." Here, teachers find projects from classrooms around the world or post their ideas of connections they would like to start.

One thing seems certain: once a teacher starts down the road of including social media tools in teaching, it seems to take off in unanticipated directions. For example Tara Seale reports:

> I have discovered that in an English classroom, Nings are useful in engaging students who are involved in a lengthy, difficult read. My ninth grade English students participated in a Ning called Verona Lifestyles, which I created specifically for the class as we read *Romeo and Juliet*. Students signed up and became a member of the Ning as a character from the play. My students responded to and posted blogs and forum comments on the Ning while in character. Not only did the Ning activity increase the students' interest in the play, but students were forced to closely read the play to understand the complexity and motivations of their character in order to create a believable persona. Incorporating this fun, engaging, and creative activity balanced out the difficulty students were having in trying to interpret the archaic language of the play, kind of a reward for their hard work. (T. Seale, personal communication, August 2009) [Note: this site is no longer active but represents a creative way for a teacher to use a Ning.]

A middle school teacher, Sondra, reports:

> We are just starting to experiment with Nings in some middle school classrooms. The first to try it was a seventh grade English teacher who wisely invited only 21 of his 84 students to join the Ning. These students read a "challenging" novel, *The Red Scarf*

*Girl,* and used the Ning to discuss it. The teacher is now planning to expand the Ning to include all students in his "cluster." He will assign each student to one of 12 different science fiction novels, and create groups in the Ning to discuss each book. Last year we used blogs for his Science Fiction Genre Study Groups.

The Ning idea is contagious! Now the Social Studies teacher who works with the same "cluster" of 84 students is planning an SS Ning! This cluster is unique in our school because the students are part of a 1:1 pilot program; each leases his own iBook from our school. The students take the iBooks from class to class and may take them home.

We also have a sixth grade teacher who is planning on introducing a Ning within the next few weeks. This will raise interesting issues around access, as these students do not have their own iBooks. We do have mobile carts of 14 iBooks which teachers can schedule for classroom use, and we have two computer labs. (Sondra, blog post, January 17, 2008)

An example of how students might participate in networking projects is offered by Owen and colleagues (2006):

A Year 13 student of English literature writes an essay on one of her Jane Austen set readings. Before she submits it for marking by her teachers she decides to submit her essay for peer assessment using a fan fiction web resource. Twenty-four hours later the student has constructive feedback from five other Jane Austen fans and she is able to improve her essay. (p. 8)

Sometimes the Ning is the place for thinking out loud. Peter Dawson reaped many responses when he set out "to establish some working projects with like-minded primary teachers around the world" (http://globaleducation.ning.com/group/primaryteacherscollaborating/forum/topics/717180:Topic:5608):

Also, there's a teacher in this Ning, Elaine Wrenn, who used to do a project called Communities Around the World. I think there was a theme each month like playgrounds and kids compared their playgrounds around the world. I wonder if we could do something simple like that … and post pictures to a Flickr group for discussion purposes. Maybe teachers then could record the discussions and we could post them online somewhere for other classes to listen to. (L. Gray, blog comment, July 11, 2007)

Paul Harrington commented:

A European Project that we are involved in called Play to Learn is targeted at looking for similarities and differences between the way children play both in school and at home—communication via blogs, Skype, and podcasting—but I think that using VoiceThread could be really good for a project like this. I look forward to your thoughts … we are in South Wales, UK. (P. Harrington, blog comment, September 24, 2007)

Here is one more example of the ways in which the Ning supports educators connecting to each other to expand their students' curricular experiences. Nerine Chalmers (http://flatclassrooms.ning.com/profile/NerineChalmers) works at the Qatar Academy Primary School, Doha, Qatar. She wrote about her class's project. Students in Grade 5, in their field of investigation for the IB Primary Years Programme (PYP) Exhibition, are interested in investigating the notion that "a balance of work and recreation contributes to the well being of our community." They wish to create a survey and then get "responses from students in different parts of the world, as well as from students living in countries facing upheaval and challenge. If students at your school would be interested in responding, please let me know. Thank you." The opportunities are obvious and exciting.

## *How* Do You Get Started with Ning?

It is always an adventure to try a new Web 2.0 tool. Happily, social networking tools are almost foolproof. From Ning (www.ning.com) click on the Try It for Free button and choose a plan (www.ning.com/pricing). The first 14 days are free. After choosing a plan, you will see the screen in Figure 5.1:

**Figure 5.1** | Create a Ning network

Enter the name for your Ning, and pick a name for your website. That is all it takes. Next you will want to consider how your network will work. The following list will help you determine the ways you want your network to operate. Before you start, you might want to plan a color scheme, find graphics that represent your network, and create a few introductory and welcoming messages.

## Some Things to Think About
## Before You Get Started with a Ning

- Your Ning network can either be open or closed. If it's closed, members can join only by your invitation.

- Ning allows you to edit comments posted by members (e.g., the students in your classroom) of the network. Therefore, teachers can remove inappropriate comments and materials.

- Because it is a social networking site, Ning may be blocked in your school district. Check with your tech support person to get the site opened.

- Although most unwanted ads are filtered, every now and then an irritating (and sometimes inappropriate) ad could pop up on your screen. A fee-based premium network allows you to restrict ads.

- If you decide a Ning is not appropriate for use with students, you might want to consider an alternative use. A Ning can be a strong communication tool for team building or staff development.

- Ning does have an age restriction: students must be 13 or older to join. If your students are younger than 13, consider using a Ning as a mode of communication with the parents or guardians of the students in your classroom.

- Finally, you may want to establish rules for your students in working with the Ning in the classroom. It also makes sense that you inform the parents about your plans and about the rules. Later, once the students have become adept at working with Nings, you and they may want to revise the guidelines, or customize them.

We found the following rules for participating in a classroom Ning in a posting by Michael Umphrey, but when he was contacted, he wrote the following:

> I don't think I can give you permission—not because I mind if you use it but because my part in it doesn't really rise to the level of making it my intellectual property. A teacher asked permission to use it on her Ning, and I told her that I'd created it in a few minutes by copying, pasting, splicing, and editing a few documents from the web, without enough investment to even note where the pieces came from.

Thus, we present the rules here as an example of the way things evolve in our social web, and as a good place to start.

# Umphrey's Ning Rules for Students

Michael Umphrey

The school standards of language and conduct apply to this forum.

1.  **Respect.** We are polite, kind, and appropriate at all times. Remember that many students and Mr. Umphrey will view your comments.

2.  **Inclusion.** Anyone is welcome to comment or join a discussion as long as he or she is respectful.

3a. **Learning (in this forum).** It's OK to have fun in this space, but if others are having a learning conversation, either add to it positively or make your comments in a new post.

3b. **Learning (in class dialogues and blogs).** These are places to reflect and learn. You are encouraged to: ask questions; answer questions; share your learning; synthesize ideas; plan projects or assignments; and reflect on the process of learning.

4.  **Safety.** In general, be reserved about revealing private details on websites. You don't need to use your full name, but use enough of it so that everyone in English 11 will know who you are. Though this is a password-protected site, it is digital information that anyone could copy, forward, save to hard drive, and so forth. Anything you type into a digital forum may last forever, so respect your own and others' privacy.

5.  **Decorating your personal space.** Arrange your personal site to your taste, but keep it wholesome. It may be your choice to walk on the dark side, but one of the purposes of this site is to add to the world's light. Please, no gross, disgusting, immoral, or irreverent photographs. Also, don't put up a background that makes your text hard to read. Communication is a primary purpose of this site, and design should enhance, rather than obstruct, communication.

> 6. **Formality.** The level of usage here is "informal standard English"—which is what is used in business, government, and education for everyday work. No texting abbreviations. Use complete sentences and standard spelling.
>
> I'll ban people who ignore these rules. When a person is banned, the program deletes all the person's content and it cannot be recovered.

This quotation from Owen and associates (2006) summarizes this chapter extremely well:

> We are increasingly witnessing a change in the view of what education is for, with a growing emphasis on the need to support young people not only to acquire knowledge and information, but to develop the resources and skills necessary to engage with social and technical change, and to continue learning throughout the rest of their lives. In the technological arena, we are witnessing the rapid proliferation of technologies which are less about "narrowcasting" to individuals, than the creation of communities and resources in which individuals come together to learn, collaborate and build knowledge (social software). It is the intersection of these two trends which, we believe, offers significant potential for the development of new approaches to education. (p. 7)

We want to provide our students with engaging, important, and valuable information and content; and we also want to help them see where and how they fit into the larger world. This chapter has offered an overview of social networking and the ways in which it is having an impact on our learners, and on our teachers.

# *Where* Can You Find More Information about Social Networking?

For a good overview, try this video on Social Networking in Plain English:
www.youtube.com/watch?v=6a_KF7TYKVc

Go to Social Networking, a website that describes all aspects of social networking:
www.whatissocialnetworking.com

Join more than 28,000 other educators at Classroom 2.0:
www.classroom20.com

Explore your options on Social Networking for Teachers:
www.huffingtonpost.com/2013/01/08/teachers-gravitate-to-soc_n_2433747.html

Or, go to the TeachAde site for educators:
www.teachade.com

Perhaps bringing about social change is of interest. Try this educational community:
www.teachingforchange.org

# 6

# Visual Learning Tools

## *What* Are Visual Learning Tools?

Today's students view and communicate information through personal displays that include computer monitors, smartphones, handhelds, and television. They learn and spread information using new media such as YouTube, photo sites, and online presentation tools that feature visual displays.

The old adage is that a picture is worth a thousand words is no longer accurate. For today's young people, the picture is all. When words matter, it is often in text messages or 140-character communiqués such as on Twitter.

With so much emphasis on visual media, students need skills to understand the power of the various media and skills to use media to communicate. And many students are visual learners for whom seeing—whether tutorials, diagrams, or videos—helps them learn.

Visual or media literacy involves both the ability to understand and interpret and the ability to create visual messages: students must develop the skill to process and analyze information delivered through images as well as understand the impact images have on a viewer. They should understand that text and images affect readers differently.

Students have always learned by reviewing photos, maps, diagrams, charts, graphs, and tables. However, because there are more ways now than ever before to get information visually—including web-delivered images, videos, and presentations—and because visual communication is so commonplace for this digital generation, students must develop the ability to think critically about the image presented and decode its meaning. They should be aware of the effect the image was designed to produce, and they should analyze the extent and ways in which it successfully accomplishes the intended effect, both while watching visual media and while creating it.

## Common Core Standards and Visual Learning

Recently, an effort has been made to implement common standards for learners throughout the United States. The mission statement of this effort explains its goals:

> The Common Core State Standards provide a consistent, clear understanding of what students are expected to learn, so teachers and parents know what they need to do to help them. The standards are designed to be robust and relevant to the real world, reflecting the knowledge and skills that our young people need for success in college and careers. (Common Core State Standards, 2013, n.p.)

Visual learning tools—graphic organizers, concept maps, mind maps, webs, and idea maps—help students to write and learn more effectively. They can apply these skills across all curriculum areas, especially with the English Language Arts standards for reading and writing. Some of these tools are Webspiration (www.mywebspiration.com), Bubbl.us (www.bubbl.us), Pinterest (www.pinterest.com), and Gliffy (www.gliffy.com).

Students can use visual learning tools to satisfy the reading requirements for understanding many aspects of literature and nonfiction. The requirements state that a student is expected to discern meaning, theme, plot, and more from the text, make connections among ideas and between texts, and evaluate to interpret and understand text.

Students can use these tools to improve writing skills by pre-writing, brainstorming, organizing, and starting first drafts to satisfy the writing requirements. The requirements for the writing strand state that a student is expected to plan, draft, revise, edit, and publish writing; develop a reading-writing connection; and research to build and present knowledge.

Bubbl.us allows students to create colorful brainstorms and mind maps online. Gliffy is online diagramming software that allows students to create professional-looking flowcharts, diagrams, technical drawings, and more. Pinterest is a virtual pin or bulletin board for assembling creative ideas and information in a virtual graphical space. Webspiration is the online version of Inspiration. Students can create, organize, and share ideas visually.

# *Why* Are Visual Learning Tools Useful?

Students must learn how to view all types of media to understand and analyze the information they see throughout their lives. Teachers can help students refine their analytical skills with practice. Providing prompts for students before they watch a video helps them know what to look for and enhances learning. "Watch for …," "Listen for …," and "Be ready to discuss three things you learned" are examples of lead-ins to get students thinking about what they see.

In addition, students must learn how to create meaning and communicate with visual tools. They can create digital media projects using video clips, video podcasting, and screencasting (screen capture with audio narration). Teachers can use images and visual presentations in the curriculum and encourage students to create presentations that develop the skills of inquiry, creativity, and higher-order thinking. Students should be able to create a product that demonstrates their knowledge of the subject matter, the ability to communicate that information visually, and the ability to make an impact on the audience. Skills include using visual means creatively to convey or enhance meaning.

Teachers can use video to record student progress in specific areas during the year. With a webcam or even a cell phone, teachers—and classmates too—can record students reading, solving math equations, and participating in class at several intervals during the year to gauge progress and to use in a virtual portfolio.

The Partnership for 21st Century Skills (2004) includes media literacy as an essential skill, demonstrated by the ability to analyze media and create media products.

According to the Partnership's statement, to analyze, students should be able to:

- Understand both how and why media messages are constructed, and for what purposes

- Examine how individuals interpret messages differently, how values and points of view are included or excluded, and how media can influence beliefs and behaviors

- Apply a fundamental understanding of the ethical/legal issues surrounding the access and use of media (p. 5)

Further, to create media products, students should be able to:

- Understand and utilize the most appropriate media creation tools, characteristics and conventions

- Understand and effectively utilize the most appropriate expressions and interpretations in diverse, multi-cultural environments (p. 5)

When students work on a curricular project, they can sharpen their ability to discover relationships among ideas and to develop new concepts and insights. When they collaborate with others, they have a feedback loop for their ideas and a relationship with others that promotes using higher-order thinking skills. When they communicate and share ideas with a real audience, they take ownership of their work and develop a commitment to learning. Using photos and videos for this purpose enhances the process. The two most important methods are digital storytelling and the making of documentaries. Students can also share information by creating slideshows or screencasts using text, audio, and visual elements.

# *When* Do Teachers and Students Use Visual Learning Tools?

## Flipping Classrooms

Flipping classrooms is a model of teaching and learning that inverts the traditional structure of teacher-centered instruction in class and homework at home. The advantage for students is that they can watch an explanation and demonstration of a concept on their computers at their convenience and use classroom time to hone their skills and apply learning under the guidance of their teacher and fellow students. Teachers can differentiate instruction more easily, and students can learn at their own pace and take responsibility for their learning.

Robert Miller (2013), director of information and communication technologies for the New Canaan Public Schools, describes how one middle school teacher flips her classroom in his blog post "Flipped Learning."

> She creates small tutorials of math lessons. Her library of video lessons are posted on her website for unlimited access by her students. This has enabled her students to access extra help and/ or enrichment outside of school. Students have the opportunity to watch these video tutorials multiple times and at their own pace. Students can also contact the teacher off hours to ask

additional questions. Parents also now have the ability to see how their children are learning math and this provides greater capacity to help their children.

Miller continues to explain the benefits:

> Has learning fundamentally changed in this model? I could argue it hasn't. She is still teaching her classes in mostly the same way she was before. What she is doing is giving access to differentiated learning. Students can work at their own pace and on the content they need the most help with at the right moment. … Students in her classes are learning to take responsibility for their own learning and there is immense power in that. Students are coming to class better prepared to learn. This has changed what she needs to do during instructional time with her students, which is the heart of flipped learning. (Miller, 2013, n.p.)

Linda Gutierrez, sixth grade math teacher at Heights Middle School in Farmington, New Mexico, described the benefits in a Meru webinar:

> Six years ago my classroom was teacher-centered and I taught all content. I used a lot of time to prepare and gather resources, and I couldn't differentiate instruction to match diverse learning needs. The result was mediocre test scores. Today my classroom is student-centered with little direct instruction, just quick reviews of content, and I have a huge amount of resources. It saves me time and now it is easy to differentiate and pinpoint a diagnosis of student weaknesses and remediate. The result is better student engagement and better test scores. (Gutierrez, 2013a, n.p.)

There are two ways to provide videos for students. The first is to access high-quality videos from trusted sources or created by other educators and placed online. The other is to create one's own.

## The Ability to Rewind

Renee Owens

One of the greatest benefits of flipping with video in my classroom is the ability for students to rewind. They cannot rewind what I am saying and doing in class, but with a video that models the process, key ideas, skill, etc., they can rewind as needed. What this means is that a student who needs to hear it again, watch it again, stop and pause—can. In a heterogeneous classroom, how can you teach at the perfect pace? You will inevitably be too fast or too slow for someone.

When I flip my lessons via video—through homework or class stations—students can do more than just work at their own pace; they have more capability and support to learn at their own pace. Struggling students are not the only ones who benefit. A good flipped video will build in time to think, reflect, and practice. A student who quickly grasps the concepts may be able to skip some practice or work more quickly through tasks. Furthermore you can build in challenges or enrichment pieces.

*Renee Owens, "Flipping: Meeting the Needs of Our Students Through Flipped Homework and Flipped Centers," retrieved from www.guide2digitallearning.com.*

The Khan Academy (www.khanacademy.org) created an interactive web-based system that uses videos for learning and gives students time to practice. It has an easy-to-use progress dashboard that informs teachers, parents, mentors, and the students themselves. There are more than 4,000 videos in many subject areas and involving practice with hundreds of skills. It is free and available to everyone. Its website says, "We're on a mission to help you learn what you want, when you want, at your own pace" (Khan Academy, 2013, n.p.).

Jim Forde (2013), a science and technology teacher at Scofield Magnet Middle School in Stamford, Connecticut, says, "One of the greatest things that the web offers is the myriad video resources that can potentially enhance your lessons." He lists his five favorite sites for outstanding resources:

**NBCLearn** (www.nbclearn.com) connects professional-quality video clips with science and math concepts in an engaging way. In one video, for example, they explore the science of NHL hockey (www.nbclearn.com/portal/site/learn/science-of-nhl-hockey) that apply Newton's laws; mass, volume, and density; and vectors.

**Science 360** (www.science360.gov) is an National Science Foundation site with many STEM topics. Teachers can embed the videos on their class websites and blogs.

**TED** (www.ted.com) videos are engaging and inspiring. I try to watch one a day and share many of the science videos with students. My favorite story about using TED with kids was the day it was snowing and the buses were late picking up students. We watched a TED video on biolumines-cence. The bus arrived, but students wouldn't leave until it was over.

**YouTube Edu** (www.youtube.com/education) offers university and secondary content that is excellent. Some school districts block YouTube, but you can get an override code.

**PBS** (video.pbs.org) has award-winning Nova, Nature, and Frontline videos for students.

## Professional Development

Whether for a flipped classroom or to help other teachers or students learn a specific topic, teachers create their own videos and post them on Web 2.0 sites such as YouTube, TeacherTube, or Vimeo.

For example, when Los Angeles educator Linda Yollis taught her students how to blog, she realized that it was important to teach them how to comment effectively. She says, "When I first started blogging, I thought the posts would be the primary focus of the blog. I quickly realized that the comment section was where the blog came to life" (L. Yollis, personal communication, 2013).

The result was a video she created with her students that other teachers learn from and show their students: "How to Compose a Quality Comment." You can watch the video at http://vimeo.com/15695021.

## Classroom Integration

Students have traditionally watched videos to learn, but being the creators of visual information is now possible with today's tools. When students create knowledge from information, collaborate with others, and do hands-on learning, they engage with the subject matter and learn, understand, and remember it. They create and collaborate, research and share, and take ownership of their learning.

### Digital Storytelling

When students can organize their thoughts logically, find just the right words to express them, and communicate their ideas to others, they are demonstrating the ability to think logically. Teachers can help students improve thinking skills by encouraging them to write creatively and express themselves visually. An effective way to do this is with digital storytelling using free photo-editing tools.

Storytelling is a tradition in which ideas and customs are handed down from generation to generation. Digital stories derive their power from adding the elements of images and design to create a story that communicates in powerful ways. Digital stories are compelling forms of expression because it is so easy to make them look professionally created, share them with a wide audience, and store them in e-portfolios.

Teachers encourage students to take, edit, post, and include their own photos in their work and to use others' photos that are stored online at sites such as Flickr (www.flickr.com) using Creative Commons attributions (http://creativecommons.org).

Being visually creative enhances the power of narrative. It is easy for students to add visual elements to their stories; they can import their photos, design their documents, enter their story text, and share their digital stories by printing them or saving them as digital files to post to a web page.

## Student Presentations

One of the ways that students can demonstrate learning is by creating presentations to share with the class, parents, and even online for the community to view. As part of a virtual portfolio, a series of presentations can be a powerful way to show how well students understand concepts and apply them over time. Although the gold standard for presentation tools is Microsoft PowerPoint, schools are turning to free Web 2.0 presentation tools with interesting features for student work. A few of those tools are:

**SlideShare** (www.slideshare.com) allows students to upload documents of various types to create and share slides and even embed the presentations in a blog or on a website.

**Flipsnack** (www.flipsnack.com) allows students to take a document in any format that is converted to a PDF and create a flipbook to display a virtual presentation.

**Prezi** (www.prezi.com) is a nonlinear presentation tool that allows students to place text, images, and even videos in imaginative ways and determine the path to display. There is a free educator account.

## Animations

According to Wikipedia,

> Animation is the display of images in ways to create an illusion of movement. The position of each object in any particular image relates to the position of that object in the previous and following images so that the objects each appear to fluidly move independently of one another.

Students enjoy creating animations and can use animators as presentation tools. For younger students, Kerpoof (www.kerpoof.com) is simple to use. Its suite of creative tools for children is perfect for the elementary classroom. Teachers can create free accounts to manage their students' work.

GoAnimate (www.goanimate.com) has an intuitive interface and high-quality graphics that middle and high school students can use to create comic-strip–like characters that move and speak.

## Video Documentaries

Using video cameras or smartphones and video-editing tools can motivate students to learn. For example, making history come alive in the classroom can be a challenge, but creating video documentaries encourages students to learn about the past.

Documentary filmmaking in the classroom can produce positive effects. Students can demonstrate their individual strengths and master the skills of researching, reading, writing, and speaking as they build critical skills such as problem solving, collaboration, and the ability to gather and analyze data. With such project-based learning, students can be motivated to do their best work and be proud to share what they've created—a professional-quality documentary.

For teachers, documentary filmmaking can offer a very natural formative assessment tool. They can evaluate student learning from the perspective of applying skills rather than from remembering facts for tests. In addition, creating a documentary changes students from being spectators of history or literature, for example, to being active participants. Students study curriculum by filling in gaps, solving the mysteries, and exploring and understanding rather than memorizing. They are engaged in gathering evidence and analyzing and interpreting with the goal of presenting a story.

The ultimate achievement is for students to post their videos on a video-sharing site so that it is available not only to other students, the teacher, and parents but also to the world. YouTube is the most common, but some districts block its use. Alternatively, students can post on sites such as TeacherTube (www.teachertube.com) or Vimeo (www.vimeo.com).

> ### Publish and Critique Original Videos Safely on YouTube
>
> "In a Google Apps domain, teachers and students can create their own personal YouTube channels. To maintain your privacy, you can make them 'unlisted.' When our music students, poets, videographers, and debaters choose to publish their work for the world, we can help them decide what is appropriate. Students can engage in peer critique using the comments section below each video" (Swan, 2013, n.p.).

Whether in photographs or video, students learn to create, collaborate, and communicate effectively with digital tools. Jakes (2005) gives examples of the power that visual learning has in his article *Making a Case for Digital Storytelling:*

- A student who never talks in class develops a digital story about being afraid to talk. He describes how he likes being talked to, how he is misunderstood and lonely, and how he had to develop a new identity. He shows how this was accomplished through the internet, and as a result, he found some true friends. For a student who says nothing, he has much to say.

- A student who is physically challenged and is selectively mute tells a story and makes a breakthrough by recording the voice-over.

- A student who has Asperger's syndrome actually tells a story about his favorite hobby.

- A student reconnects with her estranged siblings through her digital story.

- A student tells of the importance of her childhood drawings as representations of her life, and what she wants that life to become.

- And there are other stories—tales of first loves, of the death of loved ones, of personal sacrifice, of accomplishment, of the importance of a place, of challenges overcome, of important moments in a life, and of the value of parents and grandparents.

## Screencasting

Screen capture software such as Snagit provides tools to create videos. Teachers can use this software to record lessons for classroom flipping or supplemental learning. Rob Zdrojewski, a middle school teacher from Amherst, New York, could teach his technology class despite being out on jury duty. While he wasn't there, substitute teachers were able to play screencasts that Rob created for his students.

Screencasting allowed Rob to give his students instruction directly, which helped eliminate confusion for both the substitute teachers and students. He included webcam video in his screencasts to give his students the impression he was right there alongside them (www.techsmith.com/education-k12-stories-jury-duty.html).

You can find a tutorial and tips and tricks on www.techsmith.com/education-tutorial-absent-video.html

**Web 2.0 Wisdom**

## Digital Images and Copyright

Copyright laws govern how we use the creative work and information of others in any form. People can copy material under some circumstances if they cite the reference or get author or copyright holder permission, or both. "Fair use" provisions of the law allow teachers and students to use these materials for educational purposes—again, with certain restrictions. In creating digital stories, students often include images created by others that are stored online.

Creative Commons (http://creativecommons.org) is a nonprofit organization that offers content creators the ability to license their work in an era of too-easy copying from the web. These free licenses stipulate which rights you reserve and which rights you waive. The website states that it "helps you share your knowledge and creativity with the world … and develops, supports, and stewards legal and technical infrastructure that maximizes digital creativity, sharing, and innovation" (Creative Commons, 2013, n.p.). It also states, "Licensing a work is as simple as selecting which of the six licenses best meets your goals, and then marking your work in some way so that others know that you have chosen to release the work under the terms of that license" (n.p.).

## Useful Tools

Because there are so many tools and so many uses for visual tools, we list a few here to help in understanding the variety of options.

### Photo and Video Tools

**Flickr** (www.flickr.com) is a photo-hosting site where people upload, tag, and store their photos, share them with others, and browse the many images and photos posted. Users can add comments and annotations.

**Jing** (www.jingproject.com) allows users to snap a picture or make a quick video of anything on a computer screen and then share it.

**Photobucket** (http://photobucket.com) is a video site that provides free, web-based versions of Adobe's video remix and editing tools.

**Photoshop.com** (www.photoshop.com) is a free version of Adobe's photo-editing toolkit available online for users to upload, organize, edit, and share photos online.

**Photo Story** (http://microsoft-photo-story.soft32.com) is Microsoft's free downloadable software that allows users to create a presentation from digital photos with narration, effects, transitions, and music.

**Photosynth** (http://photosynth.net) takes a collection of photos of a place or object, analyzes them for similarities, and displays them in a reconstructed three-dimensional space.

**Picasa** (http://picasa.google.com) is Google's software for organizing and editing digital photos. Rather than editing, organizing, and storing photos online, Picasa is available for people to download and use on their computers.

**TeacherTube** (www.teachertube.com) is a public video-sharing website similar to YouTube for teachers to share videos and tutorials online. Students can also post videos for educational purposes.

**Ustream** (www.ustream.tv) is a web-streaming site that lets people broadcast their own channels on their own or other site.

**VoiceThread** (www.voicethread.com) is a collaborative, multimedia slideshow site that holds images, documents, and videos and allows people to navigate pages and leave comments in a variety of ways.

**Windows Live Movie Maker** (www.download.live.com/moviemaker) is downloadable video-creating and editing software that is a part of Microsoft's Windows Live.

**YouTube** (www.youtube.com) is a public video-sharing website. Google provides YouTube Remixer, an online video editor on YouTube that is powered by Adobe Premiere Express. Users can remix videos on YouTube or enhance them with titles, transitions, and effects.

## Graphical Organizing Tools

**Bubbl.us** (www.bubbl.us) allows students to create colorful brainstorms and mind maps online, which they can share for viewing or collaboration. They can save the mind map in a blog or website, embed it in a blog or on a website, or print or email it.

**Gliffy** (www.gliffy.com) is online diagramming software that allows students to create professional-looking flowcharts, diagrams, technical drawings, and more.

**Pinterest** (www.pinterest.com) is a virtual pin or bulletin board for assembling creative ideas and information in a virtual graphical space. Students can amass, organize, and share information and ideas. Their boards can be public, private, or shared for collaboration.

**Webspiration** (www.mywebspiration.com) is the online version of Inspiration. Students can create and organize ideas visually and share them with a private link or embed the result in a web page, blog, or wiki.

# *Who* Is Using Visual Learning Tools for Teaching and Learning?

In addition to digital storytelling tools and tools to create video documentaries, educators are using many other creative tools in classrooms today. Here are some examples.

## Critical Thinking

Kristidel McGregor, who teaches seventh grade critical thinking and research at a magnet program for academically talented students, uses Prezi (http://prezi.com) for student presentations to enhance critical thinking skills. The Utopia Island project used Prezi for performance assessment. This collaborative project had students working in teams to determine what a perfect society would look like. McGregor says:

> One of the amazing things about Prezi is that it interfaces seamlessly with Google images and YouTube, which allows for a ton of creativity. I've had students record themselves playing their own music to include in their Prezi, or create an image video to go along with their song and embed that into their project.
>
> An advantage of using Prezi over other presentation software is that it is non-linear, which means that students create forms that fit their content. This helps them to see and make new connections both within the content and to wider knowledge, which is priceless! (K. McGregor, personal communication, June 2013)

## Doing Research

Elizabeth Kahn, library media specialist at Patrick F. Taylor Science and Technology Academy in Avondale, Louisiana, uses Instagrok (www.instagrok.com) to help students in middle through high school grades do research in any subject. She says, "After selecting a topic, I think finding quality and relevant keywords is one of the most important aspects of developing good research skills. Instagrok is a search engine, but it is very visual and uses concept maps to display results. This makes it useful in helping students develop their selected topics in a research-based assignment." She reported:

> In one instance, students in an English class were asked to write an argumentative essay on a topic related to justice. The teacher gave them broad topics from which to choose, but the students had to figure out a way to narrow their topics. Instagrok helped them do that.
>
> As the librarian, helping students develop a research paper from selecting a topic to the finished product can be arduous, especially if every student in a class has a different topic. One of the most difficult parts of the research process is in the selection of good keywords to use for searching in electronic and print resources. Using Instagrok, with its visual representation of search results, students can quickly view and select a number of keywords that they can use for further research. (Kahn, 2013a, n.p.)

## Reading Apprenticeship

Nicole Roeder, cyber English teacher at Quakertown Community High School in Quakertown, Pennsylvania, uses Screencast-O-Matic (www.screencast-o-matic.com), a one-click online screen recorder, with her students. She described her work:

> In order to integrate Reading Apprenticeship in a distance-learning environment, I teach students to use screen casting to record a think aloud activity that requires them to use meta-cognition. They use the software to talk to text and share the videos with other class members.
>
> In an asynchronous cyber environment, it is often difficult to access a student's ability to work through a text step by step because you cannot hear what's happening the way you can when conducting a read aloud/think aloud activity. Common cooperative strategies, such as a think-pair-share, are not a possibility when students work at different paces and places.

This tool has allowed the students to capture their thoughts and ideas and clearly demonstrate their aptitude. They share the videos with classmates and teachers and, as a result of this strategy, students demonstrate that they understand the importance of essential and nonessential information and that they are able to use metacognition effectively. This in turn improves their ability to read difficult texts or discern website credibility. (N. Roeder, personal communication, June 2013)

## Interactivity

Paula Naugle, fourth grade science teacher in the Jefferson Parish Public School System in Metairie, Louisiana, uses ThingLink (www.thinglink.com) to create interactive images with her students. ThingLink helps them to design and discover rich images and add music, video, text, and images, and spark their creativity in other ways. Students tell their stories, and ThingLink interactive images form a channel that others can follow. She says:

My students learned how to take a picture and turn it into an interactive experience in a project about animals. They learned how to give credit for the image they used and had to learn how to link to other sites that included information about their chosen animal. They also had to learn how to take the generated embed code from ThingLink and add it to their blogs. (P. Naugle, personal communication, June 2013)

## Curriculum Design for Blended Learning

Julie Willcott, science teacher at Foxcroft Academy in Dover-Foxcroft, Maine, teaches physics to 11th graders and chemistry to 10th graders. She curates the materials and posts them in iTunes U. Students have access anywhere anytime. Her school has a 1:1 iPad program to facilitate this, although a computer and internet access is all you need. Regarding the physics course, Willcott stated:

This semester-long course introduces high school students to the study of physics in preparation for further courses in college. The objective of this course is to investigate mechanics, specifically velocity, acceleration, forces, and energy, in both one and two dimensions. Students will develop conceptual understanding as well as skills in problem solving, scientific reasoning, and communication. Students do lab activities in addition to these assignments.

She also said:

This semester-long course introduces high school students to the study of chemistry in preparation for further courses in college. The objective of this course is to investigate the properties of atoms, chemical bonding, and chemical reactions. Students will develop conceptual understanding as well as skills in problem solving, scientific reasoning, and communication. Students in that class will do lab activities in addition to these assignments.

Students are empowered to be in charge of their own learning. They can move ahead or review at their own pace. In addition, a variety of materials (suitable for a variety of learning styles, preferences, etc.) are incorporated into the curriculum. Students still experience face-to-face time with labs, time for questions, and enhancement based on this common understanding. (J. Willcott, personal communication, June 2013)

To see more of Julie's work, check out her class sites at http://itun.es/us/hkSuI and http://itun.es/us/L4r3G.

## Infographics

Elizabeth Kahn, library media specialist at Patrick F. Taylor Science and Technology Academy in Avondale, Louisiana, works with teachers and students to create infographics, visual representations of information and data in a format that presents complex concepts clearly and concisely. Infogram (http://Infogr.am)and Easel.ly (http://easel.ly) are the ones she recommends as she blogs about the work. "A sixth grade class created infographics using survey information from all the sixth graders, like which is your favorite ice cream flavor" (Kahn, 2013b, n.p.).

Elizabeth also shared other ways she uses infographics in her teaching. "A class of juniors and seniors taking AP Environmental Science used Infogram to create infographics illustrating various environmental land-use issues such as flooding, national parks, etc., which they had previously researched" (E. Kahn, personal communication, June 2013).

## Student-Created Videos

Cathy Swan, the technology integration teacher at New Canaan High School, in New Canaan, Connecticut, says that for visual and auditory learners, YouTube is the search engine of choice. She says:

> With its seemingly infinite selection of videos on any topic, YouTube is a must-have resource for our educators and students. But YouTube is not only a video search engine; it also offers personal video channels free to anyone who registers. We get a personal YouTube channel with every account for Google Apps for Education domain members. Students log on, select YouTube from the More drop-down menu, and click on Upload to add an original student-made video to their video channel. Or they can sit at any computer with a webcam, click the YouTube record button and record, then edit a video to be uploaded to their channel. Teachers use a Google form to gather URLs of student videos for easy access. Students can upload a video as Unlisted so that anyone with the link can view it. Making it public allows it to be found in search and making it private makes it restrictive, allowing only those with permission to view it. (C. Swan, personal communication, June 2013)

## Flip Tool

Emilia Carrillo, Spanish teacher and co-head of the department at the International School of Uganda and Pamoja Education, uses the TED-Ed Flip Tool (http://ed.ted.com) with students learning Spanish in Grades 11 and 12 in the International Baccalaureate Curriculum. She says,

> I use the TED-Ed tool to create engaging listening activities for my students such as this one: http://ed.ted.com/on/OekMnVHT.

[The tool] allows me to track my students' answers and performance. Lately I have designed the project "A Talk for TED" in which my higher-level students have to give a TED-Talk video about a particular issue or event and then use the tool to create comprehension questions for their peers.

The tool allows for differentiation in my classes for content and ability level. Students can work on different videos for different purposes (using the activities I created). When students create their own videos, they find a purpose in their work and strive more to complete it conscientiously. (E. Carillo, personal communication, June 2013)

A complete explanation of this lesson can be found at http://spanish4teachers. org/techblog/ted-ed-flip-tool-updates.

## Home-School Connection

Erin Jackle and Stephanie Hopkins, early childhood special education teachers in School District U-46 in Elgin, Illinois, use technology to connect to parents. They say, "Parents are their child's first and most important (best) teachers; therefore, parent involvement is critical for school success." They use visual learning tools to connect with families and go on to describe some of their tools:

**Animoto.** Slideshows are a great way for students to share their work at home. By viewing slideshows as a family, our students are able to talk about their day with their families. Animoto is our current favorite for creating slideshows because there is an option for mobile-friendly short slideshows that do not use Flash. It also has an app so slideshows can be created directly from a smartphone or tablet. We have sent home photos of students working together on a project, a video clip of a student retelling a story, photos of artwork, or videos of events in our classroom such as classroom caterpillars turning into butterflies.

**Pinterest.** We use Pinterest to share everything from age appropriate crafts and recipes, to favorite read alouds, academic games, and developmental information. Pins can give parents ways to reinforce what their child is learning in the classroom. Because Pinterest is visually based, it is a great way to connect with parents who do not speak English as a first language.

**YouTube.** Parents who work during the day may not be able to visit the classroom, but through YouTube they feel connected with their child's day and can carry over many strategies at home. We have a YouTube channel to share our videos with families of us reading and signing popular children's stories, classroom books, and songs. Students enjoy watching these videos too and they are a great way to connect what is happening at school with what is happening at home. In addition, we use them to model reading strategies to parents such as voice inflection, asking meaningful questions, and pointing out clues in the pictures.

We also use YouTube to upload longer videos such as class presentations, school sings, and even student participation in a particular lesson. Just like YouTube can be used to "flip the classroom" with older students, YouTube videos are a wonderful way to flip parent education. Parents who may not be able to make it to parent-education events at school watch videos of these same presentations on YouTube. (E. Jackle & S. Hopkins, personal communication, June 2013)

## Mystery Skype

Shawn Storm, sixth grade RELA/social studies teacher in Quakertown, Pennsylvania, found a way to make mapping fascinating by adding a human element. He says, "This past school year I came across one of the most exciting ways to engage my students with geography; it's called Mystery Skype." He elaborated his use of this tool:

Imagine your students speaking with classes in any of the 50 states, Canada, Mexico, Australia, or even Sarajevo? That's what my students did this year. The format of a Mystery Skype can take on any type—but the premise is simple—figure out where the classroom you are speaking with is located using only yes/no questions.

There are several ways to make it work—from assigning jobs to your students (greeters, researchers, question keepers, mappers), to keeping it an open format.

I even had one Skype session where we had entertainers—students who sang, played instruments, and told jokes—to keep the session moving when the classes were researching.

Mystery Skype is all about authentic learning—it works on geography, communication, computer, research, and critical thinking skills. Students can use Mystery Skype to showcase other subject areas—Mystery Author (English), Mystery Element (science), Mystery Inventor, etc.

If you're interested in Mystery Skypes, the best place to look is Twitter and search #mysteryskype—it's a great place to make connections and set up the Mystery Skypes. Mystery Skype has helped to show my classroom that their learning goes beyond our classroom walls. (S. Storm, personal communication, June 2013)

## Information Literacy

Kevin Hagen, teacher librarian at George Washington Bush Middle School in Tumwater, Washington, uses Animoto for a unit on media literacy with seventh grade students. First students discuss what advertisers do to get our attention. Then they choose a favorite book and use Animoto and PowerPoint to create a book trailer. Hagen says, "They learn about the research and devices that advertisers use to decide how to market products to us and how to use the movie-making tool Animoto to create their own marketing video" (K. Hagen, personal communication, June 2013).

## Participatory Videos

Videos are traditionally linear and directive. In the classroom, they are designed to dispense information or teach the viewer. However, great lessons are rarely passive. Bill Selak, fourth and fifth grade teacher at Workman Elementary School in West Covina, California, says:

Using the annotations feature in YouTube, teachers can create videos that require participation. At its most basic, students are given four choices, and they select the correct answer. If an incorrect choice is made, students watch a video that reteaches the concept. If the correct choice is made, the video continues to the next step, or the next problem. Students have control over the learning path. They can rewatch videos, and select other videos to watch in an interactive way. (B. Selak, personal communication, June 2013)

Anne Mirtschin, who teaches Grades 4 through 12 at Hawkesdale P12 College in southwest Victoria, Australia, uses Twitter with her students. It is a rural prep to Year 12 school that is culturally and geographically isolated, but students are connected to the world using digital tools. Anne says:

I often use Skype in my classroom because it allows for video-conferencing and sharing files like presentations with other classes and is globally user friendly. We use it for sharing class-room activities in history and geography to learn about cultures and languages, and to bring in expert speakers such as authors and scientists. We also use Skype to bring in students who are absent from school, who are ill or who want to learn a subject that another school offers. Learning from nonsynchronous global projects is made richer with videoconferencing linkups with partner schools.

During International Peace Day, I spoke to special students in Russia about what world peace means to us in Australia, and students who could not get to the school watched via Skype.

My students pushed the boundaries in learning Scratch and wanted to do more than I could help them with. We Skyped in Lorraine Leo, a teacher from Boston, and a university lecturer, Yoshiro Myata from Japan, to solve problems with individual Year 8 students who were programming in Scratch.

Students from Ipoh, Malaysia, have often Skyped in to share cultural information about Chinese, Indian, and Malay peoples, and my students learned how to fold paper money for traditional Chinese marriages, dance some Malay steps, watched shadow puppet shows, and more. Our students learn Mandarin Chinese as their second language and can practise with Chinese counterparts in Malaysia.

Year 9/10 ICT students have learned how to create games in MS Kodu with Sarveesh, a student from Kuala Lumpur, using Skype. He got my students to play his award-winning game and provide feedback for further improvement.

I also use Skype for "Show 'n Tell" with my Year 3/4 students; they individually shared their book character costumes for Bookweek with students from Taiwan. Introductions had to be made in Chinese and English.

Learning and connections go beyond the classroom. When my Year 4/5 class participated in the International Dot Day project, they did not have the book, *The Dot,* in our library. So Chrissy Hellier and her class from Bangkok read the book to us over Skype.

My students have taken classes using Skype with Year 7 German students who were studying healthy foods in science. They discussed the food in our student lunchboxes, our canteen, and the school vegetable garden. This led to a number of collaborative projects and then brought in the wider school community with our school canteen manager linking up with the German canteen manager. A German/English interpreter had to be present over Skype as the managers discussed and swapped menus for a German canteen food day in our school and an Australian canteen food day in the German school. Year 7 German students were responsible for translating the recipes, as they are learning English.

We also used Skype to bring in an author from New York at lunchtimes to talk to students who are passionate about writing. Over the last two years for a 6- to 10-week period, they have met over Skype. Students received writing assignments, completed the tasks, uploaded them to collaborative notes in Evernote, and received feedback and evaluation.

Skype brings a textbook to life, especially when connecting with students from other cultures. They hear accents and different names, see different races, see different manners of dress, understand the cultures better, gain greater empathy for those who are different to themselves, and increase in personal confidence and oral communication. They learn to use body language, the text chat, and other skills to communicate over a web camera, especially when working with students who do not speak English as a first or even second language. (A. Mirtschin, personal communication, July 2013)

## Ask an Expert

Sandy Wisneski, Grades 6–8 teacher at Catalyst Charter Middle School in Ripon, Wisconsin, uses project-based learning throughout the year and believes that real-life situations are important to project-based learning. She reports,

In Ask an Expert (http://catalystchannel.blogspot.com/2013/04/ask-expert.html), students have an opportunity to Skype with an engineer. For example, my students needed background information to make decisions when planning a paper roller coaster. There were plenty of videos and websites that have information about Newton's laws, but they wanted to get the information from someone who experiences them daily. The class decided to find experts on roller coasters and asked an engineer at Great America in Gurnee, Illinois. The folks at Great America were willing to Skype with us and answer our questions.

Before the actual Skype, students submitted their best questions to a Google form. We selected the "deepest" questions to be shared with the expert. Students practiced asking their questions and discussed netiquette before the event. The Skype was a firsthand opportunity to get information from engineers who design and work with the coasters. The people at Great America offered insights into their jobs, and they were patient and gave the students an experience that made a difference to their learning. (S. Wisneski, personal communication, 2013)

## A No-Ended Project

Tóthné Bán Gyöngyi, a teacher in the Primary School Balatonboglár, Hungary, uses Skype with students in Grades 2–8 to communicate with other students around the world. Tóthné says:

> We like to find friends in other parts of the world and meet them online via Skype. We find possible partners and look for where they live. We get as much information as we can about their cultures and then plan our meetings. We decide what to talk about, what game to play together, and what to sing.
>
> During the meeting, we talk, we practice English, play games, play musical instruments, sing, or make quizzes. After the sessions, we record all the new information we got. We always learn something new. In some cases we collaborate on our or their Wikispaces or Google sites.
>
> This work is so interesting and exciting for us because we live in a very small country in the middle of Europe. We don't have the possibility to travel or to meet other people. We can't go … but this way the world can come into our classroom. It's fantastic! We can meet other cultures and speak to students online and even write to them. We can talk about Hungary, too. As a result of this exciting work, my small students know more about the world. They know how other students live, celebrate, and play in other places. (T. Bán Gyöngyi, personal communication, July 2013)

# *How* Do You Get Started with Visual Learning Tools?

With the large number of options for visual learning, there are many choices. For the purpose of simplicity, we chose to focus on a photo-editing tool, Google's Picasa, and a video-editing tool, Windows Live Movie Maker. Both are downloaded and manipulated on a computer rather than online and are most often used on PCs; however, Macintosh users have free photo- and video-editing software included on their computers (Picasa is also available for Macs).

## Steps for Digital Storytelling

- Brainstorm and develop a topic and purpose for writing.

- Discuss expectations and assessment of digital stories.

- Create a storyboard or outline for the story line.

- Discuss how images can help communicate a story and enhance the message.

- Use a digital camera to capture photos or find photos online that are free and available to use (attribute photos that were online).

- Identify elements of digital stories.

- Use editing tools to edit images and create the digital story.

---

### Six Elements of Digital Stories

1. **Voice.** Write in the first or third person

2. **Character.** List the traits your main character demonstrates

3. **Setting.** Describe where the story takes place

4. **Conflict.** Show a disagreement or struggle

5. **Visual.** Use photos or other images to enhance the story's meaning

6. **Pacing.** Set the stage by using rising action, create drama using conflict, and use falling action to lead to resolution

---

## Photo Editing with Picasa

Download and install Picasa on your computer (Figure 6.1). Watch as Picasa scans your hard drive and displays folders with your images. Note for Macintosh users: Picasa displays photos from the iPhoto Library as read-only files.

You import new photos from cameras, CDs, memory cards, and so forth by clicking the Import button, selecting the device, and selecting specific images or all of the photos. You can edit your photos by double-clicking a photo to open the Edit Photo screen. Use the editing tools on the left-hand side of the screen. These include Basic Fixes, for simple edits; Tuning, to control the color and adjust the lighting; Effects, where you can apply any of 12 effects; and Make a Caption, for adding captions.

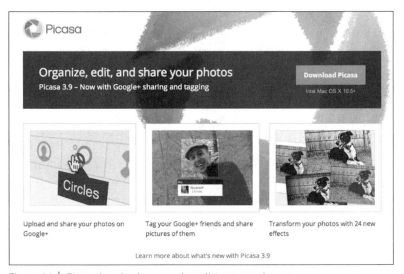

Figure 6.1 | Picasa download screen—http://picasa.google.com

## Steps for Video Documentary Making

Regardless of the topic or tools used, these are the basic tasks that need to be done in the production and delivery of a video documentary. Although some are obviously sequential steps, others may actually be done out of order or as many times as needed throughout the process.

- Conduct background research.

- Discuss expectations and assessment of videos.

- Brainstorm and develop a topic, keeping in mind the purpose for doing it.

- Create a storyboard or outline for the project.

- Discuss ways to communicate the story using video.

- Practice filming techniques.

- Capture the video on a video camera.

- Transfer the video (and audio, if captured) to a computer.

- Use video-editing tools to edit the video clip, and add effects such as fades, wipes, and dissolves.

- Enhance movies with music, voice-overs, and sound effects.

- Save the movie and link to it or embed it in a blog or wiki or on a web page, or post it on YouTube (or TeacherTube or other video-sharing site).

## Creating a Video with Windows Movie Maker

A good way to get started is to let Movie Maker create a movie automatically using the AutoMovie feature. Then you can learn how to do your own editing and moviemaking.

1. Connect your camera to your computer and download your movies into Movie Maker.

2. In the Movie Tasks panel, under 2. Edit Movie, click Make an AutoMovie.

3. On the Select an AutoMovie Editing Style page, click on a style. Movie Maker will use this style to create your movie.

4. Under More options, click Enter a Title for the Movie.

5. Type a title.

6. If you have music on your computer that you want to use as background, click More Options under Select Audio or Background Music. Click Browse and select a song title.

7. Click Done. AutoMovie will edit your video.

8. Click Play on the Preview monitor.

# *Where* Can You Find More Information about Visual Learning Tools?

Free interactive, online tools from Intel:
www.intel.com/education/tools

Creative Commons:
http://creativecommons.org

The WNET National Teacher Training Institute explains how to use educational video and offers short videos that demonstrate their use:
www.thirteen.org/edonline/ntti/resources/video2.html

30 of the Best Educational Tools for Auditory, Visual, and Kinesthetic Learners:
http://diplomaguide.com/articles/30_of_the_Best_Educational_Tools_for_Auditory_Visual_and_Kinesthetic_Learners.html

# 7

# Virtual Environments

## *What* Are Virtual Environments?

Virtual environments can be excellent for teaching and learning! This is an exciting step into the world of Web 2.0 and offers you and your students the opportunity to teach and learn in a new way.

Just as with any application or tool, the effectiveness and appropriateness of a virtual environment depends on what your educational goal is, what the learners are doing and why, and how you can assess their learning outcomes. In general, virtual environments are all around us, and it is important to consider them as one tool in your educational repertoire.

Multiuser virtual environments (MUVEs) have been a popular form of multimedia-based entertainment for some time. However, attention has recently turned to exploring their use to support learning, and groups have been creating MUVEs and investigating their effectiveness both for professional development and for curricular activities. Meadows (2008) defines *virtual worlds* as "online interactive systems in which multiple people, sometimes millions of people, share in the development of an interactive narrative" (p. 34). We know that environments such as these offer individuals and groups the possibility for creativity, collaboration, and communication.

## *Why* Are Virtual Environments Useful Tools?

Students do many things these days in the world of virtual environments. They invent extensive and creative lives for themselves in which they play, build, interact, and explore. The best known and currently most popular of these environments is Second Life (SL). It is not the same as World of Warcraft (WoW) or other game-oriented multiuser environments in which the goal is to win something or to play against others. Second Life is a 3D user-created world that is used for multiple purposes but is most particularly focused on social interaction.

Education is making bold steps into the world of virtual environments in several ways. Second Life was developed by Linden Lab and launched on June 23, 2003. According to Burgess and Caverly (2009), in 2009, more than 200 postsecondary institutions had created a presence in Second Life. You can find a list of universities that have registered as using Second Life here: http://wiki.secondlife.com/wiki/Second_Life_Education_Directory. In a systematic review of published studies concerning the uses and application of Second Life in K–12 and higher education settings, Inman, Wright, and Hartman (2010) reported, "Second Life is currently predominantly the domain of higher education, with 23 out of the identified 27 studies conducted by higher education faculty or in the context of a higher education classroom or with higher education students" (p. 55).

Second Life is accessible via any broadband internet connection. Interested users are required to download a free Second Life Viewer, a client software package that enables individuals to create an avatar and become a "resident" of SL. Once you become a resident, you can do many things: meet others, join groups and socialize, participate in activities and professional development opportunities, build a "location" for living, and even buy and sell property. Although joining SL is free, there is a cost for some activities.

As you create your avatar, or persona, it is possible to reinvent yourself. Your avatar is then free to wander the many 3D locations, including seaside towns, educational islands, or virtual worlds that others have designed. SL users (termed residents) create most of the "in-world" environments using built-in tools (Atkinson, 2008). The result is a place to wander, socialize, build, and learn.

Built into the software is a 3D modeling tool based on simple geometric shapes that allows a resident to build virtual objects. This can be used in combination with the Linden Scripting Language, which can be used to add functionality to objects. More complex 3D sculpted primitives (also known as sculpted prims and sculpties), textures for clothing or other objects, and animations and gestures can be created using external software. The Second Life terms of service ensure that users retain copyright for any content they create, and the server and client provide simple digital rights management functions.

Just how popular is Second Life? According to Linden Labs, more than 30 million user hours are logged each month (Voyager, 2013). The estimate is that approximately 33 million individuals have signed up for SL accounts and typically 57,000 to 61,000 people are logged on at any given time during peak times. Large corporations such as IBM, Sony, Sears, and Mercedes-Benz have devoted enormous resources to create Second Life islands, and many celebrities actually have live performances through their avatars (Atkinson, 2008). Some believe that Second Life and other virtual environments will replace the web as we have known it. A recent (June 2013) YouTube interview with Rod Humble, the CEO of Second Life, is available at www.youtube.com/watch?v=kwNCU3RGruE.

As mentioned, the number of individuals who use virtual environments has been growing exponentially, but that does not necessarily translate into its use by educators for their own development or in their professional practice. What, then, are the educational benefits or reasons that these are being used? Is it really the next big thing or the educators' silver bullet we have all been searching for? Kelton (2008) suggests that it may be something worth considering:

> Just as once many in higher education loudly proclaimed that the internet was of no practical use and was filled with questionable material and marketing, so too do critics today have their doubts about virtual worlds. But the web grew into a vital part of our lives, and a growing number of people believe that virtual worlds will do so the same. (p. 22)

According to Dede, Dieterle, Clarke, Ketelhut, and Nelson (2007), students may no longer "see face-to-face learning as the gold standard for education" (p. 339). They continue: "Their participation in multifaceted, distributed, and mediated learning experiences outside of classrooms and courses causes them to see more traditional school learning as rather mundane because it is based solely on face-to-face learning" (p. 339).

Barab, Thomas, Dodge, Carteaux, and Tuzun (2005) suggest:

> This work sits at the intersection of education, entertainment, and social commitment and suggests an expansive focus for instructional designers. The focus is on engaging classroom culture and relevant aspects of student life to inspire participation consistent with social commitments and educational goals interpreted locally. (p. 86)

Barab et al. (2005) also state that this is "a product that is not a game, yet remains engaging, is not a lesson, yet fosters learning, is not evangelical, yet nurtures a social agenda" (p. 88).

More important research has begun to show that students may learn in this environment. Hickey, Ingram-Goble, and Jameson (2009) reported that their research does suggest gains in learning. In two studies of Quest Atlantis, they found sixth grade students making "larger gains in understanding and achievement" than in classes that used expository text to learn the same concepts and skills (p. 187). In a study of a similar type of project, Ketelhut (2007) found that her results "suggest that embedding science inquiry curricula in novel platforms like a MUVE might act as a catalyst for change in students' self-efficacy and learning processes" (p. 99).

In addition, many educators have discovered virtual environments for their own growth and learning. At the ISTE NECC 2009 conference, one presentation was by The Virtual Pioneers, a group of social studies educators using Second Life to learn, collaborate, and share information to enhance their professional development and professional network. Once educators began to recognize the power of these environments, their explorations grew and evolved.

# *When* Do Teachers Use Virtual Environments?

## Classroom Integration

Teachers are using virtual environments in a wide variety of ways to support learning outcomes. For students, educational MUVEs are designed to engage minds, promote learning, and encourage creative thinking. They have typically been designed to support inquiry-based learning and conceptual understanding. The activities that accompany these environments promote the notion that, as in the real world of complex issues, there are no simple, single, or right/wrong answers; rather, they encourage divergent and exploratory thinking. Students using educational MUVEs frequently are required to gather information offline, and usually there is an expectation of a final product that may take many forms. Inman et al. (2010) suggest that "potential uses of Second Life include role-play, game and simulation creation, implementation within distance education programs, and the ability to encourage student-centered learning activities" (p. 44).

For example, researchers and educators at Loyalist College used Second Life as an educational tool to train Justice Students in how to interview travelers at international borders. Degast-Kennedy reportedly interviewed her students after they had completed their Second Life training and found that her students' scores increased by 28% when compared to the previous year when Second Life was not used (Hudson & Degast-Kennedy, 2009). One type of activity is known as epistemic games; they are "explicitly based on theory of learning in the digital age and are designed to allow learners to develop domain-specific expertise under realistic constraints" (Rupp et al., 2009, p. 4). The goal is to have learners experience what it is like to really think and act like "journalists, artists, business managers, or engineers by using digital learning technologies to solve realistic complex performance tasks" (p. 4). Designers develop a game that mimics the core experiences that learners outside the gaming environment would have in a professional practicum in a particular field. The experiences that epistemic games afford and make accessible to learners are characterized by a blend of individual and collaborative work in both real-life and virtual settings.

One example of an educational MUVE is the River City Project, described as "a multi-user virtual environment for learning scientific inquiry and 21st century skills" (http://rivercity.activeworlds.com). With funding from the National Science Foundation, researchers at Harvard "developed an interactive computer simulation for middle grades science students to learn scientific inquiry and 21st century skills. River City has the look and feel of a videogame but contains content developed from National Science Education Standards, National Educational Technology Standards, and 21st Century Skills" (http://rivercity.activeworlds.com). The River City Project was designed to represent a virtual 19th-century American town; the town happens to be plagued by disease. The simulation requires students to work in teams, study the materials presented, and then develop a hypothesis regarding the cause of the disease. They have the ability to read documents, examine photographs, visit the hospital, and interview River City citizens. Virtual agents are available to provide guidance, but the students determine the approach they will take (Ketelhut, 2007).

Another popular educational MUVE is Atlantis Remixed (http://atlantis-remixed.org). Atlantis Remixed is an extension of Quest Atlantis. Quest Atlantis was a virtual environment for students aged 9–12 that immersed them in educational "quests." In Quest Atlantis, students worked to change the doomed future of the mythical city of Atlantis through conducting environmental study, interviewing members of the community, studying other cultures, and developing action plans. Atlantis Remixed builds upon these activities and is currently in beta testing. However, the program now reportedly has over 60,000 players worldwide and was developed to immerse children 9–16 years in transformational play that includes online and offline learning activities. The developers of Quest Atlantis and Atlantis Remixed have created a compelling storyline that was specifically designed to inspire social action. Barab et al. (2005) conducted research on the original Quest Atlantis and concluded, "We now see ourselves in the business of supporting the emergence of sociotechnical structures so as to support a common inter-subjective experience, not simply designing technical artifacts" (p. 104). Lim, Nonis, and Hedberg (2006) also studied this environment and found growth in learning among the students who participated.

Research suggests that educational MUVEs should not focus solely on the virtual environment; learners still do best when they have ongoing support from the teacher and built-in time (and obligations) for self-reflection. As with most educational computer-based games, MUVEs are more effective in supporting learning when embedded in ongoing instruction.

The National Robotics Engineering Center at Carnegie Mellon University in Pittsburgh, Pennsylvania, has developed an interesting online and interactive application that allows students to work with robotics in the classroom. Robot Virtual Worlds (RVW) "is a high-end simulation environment that enables students, without robots, to learn programming (http://robotvirtual-worlds.com)." Jason McKenna, a K–8 gifted support teacher in the Hopewell Area School District in Pennsylvania, uses RVW in his STEM classes and writes about his experiences on the Robotics Academy Blog (http://robotics-academy.org/blog/2013/05/16/a-teachers-pov-robotics-in-a-stem-classroom). McKenna writes:

> As teachers, we are constantly looking for ways to make the subjects that we are teaching relevant. Students are always asking when they will ever use a particular concept, or how what they are learning applies to a real life scenario. Admittedly, teachers sometimes have a hard time answering those questions.
>
> Thankfully, teaching robotics and computer programming puts those questions to rest. Because technology is so ubiquitous in students' lives, students will immediately see the benefits of learning how to program. Moreover, robotics is the perfect

platform to show the application of math and science concepts to everyday scenarios.

In addition to all of that stuff that we educators like to talk about, students just have fun programming a robot to do something. Add in the allure of some competition, and you have yourself a pretty engaged classroom.

To learn more about the Robot Virtual World software, check out this informative YouTube video: www.youtube.com/watch?v=jHSmG1eTg_s.

Another example of an educational MUVE is Mission US (www.mission-us.org). Mission US was developed for elementary students studying social studies and is a free multimedia project that engages students in U.S. history through interactive gaming. For example, in Mission 1: "For Crown or Colony?" students or players act as a printer's apprentice in 1770 Boston. In this capacity, they encounter patriots and loyalists and are exposed to social and political unrest stemming from the aftereffects of the Boston Massacre. Students and players are then faced with determining their allegiances to the crown or colony.

In the Brooklyn High School for Global Citizenship, funding from the Motorola Innovation Generation grant allowed educators to develop a new curriculum for a freshman physical science class that takes advantage of the characteristics of the virtual world in Second Life. The curriculum is designed to be well aligned to the state curriculum standards and to supplement face-to-face teaching and learning, yet their goal is to "teach the kids how to be citizen-scientists in the future" (Czarnecki, 2008, p. 14). For example, one activity required the students to tour a virtual Naples, Italy, and conduct a survey of a trash dump, which they used to make comparisons with their own real-life trash dump.

Specific educational strategies that are supported in Second Life and that work well include creating interactive workshops, scavenger hunts, and quizzes. Others include having students demonstrate their knowledge and connections through photography shows, role playing, machinima (animated movies), and contests. Guests may enter using the persona of speakers, debates, or movie screenings. And finally, students can generate artifacts such as buildings, T-shirts, or other products; for example, UNC pharmacy students conduct

poster presentations in Second Life (www.youtube.com/watch?v=ksEPD8uhVk
k&feature=player_embedded#at=11).

You might like to read more about how one school is using Second Life to
assist students in their real life (http://pharmacy.unc.edu/news/a-closer-look/
using-second-life-to-help-students-in-real-life).

Individuals involved in teaching art education are also exploring the potential
in the virtual worlds. Art educators have considered the creation of art, online
art exhibitions, performance art, and education about the creation of art and
what it means to have visual culture (Liao, 2008). These ideas have translated
into a variety of activities in which budding artists share their developing and
completed works and have the opportunity to give and receive feedback on
emerging efforts. Liao also suggests that the way in which avatars are created
and presented is a form of art.

Imagine a "social studies class examining immigration building a virtual Ellis
Island, complete with the Statue of Liberty and Lower East Side tenements"
(Czarnecki & Gullett, 2007, p. 36). Consider students building an avalanche
or learning math by shopping in virtual environments, or using 3D rays in a
geometry unit as students work on their angles, proofs, and demonstrations
of conceptual understanding. Or perhaps consider the impact on students who
can explore a green library launched in 2009 called Emerald City and learn
about ecological issues through an interactive platform (saving both trees,
space, and heat!). A teacher or library/media instructor can log in and allow
their students to explore or hear a lecture. "One upcoming program will
cover photovoltaics, the science behind converting sunlight into electricity"
(Barack, 2009, p. 13).

EcoMUVE (http://ecomuve.gse.harvard.edu) is another exciting curriculum research project that was developed at the Harvard Graduate School
of Education. This project has received funding from the National Science
Foundation and Qualcomm's Wireless Reach initiative. EcoMUVE uses immersive virtual environments to teach middle school students about ecosystems
and causal patterns. "The goal of the EcoMUVE project is to help students
develop a deeper understanding of ecosystems and causal patterns with a
curriculum that uses Multi-User Virtual Environments" (http://ecomuve.gse.
harvard.edu). Here is a YouTube video demonstrating the educational applications of this project: www.youtube.com/watch?v=afrp81u-skU.

Finally, Jibe (http://reactiongrid.com/what.aspx) is a new MUVE platform that was created by ReactionGrid. Within Jibe, you can create, publish, and monitor your own virtual world. Users create an avatar to explore this world and can even explore other users' virtual worlds. Jibe is similar to Second Life. It can be embedded on web pages and can also be accessed from mobile devices. Currently, Boston College, Cedar Crest Academy, Chanchung American International School, Colorado Mountain College, George Mason University, Georgia Tech, Hong Kong Polytechnic, Future University Japan, Purdue, and Rutgers University use Jibe.

## Professional Development

Teachers are social, and they are universally eager to develop their connectivity on two levels. First, educators want to improve their practice, reflect on their activities, and learn from others. These goals may have encouraged them to explore virtual environments such as Second Life. But it is also true that humans, as individuals, have an innate desire to share, communicate, and grow on a personal level. People from all over the world who share interests have found the Second Life environment to be richer, more creative, and more expressive than other tools, even other Web 2.0 tools.

A variety of sites have evolved to introduce and support teachers who wish to explore the qualities and characteristics of Second Life. The Teaching Village is a website for educators interested in exploring virtual worlds. Its motto is "We're better when we work together," and they support teachers as they learn. Barbara (www.teachingvillage.org/2009/07/13/why-every-language-teacher-needs-a-second-life) writes, "Considering that I thought an avatar was a deity in Hindu Mythology, I think it's fair to say that my learning curve was pretty steep." She goes on to describe her exposure and growth in this environment and appears genuinely delighted that members of her learning community come from many countries and speak many languages.

Other sites offer introductions to all the possibilities. A list of ways to use Second Life in education can be found at How and Why to use Second Life for Education (http://scienceroll.com/2007/09/19/how-and-why-to-use-second-life-for-education). Other information and connections to those using it can be found at EduTech Wiki (http://edutechwiki.unige.ch/en/Second_Life).

# Using Virtual Realities for Skill Acquisition, Maintenance, and Refinement in Teacher Education

Melissa D. Hartley

In the spring of 2011, Barbara L. Ludlow had the idea to incorporate Second Life (SL) into teacher preparation courses in the online programs in the Department of Special Education at West Virginia University. We initially attempted to use SL in campus-based undergraduate courses, and the instruction for students to learn how to use the technology happened face-to-face within a "brick and mortar" classroom. Based on the success of these initial experiences, we decided to test whether providing online graduate students with instructions for how to use SL could enable those students to learn to use the technology independently, so that classroom instruction in online classes could occur within Second Life. Because of the interactive nature of SL, the idea was to use it as a platform for role-playing exercises to practice skills within my course on Collaboration, Consultation, and Inclusion. Ludlow requested volunteers from the online graduate programs, and provided the students with instructions for getting started within Second Life. The students then met with us within SL, and their success led to incorporating the use of SL in online graduate courses on a regular basis.

When class sessions were initially held within SL, there were many learning opportunities in how to improve delivery of instruction within the virtual reality (Hartley, Ludlow, & Duff, 2013). At first, Wimba Live Classroom, an online conferencing tool, remained the primary educational platform for live, interactive, real-time online instruction. However, with time, the use of the online conferencing tool decreased, and the use of SL increased, with SL becoming the primary tool for live class sessions. Because SL is interactive, its use as an educational platform is valuable for practicing skills needed by both preservice and inservice teachers. Across the semester, many skills are practiced, including working through steps of the interpersonal problem-solving model, effective communication skills (paraphrasing, reflecting, offering support, using general openings, stating the implied, clarifying, etc.), team development, co-teaching, using statements and asking questions, and responding to conflict and resistance. To view video clips of sample class sessions, and students working within SL, see http://drhartleywvu-slvideos. blogspot.com.

When SL was initially used in the online graduate program, there were approximately 50 students each semester using SL in their classes. In the 2013–14 academic year, there will be approximately 125 students each semester using SL as the educational platform for their courses. Feedback from students in course evaluations has been very positive, with student comments such as the following:

"This was an excellent learning experience and allowed us to actually collaborate and learn a lot more through an online class."

"While I admit I thought Second Life was crazy at first, I have found this has been my favorite class."

"At first I was nervous about Second Life, but after using the program, I think it's a wonderful way to hold online class."

"I really enjoyed this class, and I think taking it in Second Life made it much more enjoyable."

"I think all online classes should be held in Second Life. Loved it!"

Currently, we are working as part of an international research team investigating the use of SL in education. During spring 2013, Anders Morch, Valentina Caruso, and Ingvill Thomassen from the University of Oslo collected data during my class sessions to investigate role-playing and interactions. Nine class sessions were observed and screen recorded. Learning activities during these recorded sessions included interactive lecture, small-group role-play activities, individual activities, small-group problem-solving activities, small-group practice of collaborative skills (i.e., active listening, conflict resolution, effective communication, etc.), and group presentations by students in class. In examining the educational use of SL, a sociocultural approach framed this study, by investigating the following questions:

- What features of Second Life support collaborative learning?

- How can social interaction in SL affect learning?

- How do the artifacts in SL facilitate role-playing activities among the learners?

- How does the teacher facilitate social interaction in learning activities?

- How might SL foster social interaction through relevant learning activities?

Results are currently being analyzed through a mixed-methods approach. An interaction analysis is being used to analyze the interaction data from the screen recordings of the nine observations. In addition to the interaction analysis, participants were interviewed, and also responded to an online survey with Likert-type questions, and the option for elaboration through open-ended responses.

*Melissa D. Hartley, Ph.D., is a teaching assistant professor in the Department of Special Education at West Virginia University. Her research interests include using virtual reality simulations in teacher preparation for preservice and inservice teachers, focusing on acquisition, maintenance, and refinement of skills.*

Many school districts, states, and organizations have set up locations in Second Life. You will find islands for library media professionals, high school science teachers, and primary generalists. Organizations offering every type of learning abound.

# *Who* Is Using Virtual Environments for Teaching and Learning?

Of course, Second Life is not the only virtual environment for learners and children. Another very popular environment is Webkinz (www.webkinz.com). A gift of a stuffed animal used to be just that; the recipient gave it a name and perhaps talked to it. Not any more! If you purchase a Webkinz stuffed animal—and Webkinz animals come in all manner of shapes and sizes—you also get a code. The recipient goes online and registers the animal. Once there, the resident can do many of the things that those in Second Life can do, but this environment is targeted more to preteens.

You can teleport to another location, take classes in a school, own a home and start a garden, and also take your pet to the veterinarian so that it remains healthy (the instructions to parents do say that although a pet who is not cared for may become ill, none are ever allowed to die!). An interview with a Webkinz-active 10-year-old girl resulted in this information:

> It is a lot of fun. You get away from the real world, and my friends helped me know what to do and how to do things. I have a beagle, a cat, and a salamander. I like to take care of them, and take care of my house and garden. I bathe my animals, brush their teeth, and tend to my plants in my garden. I get around by teleporting myself, and I can see if any of my friends are on when I am. You can send messages but they can only be certain safe things and no bad words. (Cassie, personal communication, August 2009)

For other youngsters, Club Penguin is the favorite virtual environment (www.clubpenguin.com). Club Penguin tells parents that it is a virtual world for kids dedicated to safety and creativity. Although advanced features have a subscription fee associated with them, children can explore the environment for free. The website also states, "We value social involvement and encourage the kids who play Club Penguin to get involved in projects that support developing communities, and help children and families around the world" (www.clubpenguin.com/parents).

Members of Club Penguin also create their penguin avatar, and they have a wide variety of learning adventures, places to visit, and things to do. These include coloring, contests, online votes, and many other ways to engage with friends socially. Members can become tour guides and earn coins, but you must pass a test about Club Penguin to be selected. As with other virtual environments, there is a store where you can spend your coins, find penguin paraphernalia, and decorate your home.

Even though Webkinz and Club Penguin are for children, they can also be easy entry points for adults. Lisa Cundiff, from Kansas, reported that she "introduced teachers/administrators to the use of Webkinz as a way of learning basic social networking skills, information literacy, skills building, and responsibility" (L. Cundiff, personal communication, August 2009).

These are not necessarily the same as guided educational experiences that are completed within a school curriculum. For example, South Greenville Elementary School in North Carolina (www.pittschools.org/sge) has 670 students, but a small group of advanced students take part in a Young Einstein Club for Grades 3–5. In this project students worked to plan, design, and construct a space compound, located on a distant planet named VRLAB. The students used virtual reality software to build the compound and walk around in it. Students were responsible for including a specific set of objectives and criteria in their compound creation. This activity allowed students to construct an imaginative virtual environment while being guided by the objectives and criteria of the project.

SecretBuilders (www.secretbuilders.com) is a virtual world where kids can develop an online presence and live, learn, and play in an interactive educational setting. Kelly Tenkley (http://ilearntechnology.com/?tag=kelly-tenkely), a Grade 3–5 technology teacher and technology integration specialist and instructional coach for elementary teachers in Colorado, uses SecretBuilders regularly in her teaching. You can learn more about this on one of the site's community blogs (http://blog.secretbuilders.com/2009/12/how-teacher-uses-secretbuilders-in-her.html).

Tenkley has reportedly used SecretBuilders for interactive online assignments. For example, she assigned her students to conduct interviews of scientific characters (which are created and maintained by the site) when her students were studying famous scientists. Once the interviews were completed, she assigned her students to create articles acting as newspaper journalists on SecretBuilders' online magazine called The Crooked Pencil (www.secretbuilders.com/crooked-pencil.html). These articles were then published on the site where other students could read and comment about them. According to Tenkley:

> What I really think is neat about SecretBuilders is a virtual world, but it goes beyond just the play of most virtual worlds, and it actually teaches students about history and historical

figures and literary figures. It does that through interaction. Kids can actually interact with the historical figures in the virtual world and learn about them (http://blog.secretbuilders. com/2009/12/how-teacher-uses-secretbuilders-in-her.html)

Also, you can see a video of Tenkley describing her experiences with the site: www.youtube.com/watch?v=O4RkXzq5Skw.

Space Heroes Universe (www.spaceheroes.com) was designed to help kids develop thinking in the areas of resource management and logistics, motor skill enhancement, and social communication. Space Heroes Universe is a fun online adventure that does well in simulating real-life skills such as teamwork and frames these experiences in an exciting and interactive world. The game has also been praised for its entertainment value. For example, players can dance, start a band, compete against each other, and explore the vast universe. Space Heroes has received favorable feedback from both teachers and parents and has also received recognition from game reviewers. To learn more about Space Heroes Universe, go here: www.spaceheroes.com/kudos.do#aparents.

Minecraft (http://minecraft.net) is an immensely popular online gaming environment that may have powerful educational applications as well. Minecraft is simply a game about breaking and placing blocks. In the early stages, users built structures to protect against damaging monsters. However, as the game grew in scope, users began to collaborate when creating block structures and strategies against block-breaking monsters. Basically, the game has become a collaborative version of online Lego. By June of 2013, nearly 11 million users had purchased the game. To see how Minecraft is being marketed and used as an educational tool, please go here: http://minecraftedu.com/page.

The University of Luebeck, in Germany, designed a study in which a third grade class used virtual reality. The learners created an environment known as a "mixed reality world," in which real and virtual worlds are merged to produce a new environment where real and digital objects can co-exist. The class's goal was to incorporate computer science into the study of arts. The children used Lego software to animate and interact with things they had previously created. They were thus able to mix the ways of thinking about these two areas and experienced true interactive learning.

Opportunities abound for students to experience educational opportunities in a virtual environment. For example, the University of Cincinnati planned a Second Life adventure to celebrate the 200-year anniversary of the publication of Charles Darwin's *On the Origin of Species* (Collins, 2008). Although the university planned many on-campus activities, they extended those by recreating Darwin's historic journey, including representing indigenous species in their natural habitat. Because they used actual photographs, videos, and other materials collected by students on trips to the Galapagos, their Second Life site offers authentic opportunities for learners throughout the world to explore and interact while learning the history of the adventure.

What might the longer view of virtual worlds be for educators and learners in the next many years? Kelton (2008) reminds us:

> The educational aspect of virtual worlds has attracted a diversity of people and organizations. Government agencies (such as NOAA) and programs offering hazmat or other simulated training, students taking both credit and noncredit classes, and people from all around the world coming together in the same place, at the same time, to work on a shared idea or project— many of these efforts are simply not feasible in the non-digital world. (p. 22)

Although research into the use of virtual environments is only beginning to be seen in the literature base, Leese (2009) did report that freshmen were able to stay involved in their class and with their colleagues between face-to-face sessions through the use of a virtual setting and carefully structured environments. Unfortunately, we may need to wait for a robust body of research that actually provides useful information on the affordances and constraints of using these environments.

Wagner (2008) reports that users can practice new behaviors and repeat them, in safe but productive environments. This research study resulted in more engagement than expected by the instructor, and enthusiasm from the students. "Users thus create their own experiences and construct their own knowledge. Different from much of classroom learning, the experience is immersive and learning-by-doing" (p. 263).

Second Life has some of the same issues that the web has, or for that matter, that life itself has (Botterbusch & Talab, 2009). For example, individuals can have multiple or false identities, offer illicit materials, or take part in spamming. There have been some reports of harassment, vandalism, and unauthorized use of information.

In 2008, Google experimented with Lively, which was designed to be "a free, browser-based virtual environment with tight integration to MySpace, Facebook, OpenSocial, and Google gadgets like Picasa and YouTube" (Updated Breaking News, 2008). Lively closed January 1, 2009. It is important to recognize that although Second Life is now the most heavily populated and robust virtual environment, this may not always be the case.

# *How* Do You Get Started with Virtual Environments?

It is worth the time to get familiar with Second Life (http://secondlife.com) as a start to your efforts in the virtual world. And we strongly recommend that, as an educator, you become very familiar with Second Life before you begin designing instructional activities that take advantage of its affordances. The place to begin is at Orientation Island Public, where you can learn to fly, modify your avatar, and even make sure you are appropriately dressed. You have the ability to ask questions of the numerous Second Life Mentors, who can answer them as well as show you around. You can also stop at InfoHubs, where you can get information about specific aspects of thriving in Second Life.

There are three main ways to communicate: chat, instant messaging, and voice. You can chat by typing text into a text box at the bottom of your screen, much as you might do in a variety of technology environments; however, it can be read by anyone in the immediate vicinity. An instant message is private and can be sent to someone online synchronously; if they are not online, they will get your message in an email. Finally, you can speak to others, but it is best to have a headset and microphone system to be effective. It is worth noting that nothing in Second Life is really private; others may save and print your chats.

Soon you will have mastered teleporting (a great way to move where you want to go quickly). You can then learn how to search for specific things you are interested in—for example, other teachers. The International Society for Technology in Education (ISTE) Special Interest Group for Virtual Environments (SIGVE) maintains a Second Life presence with help, guides, and many discussions taking place. That may also be a way to find others interested in topics similar to your own.

Another well-established island is Jokaydia, which was developed by two Australians. It is a community of educators and artists who are dedicated to finding ways to use Second Life in education and the arts. The Discovery Educator Network (DEN) has also been established. In this area educators can connect and share with each other, exchange ideas, and often create innovative cross-cultural and cross-curricular projects.

Beth Knittle (2008) recommends the following as great places to begin your exploration of Second Life:

Genome Project: http://slurl.com/secondlife/Genome/158/119/29

ISTE SIGVE Island: http://maps.secondlife.com/index.php?q=ISTE&s=Places

Jokaydia: http://slurl.com/secondlife/jokaydia/113/150/23

Okeanos, a NOAA Island in Second Life: http://slurl.com/secondlife/Okeanos/64/217/30/

Paris 1900s: http://slurl.com/secondlife/Paris%201900/44/169/24

Roma (Ancient Rome): http://slurl.com/secondlife/ROMA/215/25/22

Explore Vasser's creation of the Sistine Chapel in SL: www.vassar.edu/headlines/2007/sistine-chapel.html

# *Where* Can You Find More Information about Virtual Environments?

There are many video introductions to Second Life. For example, www.youtube.com/watch?v=edUV0_FOl0M shows ways to move smoothly and with relative ease. Here are some more:

New Media Consortium virtual tour:
> www.youtube.com/watch?v=S9VZKTT6gZ8

Great Information for Educators using MUVEs:
> www.cited.org/index.aspx?page_id=159

For an excellent overview of SL (click on the hotlinks in the presentation to view the embedded videos):
> www.slideshare.net/sreljic/aect2007sreljic

Pros and Cons of Second Life in Education:
> http://sites.google.com/site/comminicationinsecondlife/second-life/pros-and-cons

8 Ways to Introduce Second Life for Educators:
> www.ctrlaltteach.com/8-ways-to-introduce-second-life-for-educators/#.UwqSi3mQbw

Second Life Science Islands:
> http://secondlife.com/destinations/science

Online Leadership for Global Kids:
> olpglobalkids.org

Global Kids Science—Students' Houses (Machinima):
> www.youtube.com/watch?v=yRkcT3PjYyM

Best Practices in Using Virtual Worlds for Education:
> http://olpglobalkids.org/pdfs/BestPractices.pdf

# 8

# Wikis and Other Collaboration Tools

## *What* Is a Wiki?

Wikis are web pages that students can use to write, edit, and add elements, such as images and video, to create collaborative projects. When the assignments are tailored well, the projects involve a group of students in researching, synthesizing, and analyzing information, writing about what they've learned, and evaluating and editing one another's work. The end result is a product that all members of the group believe is their best work.

The most well known wiki in public use is Wikipedia, a collaborative ency-clopedia that includes an enormous amount of information. It is constantly updated. Contributors and evaluators monitor and edit the entries, which serves as a way to authenticate the contents so that people can trust the infor-mation. The most popular wikis in education are PBworks and Wikispaces.

Although wikis continue to be popular for collaboration, there are many other collaborative tools that students and teachers are using in classrooms today with great success. The emergence of new tools demonstrates how important collaboration has become for student achievement. In fact, there is widespread recognition that collaboration is essential to learning, and it is key in the Common Core State Standards. With Common Core driving so much of what teachers do, collaboration tools have become more important in the mix of how teachers encourage students to learn.

The Common Core State Standards Initiative includes Comprehension and Collaboration in the ELA standards with the mandate for students to "prepare for and participate effectively in a range of conversations and collaborations with diverse partners, building on others' ideas and expressing their own clearly and persuasively" (Common Core State Standards, 2013b, n.p.).

With collaborative learning, educators create small groups of students who work together on a project, problem, or task. Students in the group feel responsible for one another's work and discuss and provide feedback to each other. Through collaboration students acquire the career skill of teamwork and learn that working with peers provides a good way to achieve superior results.

Technology enhances the options for students to work collaboratively in that they can be together in the same classroom or half a world away and still communicate and build a presentation or other evidence of their work. Wikis were perhaps the first classroom tool for collaboration because students could share a single document and teachers could monitor individual contributions. Recently, schools have adopted cloud-based tools such as Microsoft's Office 365 for students to use for collaborative work.

# *Why* Is a Collaboration Tool a Useful Tool?

Class assignments that include elements of project-based learning, collaboration, authentic work, and an audience can help students develop and refine higher-level thinking skills. Wikis are good tools to use for such assignments.

The possibilities for classroom uses include group collaboration and problem solving, peer editing during the writing process, and electronic portfolios. Students produce a shared document online by writing, editing, and revising it in their own class, across a grade, school, district, or with others. They can work from anywhere, which means they are able to contribute anytime rather than being limited to the school day or class period. If they are creating work that others will use to learn about the topic, both the task and the audience are authentic.

Students read and build on each other's work in these collaborative online environments because they can do research, analyze what they've read, and synthesize it into useful knowledge before contributing their work. The group then reflects on it, and finally they discuss and edit it—with the knowledge that changing anything is easy, and that it can easily be changed back because previous versions are saved.

An example would be a team writing assignment in which students research a topic in the curriculum, analyze what they find, enter their syntheses into the wiki, and consult with one another to make sure the topic is covered thoroughly and accurately. They can use peer editing to make sure the writing is clear and concise.

Because everyone in the group can add, edit, delete, or change the contents, this makes the process democratic. Changes are visible instantly, which encourages responsibility for one's actions and accountability to the group. In addition, it is possible for the teacher to track the work done by each student in a collaborative effort, which encourages a high level of contribution and quality performance.

# *When* Do Teachers Use Collaboration Tools?

## Classroom Integration

Carnegie Mellon's Eberly Center for Teaching Excellence and Educational Innovation defines collaborative learning as "people working together to solve a problem, create a product, or derive meaning from a body of material" (Eberly Center for Teaching Excellence and Educational Innovation, 2013, n.p.). A central question or problem serves to organize and drive activities, as well as to encourage application, analysis, and synthesis of course material. They list the functions of collaborative tools as to:

- Facilitate real-time and asynchronous text, voice, and video communication

- Assist in basic project management activities

- Support co-creation by enabling groups to modify output in real time or asynchronously

- Facilitate consensus-building through group discussions and polling

- Simplify and streamline resource management

- Enable local and remote presentation and archiving of completed projects

The Common Core K–12 standards define what students should understand and be able to do by the end of each grade. The first of three Anchor standards for English Language Arts is Comprehension and Collaboration. The most common uses for collaboration tools are student writing, projects, web searches, whiteboards, backchannels, and other voice conversations, as well as for homework and study groups. Some popular tools for these purposes follow.

## Writing

**Draft** (http://draftin.com) is a simple writing editor that has collaborative tools that lets students post their work then invite peers to edit and comment.

**Google Drive** (http://drive.google.com) provides a collaborative work space for students to write and work in teams.

**Hackpad** (http://hackpad.com) helps students to develop collaborative note-taking skills and write outlines.

**My Simple Surface** (http://mysimplesurface.com) works on the principle of writing surfaces. Students create as many surfaces as they need and link them to one another. They can manage large projects with linked surfaces. Students can organize the surfaces, edit one another's work, and share the results.

**Primarypad** (http://primarypad.com) is an online word processor designed for classrooms so that students and teachers can work together on documents in real time.

**Titanpad** (http://titanpad.com) allows people to work on the same document simultaneously.

**Zoho Docs** (www.zoho.com/docs) is an online word processor, spreadsheet, and presentation tool that allows students to create and share documents online in real time.

## Projects

**Wizehive** (www.wizehive.com) allows students to share files, manage projects, track their activity, and collaborate with others. It provides a secure and private collaborative workspace that includes several tools that students use on a single platform.

## Web Search

**ChannelME** (www.crunchbase.com/company/channel-me) allows several students to browse a website simultaneously. They can see the content of a web page in real time and chat about the work.

**Search Team** (http://searchteam.com) is a simple tool that allows small groups of students to search and retrieve the best search results together.

## Whiteboards

**CoSketch** (http://cosketch.com) is a multiuser online whiteboard that allows students to visualize and share ideas as images in real time.

**Scribblar** (www.scribblar.com) is a great, simple, multiuser whiteboard with live audio, image collaboration, and text chat.

**Twiddla** (www.twiddla.com) is an online playground where students can mark up web pages, graphics, and photos or brainstorm.

## Backchannels and Other Conversations

**Chatzy** (www.chatzy.com) provides students with free private chats.

**NeatChat** (www.neatchat.com) allows students to have an online conversation with a group or team.

**Skype in Education** (http://education.skype.com) is designed for teachers and students and is a free global community of educators who exchange resources.

**Stinto** (http://stinto.net) lets students create a chat and invite others to join.

**TodaysMeet** (www.todaysmeet.com) provides a backchannel to connect with others in real time. Students can use the live stream to make comments, ask questions, and take notes.

## Homework and Study Groups

**Dweeber** (http://dweeber.com) is designed to help students work on their homework and build a community of peers.

**Thinkbinder** (http://thinkbinder.com) is a platform for students to create study groups.

## Turbo-Charged Wikis:
## Technology Embraces Cooperative Learning

Jon Orech

By infusing cooperative learning strategies, student-generated wikis become a much more productive activity. First, a teacher must establish a collaborative environment from the beginning of class. A wiki-based project should not be the first time students work together. Collaborative projects work well, but only if an environment of cooperation already exists.

The assigned project must possess two qualities. First, it must be an authentic problem or situation that must be solved collaboratively. Second, the final product must be used by another audience, preferably classmates to advance the learning of the entire class. In other words, the wiki cannot result in an assignment that is merely "turned in." Also, teachers need to remember that the wiki is only the tool to enhance learning; the problem solving is what drives the project.

In addition, teachers need to supply a system of expectations, due dates, and a constant flow of feedback throughout the development of project. They must build in time for students to meet during class to negotiate meaning in the planning and revision stages. Assessment must be a collaborative endeavor, with students having input on the rubric criteria before the completion of the project, as well as an opportunity to self-assess. Adherence to these strategies will ensure greater learning.

*Jon Orech is the Instructional Technology Coordinator for Downers Grove South High School, Downers Grove, Illinois.*

Collaboration tools, such as those just listed, and wikis provide features that are unlike most composing software and that offer interesting possibilities for learning and teaching. First, they allow people to edit someone else's work. Second, they retain previous versions that writers can revert to. Third, they keep track of everyone's individual entries and edits.

What the first option provides is the ability for true group collaboration on a document with peer editing. The second prevents the edits from permanently writing over the original, deleting words, ideas, or manners of expression that might actually have been the better way to say something. Educators must teach students how to evaluate the accuracy and appropriateness of content and revert to a previous version if content has been modified incorrectly.

The third option allows teachers to track students' work; they can see exactly how much work, and of what caliber, each member of the group contributed. If the final product and the process are graded separately, teachers can review the number of contributions as well as the quality. Students, aware that teachers can see all, are motivated to do their best.

In addition to having students read other groups' completed wikis—vetted by the teacher for accuracy, of course—on topics in the curriculum and learn content from them rather than from textbooks, teachers can invite parents and the community to read the work as a culminating activity that brings in a wider authentic audience.

If students are graded on the final product, they share a common goal and will want the work to be the best possible. When they help one another by editing and making changes to each other's work, it will be for the good of the product and the entire group.

Students learn from one another. The results, both for the learner as a thinking person and for the end product, can be greater than a single isolated learner can achieve. In addition, students engaged in providing explanations to other students can learn the subjects better themselves.

When students take ownership of both their contributions and the product as a whole, they can learn to respect the contributions and thinking of others and take pride in the results. The collaboration itself can result in creativity that learners spark in one another as they work together (and challenge one another's thinking) to improve the work.

Students share control of the environment and can monitor one another. Access is open to the collaborating students, with password protection, but only one person at a time can add content or edit. Because the earlier versions are saved, it is always possible to revert to a previous version or reconstruct content.

Unlike word processors and other desktop publishing tools, most wikis provide basic editing only, which means that students focus on the message rather than the format. Entering and editing text is easy and straightforward, and there's no real learning curve for students. Again, the focus is on the subject matter, because the tool is transparent.

Each student's work is saved, and teachers are able to track what each one has contributed to the product, both their contributions and their corrections to another student's work. Reviewing their entire body of contributions allows teachers to see how each student's thinking, writing, and editing skills have grown over time. Because of this, some teachers are using wikis as electronic portfolios for student projects.

In "Using Wikis as Electronic Portfolios," Huff (2008) explains:

> Using inquiry-based learning, I created a wiki page to pose questions, point students to resources, and encourage them to find their own answers and solutions for creating the portfolio. Then, rather than give them step-by-step directions for creating the portfolio, I chunked the project into small deadlines and guided and supported them through the process as they asked questions, experimented with different tools, and struggled with strategies for organizing the portfolios. ... I was amazed at the results: students created websites, new blogs, and combinations of the two. They weren't just stuffing papers in a manila folder: they were thinking critically and creatively, problem-solving, reflecting. (n.p.)

## Professional Development

Collaboration is an advantage for educators because, traditionally, teachers have worked in isolation with little sharing among peers. Wikis, as an easy tool to use for grade-level or subject-area teams, or for any other group collaboration, provide educators with a way to post and share information, strategies, thoughts, and lessons, and to build on one another's work. They also provide a backchannel for ongoing discussions among their peers about their work.

Vicki Phillips and Robert L. Hughes, in "Teacher Collaboration: The Essential Common-Core Ingredient," say:

> As the new standards are implemented, we must ensure that teachers are not left alone to figure out how best to teach to them. The standards are an opportunity for greater collaboration, fresher thinking, and a rearticulation of shared goals for teachers and students. By collaborating with each other and with instructional specialists through cycles of examining student work, creating hypotheses about how to implement Common Core–aligned lessons, implementing them, and making adjustments in their practice in real time, teachers can find the best ways to help their students reach these higher expectations while still maintaining individual styles and flexibility. (Phillips & Hughes, 2012, p. 32)

Administrators can use wikis with the staff. For example, principals can ask the staff to write and edit policy documents, such as internet safety rules or hallway safety procedures, using a wiki. This gives stakeholders a truly responsible role in creating the kind of document that reflects their beliefs. The best ideas will emerge as the group collaborates toward the goal of providing the document for the school.

Lisa Nielsen, Manhattan Technology Innovation Manager for the New York City Department of Education, offers a model of administrative wiki use in "Eight Ways To Use School Wikis." She explains that Jason Levy, Principal of CIS 339 in New York, posts daily notes on the school wiki so that teachers can read them when they have time. He includes announcements and reminders, attendance information, attaboys, and sometimes surveys or forms and news. The staff has to look in just one place to find out the important information.

Nielsen says,

> All teacher schedules, bell schedules, meetings, etc. can be posted right on the wiki so any staff member can locate their colleagues at anytime. This combined with the posting of staff absences and class coverage in the daily notes ensures that staff will always know where and when their colleagues can be found. (Nielsen, 2009, n.p.)

Anytime your school is having professional development, all the materials can be loaded to the wiki. No more copies to run off, folders to buy, teachers sharing if there aren't enough copies, or worrying about writing on your only copy. In addition, a discussion forum is associated with each wiki page. This is a great way to elicit feedback during professional development and to keep the conversation going afterwards.

Staff developers can use wikis with groups of educators in workshops and in preservice or inservice courses. They can use a wiki to have the educators share best practices and discuss teaching strategies. Group members can post discussion items for class in advance, add notes during the session, and edit and use the results later. They can collaborate on ideas, produce knowledge built on the thinking of each participant, and develop teamwork skills in the process.

Chad Evans (2013) says in "Collaboration Is Not a Time, It's a Mindset":

> The collaborative mindset is less about the tools we use to accomplish our goals and more about the desire to do whatever it takes to help students learn. The good news is, all of this is in our control. All of us can commit to one another to maximize the face-to-face time engaging in the deep and meaningful conversations. We can all take on the necessary roles to function as an effective and collaborative personal learning community. We can be honest and establish and support trusting relationships with one another. We can be transparent about our goals, process, and results while also maintaining and rewarding the confidence of our colleagues and their opinions. We can be open to trying new means of communicating, sharing, and working through digital tools that help keep the process and conversation ongoing between face-to-face meetings. Collaboration is an ongoing conversation. It is not a time. It is a mindset. (Evans, 2013, n.p.)

For example, in curriculum planning, teachers can set up a wiki for collaboration and assign sections for each to add content and resources (original materials as well as embedded or linked videos, presentations, and sources for research) that students would use when they study the topic. Sharing the work and being able to see what others have done helps the result be more cohesive and structured. Yet the shared responsibility takes away some of the burden, and the collaboration makes the tasks more collegial and reduces teachers' sense of isolation.

# *Who* Is Using Wikis for Teaching and Learning?

## Wikis for Everything

Wikis have become popular tools because of their versatility. For example, Audrey Colwell, first grade teacher at Slaughter Elementary School in McKinney, Texas, uses her class wiki to post important information. She says, "We use our class wiki for *everything!* I often compile resources, and then students access our wiki for learning in class or at home. We also display our learning and project products, such as picture slideshows, research PowerPoints, and more. Students can learn from home when absent, or in a 'flipped' way. It also allows for more independent learning at a student's own pace" (A. Colwell, personal communication, June 2013). Her class wiki is available at http://colwell2012-13.wikispaces.com/home.

## Eighth Grade Science Wiki

Cathy Laguna, eighth grade science teacher in the Quakertown Community School District, Pennsylvania, describes her yearlong wiki project (http://mrslagunasclass.wikispaces.com):

> At the beginning of the year I begin with a home page and an almost blank wiki. Each day, I post resources that are either needed for class or created during class. We form lab groups, and each group gets their own wiki page. Our first post to the lab group pages is about digital citizenship and what it means and looks like. Then as the students do their lab experiments, they post summaries and pictures on their lab group wiki pages.

In addition, the wiki serves as a hub to our class Diigo page, Edmodo, YouTube channel, and Flickr account. I share our progress occasionally with teachers via Twitter, which slowly increases the number of visits to our wiki. We track visits using Clustr Maps. Anything with an embed code can be incorporated into the wiki. We also post PDF files from the SmartBoard, pictures from class, Google docs and surveys, Quia web games, Wall Wishers, Edit Grids for lab data, videos of our labs, Draw.io diagrams, and anything the students suggest. If there isn't an embed code, I take a picture from the website using Jing or the snipping tool and then link the picture to the webpage so that it looks visually interesting and gives a preview of the link before students click. The table of contents feature on the wiki allows us to organize the page like a Web 2.0 journal of our school year. By the time June rolls around, the students have helped to create an incredible resource and a fun collection of memories from their eighth grade science class. (C. Laguna, personal communication, May 2013)

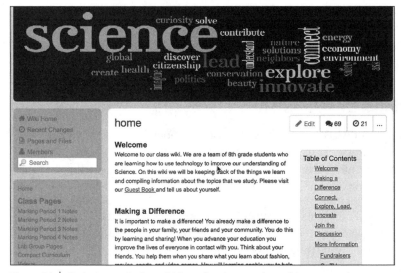

Figure 8.1 | Cathy Laguna's class wiki (http://mrslagunasclass.wikispaces.com)

## Diaries of the Latin American Revolutions

New Canaan High School's Diaries of the Latin American Revolutions, a role-playing simulation wiki, helped students write historical fiction. Students combined a historical analysis with a personal perspective for a more interesting look at revolutions. Teachers saw how each student contributed to the wiki by using the revision history feature (http://fiction.wikia.com/wiki/Diaries_of_the_Latin_American_Revolutions).

According to Kristine Goldhawk, one of the teachers involved:

> During the sophomore year, my class is dominated with various types of role-playing and simulations. I believe students who take on the personas of historical figures and "live the life" have a deeper understanding of the concepts and motivations that exist in history. While we were studying the Latin American revolutions that occurred in the 18th and 19th centuries last year, we decided to take what was a paper and pen journaling project and move it online, with the hopes of adding to it. Wikia Novelas (http://fiction.wikia.com/wiki/Fiction), a wiki based on all genres of fiction, gave us a place to do it. The students were excited when people from the outer world modified and edited the work. (K. Goldhawk, personal communication, 2013)

## Professional Development

Steven Anderson (2011), in "Back To School with Social Media," provides two examples of wiki use. He says "Recently some administrators got together on Twitter to talk about Social Media. They came up with a great reading list and more resources for other administrators and school leaders" (n.p.).

They created the Social Media Reading List wiki (http://newhampton.wikispaces.com/Social+Media+Reading+List) with the idea "to build a 'best of the web' reading/watching list for school leadership regarding using social media for school advancement."

Anderson also links readers to the Social Media Guidelines for Schools wiki (http://socialmediaguidelines.pbworks.com), a resource for creating social media policies. The wiki describes the guideline as "a collaborative project to generate Social Media Guidelines for school districts. The goal of this guideline is to provide instructional employees, staff, students, administrators, parents and the school district community direction when using social media applications both inside and outside the classroom."

## The Flat Classroom Project

Julie Lindsay, from the International School in Dhaka, Bangladesh, and Vicki Davis, from the Westwood Schools in Camilla, Georgia, won an award for their Flat Classroom Project (archived at http://flatclassroomproject.wikispaces.com).

This project was an active learning project created for students on opposite sides of the globe—Dhaka, Bangladesh and Camilla, Georgia—to discuss and experience 10 technological trends highlighted in the Thomas L. Friedman book *The World Is Flat* (2007). This telelearning activity was original in its use of Web 2.0 tools to foster communication and collaboration and to construct web spaces and share ideas. It also championed social networking as a pedagogically valid method for learning.

## Digitween Flat Classroom Project

Sandy Wisneski teaches Grades 6–8 at Catalyst Charter Middle School in Ripon, Wisconsin, a school that offers a dynamic, project-based environment. Sandy says:

> A theme of Catalyst Charter Middle School is global collaboration, and wikis are tools that support collaboration. One step in the Digitween project is for students to collaborate globally on the Digitween Wiki. Students from various schools across the globe are assigned into a group and given a current topic on digital citizenship.

> Students research their individual topic and share results in collaborative reports on the wiki. It is interesting for students to work collaboratively with other students from around the globe in this setting. They do editing in real time as students

add information to the wiki. They used information on the wiki to create an action research project that informed others of relevant topics of digital citizenship. Students learned through a real-life situation the value of collaboration and digital citizenship in the Flat Classroom Digitween project. (S. Wisneski, personal communication, July 2013)

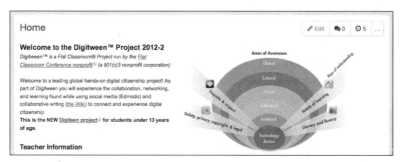

Figure 8.2 | Digitween Project website
(http://digitween12-2.flatclassroomproject.org/Home)

## Wikis to Communicate with Parents and Students

Catalyst Charter Middle School also uses a wiki as a homebase for all information and projects shared with parents and students. The wiki contains flipped videos, links to project resources, and surveys.

During projects, students refer to embedded wikis that are linked on a wiki sidebar. An example of this is the "The Ride of Your Life" wiki. The wiki leads students through various steps of the project from an entrance activity, which is a roller coaster critique (http://therideofyourlife.wikispaces.com/Coaster+Critique), to the physics of coasters (http://therideofyourlife.wikispaces.com/Workings+of+a+Coaster), to designing a coaster (http://therideofyourlife.wikispaces.com/Drawing+Your+Coaster). Wikis have been a successful communication tool because everything is hosted within the wiki. Students find rubrics for projects as well as flipped videos modeling processes. Teachers can embed surveys into the wiki for students or parents to complete. Slideshows of students are embedded within the wiki, creating a sense of pride and community.

# *How* Do You Get Started with Wikis?

There are quite a few wikis available online, so how do you choose which to use? Whether you're the tech person in the district or a classroom teacher, if it's going to be your decision, you need to decide what you need it for in order to choose. Some are simple and some are complex. Some are free and some have costs. Some have advertising and some don't.

## Fourteen Tips for Using Wikis

1. Create a culture of trust in the class.

2. Establish goals for the project.

3. Post clear instructions.

4. Establish guidelines for all processes.

5. Set deadlines (interim and final).

6. Create and display assessment rubrics.

7. Make sure project activities are meaningful.

8. Define roles for team members and work with teams to assign them.

9. Keep instructions simple for both the assignment and the wiki pages.

10. Provide examples and suggestions.

11. Decide if the wikis should be open to the public or limited to the class.

12. Remind students of copyright and licensing issues.

13. Check work regularly.

14. Provide encouragement.

## Choosing a Wiki

Consider the following questions before you decide which wiki is right for you:

- Do I need a free wiki?

- Is there a school or district policy about advertising on websites that students see and use?

- Will the school's or district's infrastructure allow access to it?

- Is it easy to set up and use?

- Does it have features that are needed, such as adding images, video, and voice?

- Is it age appropriate?

Once you've selected the wiki, you can start right in to set up your top wiki page. Once the group is set up in a wiki, the two primary functions are Edit and Save.

Figure 8.3 | Getting started editing your page (Wikispaces tutorial screen)

## Wikispaces Tutorial

The following is a tutorial to get started with Wikispaces (www.wikispaces.com), which offers free, advertising-free wikis for education. Setting up a Wikispace wiki is simple. Editing is a lot like editing in Microsoft Word. See www.wikispaces.com/content/wiki-tour.

1. Go to www.wikispaces.com.

2. Select "I'm a Teacher" or "I'm a Student."

3. Type a username.

4. Choose a password.

5. Enter your email address.

6. Click Join.

7. In "My Account," make a new wiki.

8. Select your industry from the dropdown menu. You can also choose "I prefer not to answer."

9. Choose a name for your wiki.

10. Enter your school, course and grade being taught.

11. Certify that the space is for educational use by checking that box.

12. Click Create.

13. Your wiki page will appear, and it's ready to use.

14. Click on the Edit button at the top to start writing your wiki. (Entering and editing text is similar to working in a word processor.)

15. Click on Members and Invite People to add new members to your wiki.

16. Click on Settings and Permissions to set who can view only or view and edit your wiki.

    - Public: Everyone can view and edit your pages

    - Protected: Everyone can view pages but only wiki members can edit them

    - Private: Only wiki members can view and edit pages

17. Click on Settings and Themes and Colors to edit your wiki's look and feel.

18. Click on the Help link anytime you need help.

## *Where* Can You Find More Information about Wikis?

Wikis in Plain English, TeacherTube Video:
www.teachertube.com/viewVideo.
php?video_id=20514&title=Wikis_In_Plain_English

Wiki Basics: Instructions for setting up a wiki page:
http://umwikiworkshop.wikispaces.com/Wiki_basics

7 Things You Should Know about Wikis:
www.educause.edu/eli/7ThingsYouShouldKnowAboutWikis/156807

MediaWiki is the wiki engine that was developed for Wikipedia and other Wikimedia projects, but it is free for others to use. It is server based, which means that it is protected and free of advertising.
http://mediawiki.com

Districts can set up a wiki on their own servers or use commercial wiki services such as Wikispaces (www.wikispaces.com), which offers its service free to educators and removes all advertising from its pages. Wikispaces also offers its fee-based Private Label wiki environment for a school or district, a system that provides central administration, control, and privacy. These wikis are secure because the teacher or someone at the district level determines who can view and edit.

PBworks has a free basic edition that is free for educators, and schools can password-protect their wikis.
http://pbworks.com

Content management systems such as Blackboard (www.blackboard.com) offer wiki software within their systems, which makes them secure for students.

# 9

# Mobile Apps

## *What* Is a Mobile App?

An app (short for application) is a program designed for a specific task. Recently, the term has come to refer to small (in size and scope) software for mobile devices. In schools, the push to implement 1:1 computing and the Bring Your Own Device (BYOD) movement has led to the popularity of mobile devices (tablets and smartphones).

Although the distinction between online tools and apps is blurring, in general, we see Web 2.0 tools as programs that reside (often with the files users create) in the cloud. We access them with a web browser and use them online; the software doesn't download to our computers. Most of the tools discussed in this book are Web 2.0 tools.

Apps are small programs you download from iTunes or Google Play or the Windows Store to a mobile device. They run on the device, and the files that users create reside on the device, in the cloud, or both. For example, Instagram is a photography app that allows people to take photos with a mobile device, edit and save them on the device, and upload them to the cloud.

With Web 2.0 tools, it's easy for schools to have students share computers. The software they use and files they create don't reside on the desktop or laptop. Students go to the website to run them. BYOD programs work well with mobile devices, because apps and their data can stay on the device. In this chapter, we focus on tablets rather than all mobile devices because many schools are purchasing tablets for students to use.

## A Word about Tablets

The first tablet to emerge was Apple's iPad running on the iOS operating system. Developers created apps to sell in Apple's App Store. The industry grew to include major software publishers, and today most apps are available not only for iOS but also for Google's Android operating system and Microsoft's Windows 8 operating system. Although increasing numbers of schools are using Android and Windows 8 tablets, iPads were out first, and so many of the early adopters bought iPads. It is early enough in the tablet (r)evolution that most of the educators we interviewed for this chapter tended to talk about iPad implementations. Because developers are creating the same apps for all operating systems, we can safely assume that what students do on iPads, others are doing or will do on tablets that run on other operating systems. As Coby Culbertson, director of technology for the Western Dubuque School District in Iowa, said, "We are device agnostic. It doesn't matter what device you have if people are working in the cloud" (C. Culbertson, personal communication, June 2013).

In a 2013 report, the International Data Corporation (IDC) found that:

> While personal computers are facing weak demand and reduced budgets in the U.S. education sector, tablets are experiencing exceptionally strong interest among education stakeholders, from school managers, teachers, and governments, to parents and students. ... Strong demand for these devices increased the share of tablets in the education client device market from 19.4% in 2011 to more than 35% in 2012, and that momentum will continue.
>
> Leading tablet vendors are succeeding not just because of user interest in the devices, but also because they are beginning to work in partnership with school systems to execute strategies that encompass educational content as well as the content delivery platforms. (International Data Corporation, 2013a, n.p.)

According to the forecast in IDC's Worldwide Quarterly Tablet Tracker, tablet shipments are expected to increase year after year.

> "What started as a sign of tough economic times has quickly shifted to a change in the global computing paradigm with mobile being the primary benefactor," said Ryan Reith, Program Manager for IDC's Mobility Trackers. "Tablets surpassing portables in 2013, and total PCs in 2015, marks a significant change in consumer attitudes about compute devices and the applications and ecosystems that power them. ...
>
> While Apple has been at the forefront of the tablet revolution, the current market expansion has been increasingly fueled by low-cost Android devices. ... "Apple's success in the education market has proven that tablets can be used as more than just a content consumption or gaming device." sais Jitesh Ubrani, research analyst for the worldwide quarterly Tablet Tracker, "These devices are learning companions, and as tablet prices continue to drop, the dream of having a PC for every child gets replaced with the reality that we can actually provide a tablet for every child." (IDC, 2013b, n.p.)

The chart in Figure 9.1 shows how IDC expects the market to change.

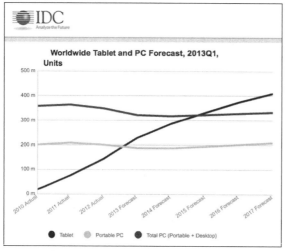

**Figure 9.1** | Worldwide Table and PC Forecast (from www.idc. com/getdoc.jsp?containerId=prUS24129713)

## Research

One of the most extensive studies on the use of tablet devices shows that there has been a significant and positive impact on learning and significant and still-developing changes in pedagogy (Webb, 2013). Findings from this British study at Longfield Academy include:

- The overwhelming majority of teachers regularly use iPads in their teaching

- iPad use is particularly strong in English, math, and science

- There is high demand from students for iPad use to be extended further

- Teachers have identified significant benefits for their workload and have also identified cost savings

- Use of the iPads is increasingly being developed for homework and beyond-school activities

- Students are more motivated when using iPads

- The quality and standard of pupil work and progress is rising

- Both staff and student feel they can work more effectively with iPads

- Levels of collaborative working have improved

- Appropriate use of apps aids learning

- Minor technical issues have arisen, often due to user error, but are readily dealt with

- Effective project management has been critical to the success of this development

The outcomes at Longfield clearly demonstrate the value of the iPad as an educational tool and the role that it can play in learning and teaching (Webb, 2013, n.p.).

## Comparison Study

The Center for Digital Education (CDE) reviewed three iPad implementations in 2011 in "The Impact of the iPad on K–12 Schools" and sought the insights of district leaders about the advantages and disadvantages of tablets compared with traditional PCs (Roscorla, 2011). Among the advantages were screen size, the touch interface, battery life, a predictable user experience, and the freedom from worrying about outlets, power cords, or battery life. In class, they excelled for communicating, e-reading, and web browsing.

The devices had disadvantages as well, and technology directors had several challenges to overcome. The biggest challenge at one of the sites was sharing the devices, which students had to do because of budget issues (Roscorla, 2011). Students at one site were surveyed on the degree to which iPads helped their learning in class; the average response was 3.38 on a scale from 1 to 5, a positive reaction but not overwhelming. Typing with the on-screen keyboard was a challenge for students, and they tended to type only short pieces. The survey question on the ease of keyboarding returned a 3.60 average. However, practice helped them adapt over time, and the class with the most access to iPads liked them better.

## Impact

Ian Wilson, a freelance Apple Professional Development Authorized Trainer based in the northwest of England, explains in "Apps v Programs for Learning" that schools have often had to limit student use of software to "an office suite plus web and mail applications" (Wilson, I., 2013, n.p.). The result is that "rather than finding applications and programs which suit the learning style of the individual, each learner has had to adapt to the software" (n.p.).

With tablets and apps, teachers and students "now look for software which meshes with their needs rather than the other way around" (n.p.). They can use apps "in an interactive and composite way." In addition, use of apps provides students with "effective, efficient and highly creative processes over which they have a high degree of control" (n.p.).

Because they carry the devices with them, students can use their apps for learning as needed. Because they take the devices home, they "can continue with the same set of apps, providing a seamless learning experience between home and school" (n.p.).

## Tablet Programs

In June 2013, Los Angeles Unified School District announced a district-wide purchase of 30,000 iPads. Before that, according to ZDNet's Eric Lai (2012) in his October 16, 2012, count of the districts with the greatest number of iPads in use (10,000 or more) the largest installations were:

| District | Units |
| --- | --- |
| San Diego Unified School District (CA) | 26,000 |
| McAllen School District (TX) | 25,000 |
| Lexington County School District 1 (SC) | 16,000 |
| Rochester District (MN) | 15,000 |
| Mansfield County Schools (TX) | 10,720 |
| Prince George's County (MD) | 10,000 |
| Chicago Public School District (IL) | 10,000 |

# New Canaan Public Schools

Robert Miller

New Canaan Public Schools first introduced iPads to the high school library program and provided special education students with them as assistive technology tools. At first we struggled with the setup and management of a larger quantity of iPads, but trial and error led to a more thorough understanding of how to implement and support our iPads successfully.

We also gave iPads to the librarians and technology integrators who would become the lead professional development experts. In the middle of last year, we offered a series of six iOS workshops for staff from December through June and focused on general use, professional productivity, instruction, assessment, and searching for apps. Teachers throughout the district who applied to participate in our pilot got iPads.

One of these teachers created a "One iPad Classroom" model with the iPad as a center in her kindergarten classroom. She taught students two to three apps to use. Students cycled through using math and reading apps. The teacher noted increased student independence and learning and the ability to work with other students more efficiently. Another teacher used the iPad Confer App to collect, analyze, report, and inform her instruction.

Last year we rolled out a cart of 30 iPads to this school. Kindergarten and first grade classrooms all received one, and the technology integrator created a differentiated approach to coaching and developing strategies for their use.

Teachers employed a model similar to the original One iPad Classroom. Classes in Grades 2–4 shared the rest of the iPads for math, reading, and writing. A weekly refresh set up the screens and folders for use by revolving groups of students.

We use an Apple volume license account to purchase and distribute the apps. Teachers with assigned iPads, which now total more than 100, can request new apps through the use of an online Google Form.

The license is sent to them for install via email. We are now gearing up to provide all kindergarten teachers two classroom iPads and all classrooms in Grades 1–5 an additional iPad. Five carts of 30 iPads each will also be rolled out as classroom sets similar to a mobile computer lab.

Much of our success grew out of individual innovation and piloting of our teachers and the ability for these teachers to share with each other.

*Robert Miller is the Director of Information and Communication Technologies for the New Canaan Public Schools.*

# *Why* Are Apps Useful Tools?

In addition to iPads, other tablets are becoming popular. Let's look at why a district would purchase tablets and see examples of how tablet implementations are working for districts around the country.

According to the San Diego Union Tribune, former district technology director Darryl LaGrace explained the purchase with:

> A factor in favor of the iPads are the fact they are "instant on," meaning there is no delay or wasted time as they boot up. They also have a larger screen than netbooks, which make them a better option to replace traditional textbooks. Also, they have an extended battery life and can utilize a large collection of educational apps that are available. (Kucher, 2012)

## Districtwide Improvement

Phil Hintz, director of technology for the Gurnee School District 56 in Illinois, talks about their iPad implementation:

> The program we are most proud of and that has made the biggest difference in the lives of all of our students in the

district is our district-wide, 2,400 iPad 1:1 Initiative for Grades PK–8. This has been what I call year zero for this initiative because we began rollout in December of 2012, but in the last 6 months, education in District 56 has totally been transformed. We have seen an extreme amount of growth in every facet of education in our district thanks to this initiative. This includes both intended and unintended successes, including such things as a complete drop in discipline issues on our buses; double digit to single digit absences at our middle school; and the need to completely revamp our technology curriculum maps for our students because skills that we used to have to wait until fourth grade to teach, we can now teach in kindergarten.

Perhaps the best evidence of how well our 1:1 iPad initiative has gone is in the results of our students and their engagement. While our principals have seen a drop from double-digit daily absentee rates down to single-digit absentee rates, teachers have been amazed at how much student work is completed and turned in (even ahead of time) even at the middle school level. Bus drivers have seen a nearly 70% drop in negative student behavior on the buses, and custodians have seen a reduction in the time it takes to clean each classroom by at least 8 minutes per classroom daily. These are just some of the many benefits we see just 6 months into the initiative.

About two weeks after our kindergartners received their iPads, one of the teachers used her iPad to take a video of what her students were doing in class. It shows one of her kindergarten students teaching the entire class of 25 kindergartners how to annotate pictures using an App called DoodleBuddy. The entire class is engaged in learning from one of their peers. When she went to help one of the students who had a question, the rest of the class stayed on task. This 50-second video paints the picture of what is going on in almost every classroom in our district (http://docs.google.com/file/d/0B9mDaXJUVfKGRm04SU1iNH d0Q1E). (P. Hintz, personal communication, July 2013)

## Achievement

A 2012 research study in Maine showed that kindergarten students using iPads scored better on literacy tests than students who didn't use the device. The Loop magazine reported:

> The study, conducted in Auburn, Maine, randomly assigned half of the district's 16 kindergarten classes to use iPads for nine weeks. In all, 129 students used an iPad, while 137 students were taught without an iPad. The 266 students were tested before and after the iPads were introduced into the classroom. ... According to the literacy test results, classes using the iPads outperformed the non-iPad students in every literacy measure they were tested on.

> "We are seeing high levels of student motivation, engagement and learning in the iPad classrooms," said Sue Dorris, principal at East Auburn Community School. "The apps, which teach and reinforce fundamental literacy concepts and skills, are engaging, interactive, and provide children with immediate feedback. What's more, teachers can customize apps to match the instructional needs of each child, so students are able to learn successfully at their own level and pace." (Dalrymple, 2012, n.p.)

## Replacing Outdated Textbooks

At Burlington High in suburban Boston, principal Patrick Larkin calls the $500 iPads a better long-term investment than textbooks, though he said the school will still use traditional texts in some courses if suitable electronic programs aren't yet available.

> I don't want to generalize because I don't want to insult people who are working hard to make those resources [Larkin said of textbooks], but they're pretty much outdated the minute they're printed and certainly by the time they're delivered. The bottom line is that the iPads will give our kids a chance to use much more relevant materials. (Amendola, 2011, n.p.)

## Communication

Tablets are well suited as communication devices. Districts have used them for student collaborations and for student-to-teacher and teacher-to-parent messaging. In addition, having a district app can make a huge difference in communications. Judson ISD in Texas created one, and Steve Young, chief technology officer, says:

> We used Conduit Mobile (http://mobile.conduit.com), a mobile development platform out of Israel, to develop the Judson ISD Connect! app for our district. They submitted our app, and we won a Bronze Lovie Award in the education category. I think school mobile app development is an area about to take off. I spent less than $1,000, plus a minor amount of staff time, to get it developed, and now we have a cool app. We presented at TCEA to a standing-room-only crowd of 150 people. Our app has news, events, sports scores, board meetings, athletic schedules, Facebook, Twitter, photos, videos, district links, Report It, and our ParentCenter, which includes grades, discipline information, bus routes, and lunch balances. Since all of us are tethered to our devices 24/7, we really wanted to include as much as we could in the app. We focused on repurposing existing web content into the app so we did not have to duplicate data entry. We are always exploring other features to add.
>
> You can check out Judson ISD Connect! in the App store. We tell people to steal from it and if you come up with better ideas, tell us. We're proud of it and we didn't have to spend a lot of time or money. I say "Go for it" to other districts. We get a lot of inquiries about it. (Young, 2013, n.p.)

## However ...

As with any new device, there's hype and great expectations. When the dust settles, smart people find the right reasons for using it. As with any new technology, the controversy centered on whether these devices would be good learning tools or distractions. And as people focused on searching for the best app, the coolest app, and the latest app, that conversation often overshadowed discussions of why they needed it.

## What You Should Look For in a Tablet

According to Kharbach (2013, n.p.), here are some of the things you need to pay heed to when opting for a tablet:

- Look for the features of each tablet. See whether it has the features you will need, like a music player, video chat capabilities (check its resolution), a good camera (check the pixels of the camera) in front and back, GPS, and a built-in eReader.

- Check what operating system it has and what version is available.

- Look at the processor and make sure it offers the speed you need.

- See the memory capacity and make sure that it is enough to store your photos, videos and music collections.

- Check the display of each tablet. See whether it has a responsive touchscreen and a beautiful resolution for viewing photos and videos in HD.

- Portability is the distinctive feature tablets bring to the computing world. See if the device is easy enough to navigate, whether it has a built-in stand to hold it for easy viewing or whether it has other accessories like a digital pen, stylus, etc.

Patrick Larkin, assistant superintendent for learning of Burlington Public Schools in Burlington, Massachusetts, who was principal of Burlington High when it initiated its tablet program, says:

> The most common question we get regarding our 1:1 initiative with iPads is—What apps do you recommend?

> While I understand that it seems like a logical question, I hate it. The reason for my disdain is that the focus of educators should be on outcomes first and not on devices or apps. Before we can answer the app question, we need to have a bit more information about what the goals are for the class and how the teacher would like to facilitate the lesson (i.e., will students work independently or collaboratively).

So when it comes to the iPad, there are over 225,000 apps in the App Store. I am not going to even get into the discussion that we should stay away from becoming app-dependent and focus on digital resources that are free and will work on any platform. (I'll leave that for a future post.)

Instead, we'll stay on the topic of not using technology for technology-sake. We need to be careful with all of the excitement over bringing shiny new devices into our schools that we do not put gadgets before goals. (Larkin, 2013, n.p.)

Nikolaos Chatzopoulos, fourth grade math and science teacher at Plato Academy, in Clearwater, Florida, poses the issue as "The 'How' vs 'Why' Of iPads In The Classroom":

One of the arguments that keeps resurfacing in the discussions surrounding the iPad in the classroom is the idea that if the iPad complicates things in the classroom, we have to move away from the question of "how to use an iPad in the classroom" and think more in terms of "why to use the iPad in the classroom."

We, like so many other educators, progressed from "searching for the perfect apps" to realizing that the iPad is a tool that can provide unique pedagogical practices in our student-centered classroom. As our questions about the iPad evolved, so did our vision about our classrooms and the role of the iPad in helping our teachers create a classroom environment that fosters innovation and creativity. Which brings me to my final point. Maybe asking "why," and "how," is not a bad thing after all.

Even more importantly, we may **have** to ask the "why" and the "how" questions first. Perhaps "how" and "why" are to be perceived as necessary steps we have to take as we go through the developmental stages of our classroom technological evolution and our understanding of the iPad as a classroom tool. (Chatzopoulos, 2013, n.p.)

# *When* Do Teachers Use Apps?

## Classroom Integration

There is an app for almost everything. Students and teachers can find hundreds of thousands of education apps at their fingertips, and most are free or low cost. Rather than list a few or dozens or even hundreds here, we're providing noteworthy resources to explore.

### New Canaan Public Schools

The rollout of New Canaan's iPad program was described earlier. As they've expanded the program, they've added apps for teacher and student use. They use an Apple volume license account to purchase and distribute the apps, and their list grows regularly. As of this writing, they use the following apps:

**All About Letters Interactive Activities** (http://itunes.apple.com/us/app/all-about-letters-interactive/id465471248?mt=8). This app allows kids to explore the whole alphabet from all angles. Animated lessons cover letter formation, letter sounds and more. This app was designed for children aged four to six years.

**Confer** (http://itunes.apple.com/us/app/confer/id387777553?mt=8). Confer is a useful note-taking app designed for teachers. It enables users to take quick notes about their students and lets users sort, group, and view their students. The app also allows users to export and import data through email, or upload it as a spreadsheet where it can be accessed anytime.

**Explain Everything** (http://itunes.apple.com/us/app/explain-everything/id431493086?mt=8). Explain Everything is a user-friendly screencasting and interactive whiteboard tool that enables users to annotate, animate, narrate, import, and export documents from basically anywhere.

**GarageBand** (http://itunes.apple.com/us/app/garageband/id408709785?mt=8). GarageBand turns the iPad, iPhone, and iPod Touch into a collection of touch instruments and a full-featured recording studio. Users can make music anywhere, save it, and share their creations with others.

**Handwriting Without Tears** (http://itunes.apple.com/us/app/handwriting-without-tears/id623327604?mt=8). This app enables students in the classroom to sign in and practice their letters and records their progress and errors. Through the Live Insights website, the instructor can access reports, view graphs, and analyze the data for each student individually or collectively as a class.

**iMovie** (http://itunes.apple.com/us/app/imovie/id377298193?mt=8). This app allows users to make HD movies from anywhere and gives users everything they need to tell their stories. Users can browse and play projects in the Marquee view or create Hollywood-style trailers and sophisticated home movies in minutes.

**iPrompts** (http://itunes.apple.com/us/app/iprompts-visual-supports-schedules/id313144705?mt=8). This app is the original picture-based prompting app for the iPhone and iPod Touch. It has been used by parents, special educators and therapists for children with disabilities, including individuals with autism, Down syndrome, and attention deficit hyperactivity disorder (ADHD).

**Keynote** (http://itunes.apple.com/us/app/keynote/id361285480?mt=8). Keynote is advertised as the most powerful presentation app ever developed for mobile devices. The app allows users to create graphs and animate transitions. Keynote works with iCloud, so your creations stay up to date whenever changes are made.

**LetterSchool** (http://itunes.apple.com/us/app/letterschool/id435476174?mt=8). LetterSchool is an amazing, intuitive game that kids can use to learn about letters and numbers, writing, counting, phonics and more.

**Lulu in the Amazon** (http://itunes.apple.com/us/app/lulu-in-the-amazon/id571916239?mt=8). This app provides users with an interactive story that demonstrates how learning can be fun. Users follow Lulu as she travels up the Amazon with friends by boat, takes her first steps in the rainforest, and meets strange new animals.

**MakeChange** (http://itunes.apple.com/us/app/make-change-not-waste/id516384696?mt=8). "Make Change, Not Waste" is a green living initiative and app that rewards Whole Foods Market shoppers with coupons for green lifestyle actions, while simultaneously raising awareness and donations to alleviate global poverty through the Whole Planet Foundation microcredit.

**Math Bingo** (http://itunes.apple.com/us/app/math-bingo/id371338715?mt=8). The object of Math Bingo is to get a pattern of five Bingo Bugs in a row by correctly answering math problems. This is a great and fun way to teach mathematics.

**Math Doodles** (http://itunes.apple.com/us/app/math-doodles/ id526959716?mt=8). Math Doodles is a mathematical puzzle game that allows users to play, explore, and experiment with mathematical concepts. Math Doodles challenges have been designed to allow for multiple solutions, which helps users develop math problem-solving skills.

**National Geographic World Atlas** (http://itunes.apple.com/us/app/national-geographic-world/id364733950?mt=8). National Geographic's award-winning World Atlas has been updated for 2013 with a new look, improved functionality, and brand-new features.

**Notability** (http://itunes.apple.com/us/app/notability-take-notes-annotate/ id360593530?mt=8). The Notability app integrates handwriting, PDF annotation, typing, recording, and organizing so users can personalize how they take notes.

**Pages** (http://itunes.apple.com/us/app/pages/id361309726?mt=8). Pages was designed specifically for the iPad, iPhone, and iPod Touch. The app allows users to create, edit, and view documents on the go. Pages works with iCloud, so documents stay up to date whenever changes are made.

**Project Gutenberg** (http://itunes.apple.com/us/app/free-audiobooks-ebooks-library/id585534682?mt=8). Project Gutenberg offers more than 40,000 free ebooks. Users can choose among free ebooks, download them, or just read them online.

**Scanner Pro** (http://itunes.apple.com/us/app/scanner-pro-by-readdle/ id333710667?mt=8). Scanner Pro is a useful app that makes your iPhone or iPad a portable scanner. The app allows users to scan receipts, whiteboards, paper notes, or any multipage document.

**Smart Notebook** (http://itunes.apple.com/us/app/smart-notebook-app-for-ipad/ id554245373?mt=8). The Smart Notebook app for the iPad is a light version of Smart Notebook collaborative learning software. Users can use this app to create basic multimedia files and complete Smart Notebook lesson activities.

Also, this app enables teachers to implement individual and collaborative learning with an iPad in Smart Notebook software with a Smart Board interactive whiteboard for small-group and class learning.

**Splashtop** (http://itunes.apple.com/us/app/splashtop-personal-remote/id382509315?mt=8). Users can use Splashtop to access their computers on the local network, and it has the best-in-class video streaming performance. With this app, users can view and edit Microsoft Office and PDF files; browse the web using IE, Chrome, and Firefox with full Flash and Java support; play 3D PC and Mac games and even access their entire media library and documents.

**Stack the States** (http://itunes.apple.com/us/app/stack-the-states/id381342267?mt=8). Stack the States has made learning about the 50 states fun and has been voted as the Best Kids App for iPad. Kids watch the states come to life in this fun and engaging game.

**StoryBuddy** (http://itunes.apple.com/us/app/storybuddy/id390538762?mt=8). StoryBuddy allows users to draw directly on the iPad's screen with their fingers and create a picture book page by page. Users can add customizable text with the built-in keyboard and even import images from their photo album. Users can also publish their story and flip through its pages like a book.

**Telling Time Free** (http://itunes.apple.com/us/app/telling-time-free/id473879314?mt=8). Telling Time Free is a telling-time app that has more than 700 different clock values. Instead of giving the users multiple choice, Telling Time Free lets the user input the time by the hour, ten minute, and minute.

## Bloom's Taxonomy

In this six-part series, Diane Darrow, library media specialist at Bel Aire Elementary in Tiburon, California, highlights apps useful for developing higher-order thinking skills in Grades K–5 that connect to the various stages on Bloom's taxonomy of learning objectives and skills (www.edutopia.org/blog/ipad-apps-elementary-blooms-taxomony-diane-darrow). She divides the article by apps for remembering, understanding, applying, analyzing, evaluating, and creating (Edutopia, 2013).

### High School iPad Apps

Every grade level and subject has different learning requirements, and high schools need apps for more advanced subjects. For an excellent list of apps in various subject areas, take a look at this list from Palm Beach Florida schools (http://schooltalkdev.palmbeach.k12.fl.us/groups/ipadpilot/wiki/70925). This includes lists for language arts and reading; math (including calculators); social studies; science; electives such as art, foreign language, and music; and general and productivity apps.

### Apps and Learning Tools for Kids

Common Sense Media reviews learning apps for various subjects, devices, age groups, rating, genre, and topic (www.commonsensemedia.org/app-reviews). They also offer advice on what you need to know about apps.

### Apps for Children with Special Needs

Apps for Children with Special Needs (http://a4cwsn.com) was set up to help families and caregivers of children with special needs and educators and therapists who support them. They produced videos that show how many products work for special-needs youngsters. In addition, they provide lists of approved software in various categories.

### Organizational Skills

Vicki Windman, a special education teacher at Clarkstown High School South, New York, and the founder of App-oplexy (http://appoplexy.wordpress.com), a website devoted to apps for special-needs children and adults, uses a few apps that are helpful for students who have trouble with organizational skills. It includes apps specifically for autism as well as special education. One of the greatest needs for all children, perhaps more so for special-needs students, is in organizational skills. She says:

> Show Me is a free tool that is not only an interactive whiteboard but also a voice recorder. We all know that inserting pictures or color code helps reinforce ideas. This is a great app for students who like to use audio, visual, and kinesthetics to help them learn, especially when trying to reinforce material for an exam.

IBrainstorm is a free drawing tool that also incorporates sticky notes on a corkboard background. Students can work with four friends and give each person an area to take notes. Once done, they can share notes by connecting up to four iPhones or iPads in a Wi-Fi-accessible area.

SimpleMind+ (mind mapping) is a free app that allows you to build a mind map, which helps students brainstorm and then arrange their ideas. Students drag and drop topics and arrange them on the Mind Map page. This app has a version with more features that sells for $6.99.

Idea Sketch is a 99-cent app that lets students draw a diagram easily—mind map, concept map, or flow chart—and convert it to a text outline and vice versa. I use Idea Sketch for brainstorming new ideas, illustrating concepts, making lists and outlines, planning presentations, creating organizational charts, and more. (Windman, 2013, n.p.)

### Apple Recommendations

Apple not only produces the iPads that schools are purchasing and sells the apps, but they also recommend specific apps for learning (www.apple.com/education/apps). These include apps for English language arts (reading and writing), mathematics, science (astronomy, earth science, chemistry, life science, and physics), history, and geography.

## Professional Development

Among the many ways that educators learn about integrating new tools such as mobile apps is to work with others to determine the educational value and practical application of tools and to create materials for them. Two new projects offer educators a way to evaluate apps, to create lessons and ideas for their use, and even to create their own apps for teaching and learning.

Graphite (www.graphite.org) is a free online guide to digital learning products compiled by and for educators by Common Sense Media (www.commonsensemedia.org), a nonprofit organization that reviews and rates digital products including apps, games, websites, and digital curricula for K–12.

Educators can search within four categories: product type (apps, console and PC games, websites); subject (language and reading, math, science, social studies, art, and hobbies); grade (PK–12); and price (free, free to try, or paid). Products can also be mapped to the Common Core and other standards. Educators can contribute their own feedback on the site, including field notes about how they use each product and what works best with their students.

Educade (www.educade.org) is a free site that provides information about web tools for educators to review. Hundreds of apps, games, and maker kits to use in classrooms are aligned with standards. Teachers can join for free and search for ways their students can learn by subject, tool, or keyword. For each tool, there is an overview, lesson plan summary, learning objectives and steps, Common Core and ISTE Standards, and a place for discussion. Those who want to try their hand at creating an educational app can use the site's template.

# *Who* Is Using Apps for Teaching and Learning?

## Recording Lessons

Brian Byrne, curriculum associate for elementary math in the Stamford Public Schools, Connecticut, recommends recording videos using the Educreations app. Teachers can use the results for classroom flipping or presenting information that students or parents can review on demand. He says:

> Educreations allows teachers to create video tutorials. The app not only records the lesson you're presenting (as you would at the whiteboard in your classroom) but also allows you to narrate by recording your voice. It lets you pull pictures from your tablet and the web with just the click of a button and directly import them into your lesson. The app lets you reposition, adjust the size, and rotate all photos. In addition, Educreations allows you to annotate and erase on the pictures and the screen. Does your lesson require grid paper, graphing paper, or lined paper? No problem, Educreations permits users to change the background they need for a particular lesson.

The real value of the Educreations app is in the sharing. The app saves all your presentations and lets you share them by a number of user-friendly methods. You can upload your presentation to Facebook, email the presentation, or even tweet the presentation by pressing a button. You can also copy the embedded code for the presentation and copy/paste it into a blog or website. Educreations is so easy to use and did I mention that it's *free*? (Byrne, 2013b, n.p.)

Brian used Educreations to develop a video on how to get started with the app, which can be found here: www.spselementarymath.blogspot.com/2013/01/educreations-best-new-app-for-teachers.html.

## Google Apps Services

Cathy Swan, technology integration teacher at New Canaan High School in New Canaan, Connecticut, works with teachers to use Google Apps in their classrooms. For example, she says,

We use iRubric, a Google Apps service that offers 283,000 searchable rubrics that we can use freely or edit. This total of rubics increases all the time; for example the number increased by 9,000 rubrics in less than one month recently. Teachers can sort the iRubric gallery of rubrics (www.rcampus.com/rubricshellc.cfm?mode=gallery&sms=publicrub) by grade level, subject, or assignment type. They can also use blank templates to create a rubric from scratch. iRubric is one part of Rcampus, a comprehensive course management platform, and our educators and students use many features of this service free of charge.

Teachers also use Lucidchart, a diagramming service on Google Apps. They use its simple drag and drop interface to create colorful flowcharts, webs, mindmaps or organizational charts in minutes. Teachers and students export these as .pdf, .jpg, .png, or visio files. They also upload the files to Google Drive. Diagrams include shapes, arrows, text boxes and user-uploaded images. (C. Swan, personal communication, June 2013)

## Documenting Learning

Karen Lirenman, Grade 1 teacher at Woodward Hill Elementary in Surrey, British Columbia, Canada, uses the iPad App Draw and Tell, a creative open-ended app, in many different aspects of learning with her students. She says:

> My students use Draw and Tell (by Duck Duck Moose), a very early primary-friendly app with simple, easy-to-use drawing and recording tools to document their learning. Draw and Tell seems like a simple child's drawing app, but it is much more than that. My students use the stickers in the app to create number patterns and math stories. They record their voices and move the stickers as they explain their thinking behind learning math. They use the drawing tools to create pictures of a favourite part in a story and what being healthy looks like. They also use Draw and Tell to add voice to their stories, or to speak to their non-digital work. Students also upload photos and annotate and add voice to them. (K. Lirenman, personal communication, July 2013)

## Reading and Writing in Chicago Public Schools

Chicago Schools' website iPad pages (http://sites.google.com/site/ipadsinchicagopublicschools/) describe how they use tools such as Dropbox, PDF Expert, and Office2HD.

All students and teachers have a free Dropbox account. Each student has a folder for reading, math, and so on, which is shared with their teachers. Only the student and his or her teachers have access to the folder and documents. PDF Expert and Office2HD are setup to sync to each student's folder. There is also a classwide folder that is shared with all students in a class and their teachers.

### Overview of Usage Scenarios

Students open Office2HD, navigate to their reading folder, create a new Word document, type a response to a prompt, and close the document. From their computer, the teacher looks in each student's folder to view, grade, and type feedback to students' responses. Students open documents in Office2HD to read feedback. No need for sending files back and forth. Students are prompted to push Save when they close the document, which syncs the files to the teacher automatically.

The teacher copies a PDF file from the textbook resources CD and pastes it into each student's science folder. Students open PDF Expert, navigate to their science folder, and open the PDF. They highlight text, draw a diagram by hand, and type short answers on the PDF. When they are done, they close the document and hit the Sync button. The teacher now has automatic access to all the edited PDFs.

The teacher records a mini-lesson video on his or her iPad and uploads it to the class-wide folder using the Dropbox app. Students open Dropbox, navigate to the classwide folder, and stream the mini-lesson video on their iPads.

For more information, check out the iPads in Chicago Public Schools blogs at http://sites.google.com/site/ipadsinchicagopublicschools/home/cps-blogs-and-other-resouces.

### Editing Student Work

Fifth grade teacher Monica Burns has students publish a variety of work on their iPads and use different apps throughout the writing process—such as Grafio Lite to create draw organizers (http://itunes.apple.com/us/app/grafio-lite-diagrams-ideas/id393111242?mt=8). She says:

> When it comes to typing up their final product we often use PaperPort Notes [http://itunes.apple.com/us/app/paperport-notes/id476134017?mt=8]. Before they send their work to print, I use the highlighter and marker tool to show them where edits and revisions need to be made. I write over their work, and send them back to their seats to make changes. The best part is that I can erase my notes once edits are made without losing any of the text on their page! [See Figure 9.2]. (Burns, 2013, n.p.)

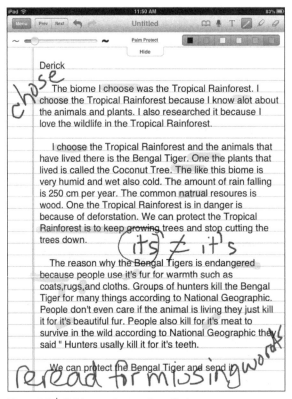

**Figure 9.2** | Editing student work on iPads

## Physical Education

Jason Hahnstadt, a physical education teacher and coach at the Joseph Sears School in Kenilworth, Illinois, uses Coach's Eye (www.coachseye.com), a mobile instant video analysis tool. He says:

> Instead of lugging around a camera, I use my iPod touch to film my students as they practice and play. I can instantly review video with my students frame-by-frame, so they immediately see what they are doing and make any necessary adjustments to their technique. This is especially helpful for our volleyball unit, because it gives me the ability to show a student exactly what they need to do to improve their serve seconds after it

hits the net—something I never before thought possible in my classroom.

I believe we are at a pivotal point in physical education. Emerging technology is our gateway to a better gym class, and I hope to encourage more "gym class flippers" to make flipping PE a common practice. After all, what better way to get students moving than to give them more time to move in class? It's not rocket science—in fact, it's just a game. (Hahnstadt, 2013, n.p.)

## *How* Do You Get Started with Apps?

Sam Gliksman says, "Well-planned technology deployments can have a transformative impact on learning" (Gliksman, 2013, n.p.). He has created "10 Steps to a Successful School iPad Program," and you can also view excerpts from his book *iPad in Education for Dummies* at www.teachthought.com/ipad-2/10-steps-to-a-successful-school-ipad-program.

## *Where* Can You Find More Information about Apps?

iPads in Education: http://ipadeducators.ning.com

iTunes: www.apple.com/itunes

Google Play: http://play.google.com/store

Windows Apps:
http://windows.microsoft.com/en-us/windows-8/apps#Cat=t1

Top 10 Sites for Educational Apps:
http://cyber-kap.blogspot.com/2012/01/top-10-sites-for-educational-apps.html

Graphite: www.graphite.org

Educade: www.educade.org

# 10 Steps to a Successful School iPad Program

Sam Gliksman

1. **Determine your readiness.** Don't consider purchasing iPads without an appropriate technical infrastructure to manage and deploy them.

2. **Communicate your objectives.** Can you explain why you're purchasing iPads and how that decision integrates into your educational vision?

3. **Focus on student-centered learning.** Moving the focus from teacher-led instruction to student-centered learning empowers students to use technology to explore, create, and innovate.

4. **Develop management strategies.** iPads require specific processes for organization and management.

5. **Forget Big Brother.** iPads aren't laptops.

6. **Use apps as tools.** The real benefit comes from selecting open-ended tools that can be mastered and used as part of dynamic and creative learning processes.

7. **Share and share alike—just not with iPads.** iPads are designed to be personal devices, and they store your personal data and files.

8. **Develop an ongoing training and support structure.** Organizational change requires adequate training and support.

9. **Connect.** The web has many helpful resources. You can easily connect and benefit from the knowledge and experience of other teachers.

10. **Embrace the unpredictable.** Technology is most effective when students are given the freedom to use it as a tool for creativity and innovation.

*Sam Gliksman is the author of iPad in Education for Dummies (For Dummies, 2013).*

# 10

# The Future of Education and the Web—What's Next?

In the first edition of this book we made a few predictions about the way the web would evolve, how education would take advantage of it, and ways in which classrooms might be transformed into environments that take advantage of the possibilities for global, personalized, and inquiry-based learning. Since then, we have seen vast changes. This chapter examines those changes, and once again we attempt to look at trends to make some assumptions about what might be unfolding.

Today's Web 2.0 has most certainly added the element of interactivity and moved users from read-only pages to read-write. Users not only retrieve information, but they create and share their own content easily and provide feedback on what others post, as well as add product reviews and find people with similar views. People write blogs, post images and videos, collaborate on documents, and socialize. The user experience is a democratic one. The most often used tools are the ones featured in the chapters of this book.

Because of the potential, in the future people will continue to use the popular applications; however, the tools may be more fully integrated and more transparent. Let's explore the current ideas around Web 3.0.

Web 3.0 is often called the semantic web and deals with the meaning of data. "Semantic web" is actually a term coined by Tim Berners-Lee, the man who is credited with inventing the World Wide Web. According to Wikipedia, the semantic web is:

> a collaborative movement led by the international standards body, the World Wide Web Consortium (W3C). The standard promotes common data formats on the World Wide Web. By encouraging the inclusion of semantic content in web pages, the Semantic Web aims at converting the current web dominated by unstructured and semi-structured documents into a "web of data." (http://en.wikipedia.org/wiki/Semantic_Web)

## Web X.0 in Education

How will the new—whatever number—web work for teaching and learning? We have seen a growth in individual use of devices; it is now possible that an inexpensive mobile phone has more power and potential than desktops of a few years ago. Students and schools find that it is more cost effective because the hardware that people now use to access it is portable and affordable: smaller, cheaper, ubiquitous, and with web access 24/7. Schools now have to respond by having information that is available, updated, and useful on that same basis. Many schools now require weekly emails to parents, homework and tests posted in online environments for learners as young as eight, and collaborative projects requiring electronic cooperation. Recent research also found that teachers have used electronic means to assist students when snow-storms prevented school for several weeks or during spring break (Schrum & Levin, 2012).

## Communication

Getting the message out is always the key to making a difference. As we saw in political situations in 2012, technology tools can play an increasingly critical role in this. In the 2012 U.S. presidential election, Barack Obama continued to take advantage of social media to energize his base, and also to raise money. Polling became more possible by including multiple methods of gathering information, and gaffes quickly went viral and frequently ended potential presidential candidacies (e.g., www.youtube.com/watch?v=ZCyTQEANlmM). In 2011, Twitter, YouTube, and other social networking tools enabled people in the Middle East, despite official censorship, to rally hundreds of thousands of citizens to protest their dictatorial governments in the "Arab Spring," while the entire world watched.

The power of communication tools can be harnessed for learning when students can reach outside the walls of classrooms into the global community. For example, learning about democracy and elections by means of student posts from around the world is more powerful when current and recent events provide the context. Reading multiple perspectives on the same event from different news sources, or Twitter accounts, provides opportunities to debate or discuss the impact of the event, as well as explore the influence of media sources. As documented in this text, educators use all means at hand to allow and encourage communications across time and distance for globally shared learning opportunities.

## Collaboration

We already see students who use wikis and online word processing tools to collaborate while creating and editing written documents and other media, and we see teachers who use social networks to find colleagues and form personal learning networks. Yet the use of tools such as these will grow, both so students can learn virtually and so teachers can create online textbooks and share other curricular materials online as learning tools for virtual schools.

When economic realities hinder districts from buying expensive and quickly outdated textbooks regularly, online versions offer advantages—from cost, to immediacy, to a fast refresh cycle, to the ability to link to primary sources. Teachers can share their expertise to create book chapters and supplemental materials that others can retrieve as needed. One website, teachthought.com (www.teachthought.com/technology/5-sources-of-open-source-textbooks), suggests multiple sources of open source textbooks.

Students can access these materials and learn from them. In addition, as student teams divide responsibility for researching information on specific aspects of a topic in order to produce collaborative projects, it may be possible for them to create knowledge, monitor and correct each other, and then post their results online for others to use.

In an interesting model of global collaboration, a team of animators from around the world created a five-minute animated film using the Wikipedia model, with each team member contributing shots and Facebook users voting on their favorites. The short, "Live Music," was picked up and distributed by Sony Pictures Entertainment to show in theaters. The trailer is online at www.facebook.com/video/video.php?v=95080051740 (Barnes, 2009).

## Mobility/Portability

Advances in chip design mean faster, smaller, and cheaper processors, which in turn mean faster, lighter, and cheaper computing devices, such as Netbooks and iPads. Schools are rapidly moving to allowing a Bring Your Own Device (BYOD) model in which most or all educational materials are in the cloud, and students have access from any device and at any time (Levin & Schrum, 2012). Many schools have changed their "no cell phone" policy, and these devices are now being used to accomplish tasks previously consigned only to desktops or laptops.

Having lower-cost devices available in classrooms will increase digital equity, providing access to technology for more children. Jenna Wortham of the New York Times cites an April 2009 report from the Pew Research Centers' Internet and American Life Project. It found that nearly half of all African Americans and English-speaking Hispanics were using cell phones (or handheld devices) to email and surf the web, whereas just 28% of white Americans reported ever using a mobile device to go online. She says, "The surge is helping to close a looming digital divide stemming from the high cost of in-home internet access, which can be prohibitive for some" (Wortham, 2009, n.p.).

Apple's iPad has demonstrated its potential for learning. Recently the Los Angeles Unified School District, the second largest school district in the country, awarded a $30 million contract to deliver iPads to each student in its schools (http://articles.latimes.com/2013/jun/18/local/la-me-0619-lausd-20130619). Schools in every corner of the globe are conducting pilot projects with iPads and other similar mobile devices.

## Personal

Personalizing learning, to whatever extent possible, means that students are able to find and learn what they need to know, when they need to learn it, and in a manner that suits them based on their learning styles or the way they like to approach learning. Some people learn visually; they may think in images and learn best from visual displays, including videos, photographs, slideshows, and online presentations. Auditory learners prefer listening and learn best from lectures and discussions that are podcast as well as from podcasts of their own notes to play back. Tactile/kinesthetic learners prefer touching objects, moving, performing, following directions using a hands-on approach, exploring the physical world, and manipulating objects (Bolliger & Supanakorn, 2011). The interactive nature of web tools allows them to get the physical sensations they need to conceptualize information.

As the technology advances, it may be possible for students to select the method by which they learn best and have the lesson appear online. An assessment component can provide feedback to the teacher on how well the student has learned the information or skill, what tasks to do next, and what approach is most likely to work.

Rather than focusing on whole-group instruction, which may still be the prevailing manner of education, schools are moving to personalized learning for at least part of each day. As an example, at the Alliance Tennenbaum Family Technology High School, a charter school on Los Angeles' east side, they are creating a new philosophy. Teachers are responsible for about one-third more learners at a time, but use a blended model to ensure that each learner gets what is needed. Headden (2013) describes a recent visit:

The school uses a hybrid model that combines online and traditional instruction and offers students three different ways to learn. On this particular fall day, 16 students are getting traditional in-person instruction in Algebra I from teacher Wendy Chaves; roughly the same number are doing math problems online; and still others are gathered in clusters of four tutoring each other. (n.p.)

## Transparent, Integrated, Intuitive

After spending part of this book providing tutorials for the various popular web tools and examples of best practices in classrooms today, it may sound strange to say that the tools may not continue to exist in their current form. But that's precisely what may happen. From whatever user interface students choose or personal start page they customize, the tools will be transparent and intuitive. All the features will be a click away and fully integrated. This new version of the web will assemble tools so that using them is intuitive.

The key to students' ability to use the tools well for learning continues to be teacher professional development: helping teachers to understand how students learn differently with collaboration and communication tools to which anyone can add features that provide more options when someone needs them.

For example, a group science report about South American weather patterns could work as follows: The group leader opens a wiki-like page in his personal start page and adds the names of the other students. The page would appear on all of their screens.

Each student looks at the widget for Google Earth and selects an appropriate country. As part of the exercise, each student wants to find out what the current weather is in a specific country from someone who lives there. Each could click a button to bring up a microblog box and send a tweet with the request. Followers could resend the message (currently known as RT, or retweeting) so that it reaches a wider audience.

The microblog box would offer the option of staying open to wait for replies, which are translated automatically. Each student could check the location of a responder on the Google Maps widget, tally his or her responses, and include the information in the wiki or Google Spreadsheet, along with any interesting comments, by copy-and-pasting the remarks and citing the author. If a reply links to a Flickr photo or YouTube video licensed for sharing on Creative Commons, a student could drag and drop it into the wiki, with attribution. At any point, any team member can insert an instant message or email to any other team member or to the whole group. If someone forgets how to figure out the data, he or she can click on a gadget and use an interactive math game that teaches mean, median, and mode. Students would also have the option of checking their online textbooks for background information, as well as searching the web with a built-in intelligent search agent.

If class time is used for such an activity, the students might be on their laptops or netbooks; after school, they might work from handheld devices or cell phones. Because everything is online, whether stored in the cloud or on a school district server, the ongoing, editable report is always available to anyone on the team. Once the activity is completed, the group leader can post the finished product to a blog, class website, or anywhere else by clicking a Make-live button and selecting where to post it. From this point, the teacher can track the contributions of each student, insert an assessment module linked to standards, and provide additional differentiated instruction modules to students whose skill in an area is weak.

## Mashups as Metaphor

Mashups are interactive web applications, services, or pages that pull in content from one or more external data sources to create entirely new services. In the past, web developers, rather than nontechnical users, wrote these programs. One example is using Google Maps to superimpose crime statistics, school information, and other data to displays geared toward real estate clients. More recently, personal start pages let users add gadgets or widgets such as email, calendars, newsfeeds, blogs, social networks, podcasts, games, photos, videos, weather, or other information they need.

These sites use application programming interfaces (APIs) from different sites to aggregate and repurpose content in a new way. The content is automatically updated every time you visit your page. Feedly (http://feedly.com/#discover) and Netvibes (www.netvibes.com) are examples. Both services are free.

## Learning Management Systems

It appears that every school relies on a learning management system (LMS) of some type to organize, teach, communicate, and store important aspects of its daily responsibilities, including the incredible increase in data reporting. Recent research suggests that although no school seems completely happy with its LMS (Schrum & Levin, 2012), most are learning to adapt and modify to make it work. Related sites specifically for education already have elements that include multiple tools and have the advantage of providing security, but there is a cost. For example, eChalk's Online Learning Environment (www.echalk.com) is a collection of web-based communication and collaboration tools that provides seamless integration with a district's existing SIS data; email system; and website content, curriculum, administrative forms, and other resources.

School Fusion (www.schoolfusion.com) helps districts build fully customized websites that include content management, online calendars, classroom websites, and personal space.

Blackboard (www.blackboard.com) provides a personalized learning experience in which teachers can create and manage content, design customized learning paths for students, and evaluate student performance. It includes online learning communities that encourage peer-to-peer participation using web-based tools across schools and throughout districts. Teachers can monitor student progress with simple evaluation and analysis. They can create online professional learning communities and store and share course materials, resources, and methods online.

As an alternative, Moodle (http://moodle.org) is a free, open-source course management system (CMS) for creating dynamic websites with tools to manage learning environments. To work, it needs to be installed on a web server somewhere—at a school, a district, or a web hosting company. Some districts use it as their platform for online courses, and others use it to supplement face-to-face courses (known as blended learning). It includes many activity modules (forums, wikis, databases, and so on) for schools to build collaborative learning communities. It can also be used as a way to deliver content to students and assess learning using assignments or quizzes. Although Moodle is free, having personnel to provide tech support is essential.

## Intelligent Search

The amount of information is growing so fast that it is becoming necessary to build an intelligent system that leverages knowledge so that people can find what they need efficiently. The web is technically a collection of words on pages with links to connect them. Google's search engine efficiently finds the links among the words that a user types into the search box, using the number of links to that page as a measure of popularity, which determines placement in the search results a user requests. However, Google doesn't understand the words and can't bring any logical thought (just processing) into play.

Advances in speed, logic, and technology are bringing the day of more intelligent searches closer. Will it ever be true artificial intelligence (AI)? No one is claiming that much power just yet, but improvements in object recognition, natural language, and the smart searching of a semantic web will improve capabilities. What that means for students is that searches will be more targeted and accurate, and the results will be relevant. Recent contenders in this category are Microsoft's Bing and Wolfram Alpha.

## Assessment

The semantic web is all about managing content and managing data, so it is possible that schools can translate the results of students' work online into quantifiable assessments. Early examples of this are schools in Montgomery County, Maryland, which maintain running records of student reading assessments, primarily on handhelds. The district believes that its ability to track test results systematically through its centralized databases helps pace both students and teachers. In one example, a teacher checks the results on her handheld to pinpoint exactly what students need to learn (Hechinger, 2009). The *Horizon Report* 2013 describes the transition of analytics, initially used as a marketing tool, into education to assist in the science of assessment. It states, "Learning analytics make data an integral part of planning, designing, and assessing learning experiences" (Johnson et al., 2013, p. 21).

Although too great an emphasis on testing has the potential to stifle creativity and may even result in eliminating the teaching of the arts or other subjects not tested, a sensible approach and authentic assessment of higher-order thinking skills can result in more student creativity using web-based tools. There are tools, though not yet Web 2.0 tools, that score student writing online and provide feedback for improvement. In recent research, students demonstrated the ways in which they kept track of their own learning, recognized the areas they needed to improve, and were able to communicate what they needed to do in order to accomplish these goals, by using their 24/7 access to their own scores and educator analysis (Schrum & Levin, 2012).

## Cloud Computing and Infrastructure

Speed and storage are the next big things to tackle. One IT director explained that adding new technology without simultaneously upgrading the bandwidth and infrastructure would almost guarantee failure and frustration (D. Townsend, personal communication, 2013). As information technology infrastructure becomes more complex, the resources needed to maintain and support it—both in equipment and in personnel—become more and more sophisticated and expensive. One answer is outsourcing to online data centers that provide warehousing and management as services. According to Wikipedia, "Typical cloud computing providers deliver common business applications online which are accessed from another web service or software like a web browser, while the software and data are stored on servers."

According to a *New York Times* article on data centers:

> Much of the daily material of our lives is now dematerialized and outsourced to a far-flung, unseen network. The stack of letters becomes the email database on the computer, which gives way to Hotmail or Gmail. The clipping sent to a friend becomes the attached PDF file, which becomes a set of shared bookmarks, hosted offsite. The photos in a box are replaced by JPEGs on a hard drive, then a hosted sharing service like Snapfish. The tilting CD tower is replaced by the MP3-laden hard drive which itself yields to a service like Pandora, music that is always "there," waiting to be heard.

But where is "there," and what does it look like?

"There" is nowadays likely to be increasingly large, powerful, energy-intensive, always on and essentially out-of-sight data centers. These centers run enormously scaled software applications with millions of users. (Vanderbilt, 2009)

Welcome to cloud computing. Cloud computing means that services and information are stored and managed on servers outside of an organization, processed quickly, and available from many different devices to result in increased efficiency with reduced costs, staff workload, and energy consumption.

The more personal PC is here in the form of smartphones and mini-laptops, and wireless networks make it possible for people to be connected almost anytime and anywhere. At the same time, we're seeing the rise of cloud computing, the vast array of interconnected machines managing the data and software that are used to run on PCs. This combination of mobile and cloud technologies continues to be one of the most significant advances in the computing universe.

Tech companies have shifted over to the cloud a lot of the software applications that businesses typically handle for themselves. Eventually, it will all work seamlessly. While businesses are the early adopters, school districts accustomed to outsourcing some elements of their infrastructure, such as data warehousing, will see benefits from these expanded systems.

## Schools in the Cloud

The opportunity to add data management as a Software-as-a-Service (SaaS) solution is already available. SaaS refers to computer applications that are delivered as a service rather than being physically installed on school servers or individual desktops. District administrators and educators—actually anyone with the right to know—can access the software from a PC web browser, or even from a mobile device. This means they can get the data they need when they need it. Because these applications are web based rather than housed on district servers, the service provider rather than the district's IT staff performs installation, upgrades, and maintenance.

Features of SaaS solutions include network-based access to, and management of, software from central locations rather than at each site; user access to applications remotely via the web or mobile device; centralized software updating, which minimizes the need for IT staff to download security and performance upgrades and new features; and integration into a larger network of communicating software for increased functionality as need develops. Companies such as SchoolDude and Century Consultants' StarBase suite already provide SaaS to thousands of school districts.

In addition, a movement toward Open Educational Resources (OER) has spread throughout the globe. In a study about the use of these resources (Hoosen, 2012), the author summarized, "There appears to be great interest in OER across all regions of the world, with several countries embarking on notable OER initiatives" (p. 25). Schools have begun to write their own texts, develop materials shared in grade level and content specific groups, and use formative assessment data for learning rather than merely as summative (Levin & Schrum, 2012).

The potential exists for online learning to scale significantly as well. Whether full-featured curriculum programs, such as Florida Virtual School, or blended learning for credit recovery, enhancement, or as part of a traditional class, the future bodes well for schools moving into the cloud in many areas. The advent of national standards (most states have signed on) could lead to national curricula; national learning materials; and assessments to evaluate learning on individual, class, school, district, state, regional, and global levels, for comparisons as well as for individualized plans to address areas of weakness. Online books and materials already reside in the cloud in such projects as Merlot (www.merlot.org) and Curriki (www.curriki.org). Cost efficiencies will be the driver into online learning.

# An Old-New Vision

It is still possible that eventually we'll end up somewhere near Apple's vision of the Knowledge Navigator, a concept described by John Sculley, former Apple Computer CEO, in his 1987 biography, *Odyssey*. The Knowledge Navigator vision is a device that can access a large networked database of hypertext information and use software agents to assist searching for information.

Apple's Knowledge Navigator included the hardware, artificial intelligence, intuitive tools, and an intelligent agent to help you, the user, learn what you need to learn, when and how you need to learn it. One in a series of videos that Apple produced demonstrating the Knowledge Navigator more than 20 years ago showed a young student who uses a handheld version of the system to prompt him while he gives a class presentation on volcanoes, eventually sending a movie of an exploding volcano to the video "blackboard."

# Everything Changes

Although predicting the future is at best an analysis of current trends, the only reality is that change happens regularly and evolutions can become revolutions, sometimes even in schools. Technology today is very different from the way it was in the 1970s, when it transitioned from corporate mainframes to personal computing, and it is also very different from the way it was when we wrote the first edition of this book. The *Horizon Report 2013* (Johnson et al., 2013) suggests the following time frame for changes:

### Time-to-Adoption Horizon: One Year or Less

Cloud Computing

Mobile Learning

### Time-to-Adoption Horizon: Two to Three Years

Learning Analytics

Open Content

### Time-to-Adoption Horizon: Four to Five Years

3D Printing

Virtual and Remote Laboratories (p. 1)

What does this mean for schools and those who support them? It's easy to see that IT departments that today run huge operations will streamline as districts move operations offsite into the cloud. Tasks such as human resources, inventories, data processing, assessment, and reporting may soon be performed online. Large and small companies use sites such as Salesforce.com and Amazon's processing power with their Elastic Compute Cloud (Amazon EC2), and there is no reason that schools can't do so as well. Instruction, too, is moving in that direction. Many districts are using thin client and server virtualization to deliver applications. It is only one step further to move the servers into the cloud. Curricular materials are online; Web 2.0 applications are replacing—and improving on—student access to information, communications, and collaborations; and some districts are moving to virtual schooling.

What does it all mean for teaching and learning? As we said at the beginning, we want to stress that web-based tools are just ways of accomplishing what needs to be done. They may be faster and cheaper, and contain the elements of motivating students and keeping them engaged in work, but, ultimately, they have to result in increased student achievement of both basic and advanced skills. And the teacher will remain the designer of curriculum, planner of activities, and the one responsible for assessing student learning and requirements. We wish you a joyful adventure as you think about the next stage of educational environments and watch them as they evolve. We leave you with this thought: Change happens; progress requires planning and thoughtfulness!

# 11

# Tools that Make a Difference

As schools open their networks to web use and allow students greater access to online tools, some lesser-known applications have become popular because they provide capabilities that make a difference in classrooms. Educators responding to our surveys mentioned some of these tools often enough to warrant discussion of their use in enhancing student learning.

This chapter deals with these interesting applications that readers say make a difference to their teaching, students' learning, and, in some cases, professional development. We invited educators to write about their favorite tools and how they use them in the classroom or professionally. We used a similar framework as in the other chapters in the book, focusing on the what, why, when, how, and where of Web 2.0.

Here are the specific tools, listed as they appear, alphabetically:

- Animoto
- BoomWriter
- Diigo
- Edmodo
- Evernote
- Lino
- Manga High
- Moodle
- Museum Box
- Netvibes
- Padlet
- Pinterest
- Planboard
- Present.me
- Skype
- SoundCloud
- Sqworl
- VoiceThread
- Voki
- Wordle

# Animoto

Christine Southard
Technology Integration Facilitator at Denton Avenue Elementary School
on Long Island, NY and NYS Local Assistive Technology Evaluator

## *What* Is Animoto?

As stated on their website: "Animoto is a web application that produces MTV-style videos using the images and music you choose. Produced in a widescreen format, Animoto videos have the visual energy of a music video and the emotional impact of a movie trailer. Best of all, no two videos are ever the same."

## *Why* Is Animoto a Useful Tool?

An Animoto video takes just minutes to create: You upload still images and videos to the application, you add music, and then you publish. You can even add text between images and spotlight images. You can use these videos to showcase lesson concepts or events in your classroom. Teachers can post or embed these videos on their school website, blog, or wiki or download them for in-class presentations. Students can also create Animoto videos to showcase their work. These videos are engaging and motivating to students when they are provided the opportunity to make their own Animoto videos!

## *When* Do You Use Animoto?

I facilitate the Broadcasting Club at my elementary school. The students in my club are in fifth grade. My students are responsible for making video commercials to advertise upcoming events at school and to showcase events after they have occurred. When creating an Animoto video, my students work independently, with a partner, or in a small group. Teachers can create Animoto videos with any age group, but younger students will require additional guidance and supervision.

Through their experience with Animoto, my students have learned how to sequence their presentations as they would an essay. Their presentations require a title, body, closing, credits, and a "thank you" when appropriate.

When creating their presentations, students always have to consider their audience. Does the audience require some background information on a particular event? Do they need any vocabulary terms defined? If so, then that information also needs to be included in the Animoto presentation. Sometimes this information shows up as text between slides.

The Animoto program allows its users to choose a themed background as well as music. My students have learned how important it is to consider the mood of their videos, and they are encouraged to choose themes and music that support the mood of their presentations.

Through this process, the students learn how English/Language Arts literacy skills play an important part in storytelling, or in their case, creating an Animoto video to share with our school and local community.

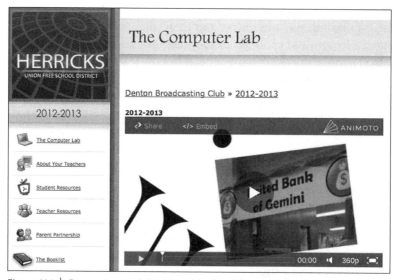

Figure 11.1 | Denton Avenue School broadcasting videos from the 2012–2013 school year (www.herricks.org/webpages/dentonlab/broadcasting. cfm?subpage=22764)

## *How* Do You Get Started with Animoto?

Educators can apply for a free Animoto Plus account for use in the classroom through the following link: http://animoto.com/education/classroom.

Creating an Animoto presentation is fast and easy. First, gather your images and/or video clips into one area, for example, a folder on your network or a USB drive. You can also gather images from various image-sharing sites such as Flickr. You can even have students draw images that you then scan or photograph.

Log in to Animoto. Click Create and then choose a style for the background. This will determine the look and feel of your video. Click Create Video.

Add your images and video clips to Animoto. You can drag the images in the order you'd like them to appear. You can also choose images to spotlight in the presentation in this section of Animoto. Spotlighted images will appear on screen for a longer period of time than the non-spotlighted images. You can also rotate, duplicate, shuffle, or delete images in this section of Animoto.

You can add text in between your images and videos by clicking Add Text. Once the text slides are created, you can drag and drop them to desired positions in your video. If you would like to get more creative with the text slides, I have taught my students to create their text pages as slides in PowerPoint. Then I export the slides as jpegs and we insert them into Animoto as images.

Music can be added to your Animoto by clicking on the music notes. Animoto provides their users with music, but you can also add your own audio files. You will be prompted by Animoto to follow their file submission terms— Animoto requires users to have the rights to any images, video clips, or music files they upload. However, an alternative to using Animoto's music files is to record your students generating their own unique audio/music and upload that audio file into Animoto. You will have the ability to trim the song and edit the pacing of the audio.

Click "Preview Video" to view your video. You can continue editing the video after previewing it or you can "Produce it" based on the prompts provided by Animoto.

Teachers can share the link to their produced video, download the video, or embed the video on their website, blog, or wiki.

## *Where* Can You Find More Information about Animoto?

Animoto Plus for education (free): http://animoto.com/education/classroom

Animoto Pro for education (paid): http://animoto.com/pro/education

# BoomWriter

David Kapuler
Author, Technology Tidbits blog

## *What* Is BoomWriter?

BoomWriter is a free and easy-to-use literacy site that has students interacting with and creating written content in a completely new way. BoomWriter is engaging for students, and teachers can easily incorporate it into the curriculum.

BoomWriter is based on a simple premise: students are presented with the first part of a story and then write what they think should happen next. Students read the anonymous submissions of their peers and then vote for the piece they think should be the next part of the story. The winner becomes the official next chapter, and the process continues until the piece is completed. Teachers then have the option of converting these stories into published books.

The BoomWriter community continues to grow and can now be found in thousands of schools spread throughout more than 50 countries worldwide!

## *Why* Is BoomWriter a Useful Tool?

BoomWriter is easy for teachers to use, and it provides a safe environment for students to be creative, because all stories are created in a closed digital environment. Teachers can go online, monitor their students' progress, and provide helpful individualized feedback and instruction from anywhere.

## *When* Do You Use BoomWriter?

BoomWriter can be used in a variety of academic settings throughout Grades 3–12, including special education and gifted and talented/challenge programs. It lets students develop their reading, writing, and assessment skills as they create and share stories while also assessing the work of their peers. BoomWriter lets students write creatively while also learning literature standards, and BoomWriter's flexible content-creating platform also allows it to be used with other types of writing and in other subject areas.

BoomWriter is strongly aligned with the Common Core's Literature Standards. It also serves as an innovative way to let students write imagined personal narrative pieces or work collaboratively to write arguments to support claims or create unit of study summaries.

BoomWriter hosts a bookstore featuring books written by kids using the site. All books are available as printed paperbacks. The bookstore can be found here: www.boomwriter.com/Bookstore.

## *How* Do You Get Started with BoomWriter?

Teachers can sign up to use BoomWriter for free at: http://boomwriter.com/Admin/Registration

BoomWriter summarizes the process as follows (http://boomwriter.com/Home/HowItWorks):

1.  It begins with a story start. A story start is the first chapter of the book. The rest of the story is up to you.

2.  You write your version of Chapter 2. Take the story where you like. The only limits are your imagination and a word count. At the same time, other BoomWriters will be writing their own version of what happens next.

3.  Submit your entry. When you're done (and before the deadline), you submit your entry for review.

4.  Vote, Vote, Vote! You and the other BoomWriters vote on the entry you think is the best.

5.  Did you win? If so, then your entry becomes the official Chapter 2 of the book. If not, don't worry because there will be many more chances for you to win.

6.  Read, write and then vote! The competitions continue until the book is finished. Then, *Boom!* you're a published author!

The end result? A real book that you, your friends, family, and the whole world can buy.

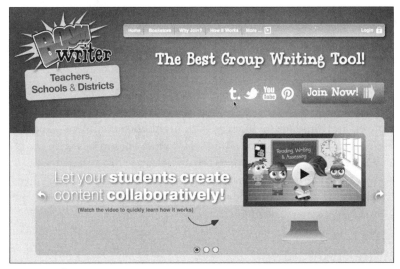

Figure 11.2 | BoomWriter page for teachers, schools, and districts

## *Where* Can You Find More Information About BoomWriter?

BoomWriter "What Do You Get?" page:
http://boomwriter.com/Home/WhyJoin

BoomWriter for Teachers, Schools, and Districts:
http://boomwriter.com/home/Schools

# Diigo

Vicki Davis
Teacher, Westwood Schools, Camilla, Georgia

## *What* Is Diigo?

Diigo (www.diigo.com) allows you to bookmark websites, index them with tags, and mark up and annotate web pages with highlights, comments, and sticky notes. You can also create groups and share your bookmarks with others. You can even use a tag "dictionary" that serves as a list of categories which can be used to index and share information that you can export as live updates for web pages, wikis, and so forth. Diigo empowers you to share your bookmarks easily via Twitter, your blog, or other social media.

## *Why* Is Diigo a Useful Tool?

Social bookmarking, or the ability to bookmark and share those bookmarks with others, has been around for quite some time, but Diigo groups have some very powerful features. One feature is the ability to use a tag dictionary that allows you to create a taxonomy or a consistent cataloging system while still being able to enjoy the "folksonomy" of simply tagging items with whatever words you wish. When you send something to a group using the handy Diigo Firefox plugin (which I highly recommend), these standard tags pop up automatically so that you can select them with a click instead of racking your brain for the proper tags to type in.

Diigo also has tools that allow us to aggregate and share bookmarks, their tags, and current information using link rolls and tag rolls; my favorite feature has to be the auto blog post. Everything that I tag "education" is rolled together and posted automatically to my Cool Cat Teacher blog, and I can send it to my blog and to Twitter automatically.

There are other powerful features, including Diigo Lists (creating lists and making web slides out of them that you can run like a PowerPoint presentation but with the added ability to interact live with the sites) and Diigo

Communities (which allows you to follow information on websites or categories of interest to you).

## *When* Do You Use Diigo?

I really understood the use for social bookmarking when I began using Diigo myself. Now I use it with my 9th and 10th grade classes as part of our award-winning Flat Classroom and Digiteen projects. I also use it to share links on my blog. It does so much more than bookmarking; it creates massive indexed catalogs of current information that can be shared in many powerful ways.

I have a special, approved educator account and can create "profileless" profiles for students if they are under age 13. They can use all the features of Diigo and share with their classmates and yet exist in a world cordoned off from all other Diigo users. This protects students, upholds the law, and provides ways to share.

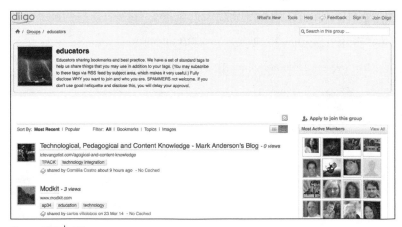

Figure 11.3 | Diigo message page

One important aspect of this is that by having some standard tags, you can use the RSS feed to populate wikis or any web page with common research topics. For example, on Digiteen, we have nine aspects of digital citizenship and have set up nine tags (plus a few extras); when a student uses the tag called digital safety, it not only goes to Diigo but also to the wiki page on that topic. This means that we can research digital citizenship and, as we bookmark the pages to the appropriate categories, we are sending current information to our wiki pages on Digital Citizenship according to our nine categories. It is a powerful research tool!

## *How* Do You Get Started with Diigo?

Go to www.diigo.com and click on the Get Started Now! button to create an account. You can also watch a video about Diigo.

## *Where* Can You Find More Information About Diigo?

You can see my Diigo list on using Diigo as a Web 2.0 research tool at www.diigo.com/list/coolcatteacher/research2.

Other sources of information:

Diigo Tutorial on Diigo's YouTube channel: www.youtube.com/watch?v=0RvAkTuL02A

Educator group: http://groups.diigo.com/group/educators

Digital citizenship group: http://groups.diigo.com/group/ad4dcss

# Edmodo

Janel Schafer
Technology and STEM instructor and coach, Northfield Community Middle School,
Northfield, New Jersey

## *What* Is Edmodo?

Edmodo (www.edmodo.com) is a free and secure learning network for
teachers, students, and schools. It provides a safe way to connect, share
content, access homework, take quizzes, complete assignments, participate
in discussions and polls, and receive class information.

## *Why* Is Edmodo a Useful Tool?

Edmodo is accessible online through any device with internet capabilities.
Students can access their account from any computer or mobile device using
free apps for iPhone, iPad, iPod touch, and Android devices. Students and
teachers are able to follow class progress whether in school or out.

## *When* Do You Use Edmodo?

Students in my Grades 5–8 computer classes sign on to the computers and
log in to Edmodo as soon as they enter the classroom. Within the students'
Edmodo classroom, they have access to a folder containing all assignments
and directions, labeled by unit. I am able to share documents, links, or videos
with any or all class groups from my teacher library right in Edmodo. Students
access shared items through their Folders tab.

Pupils work independently through quizzes and assignments and progress
through the units at their own pace. I can then move around the room and
assist students in need of help, one-on-one. Each unit includes several quizzes
and assignments that are scheduled to appear on certain dates throughout the
marking period. When a quiz is created, teachers have the option to schedule
them immediately or for some time in the future. In this way your classroom
can be completely set up in advance, for a marking period or one day out.

Pacing the assignments keeps students from going too far ahead and helps others recognize when they may be falling behind. Edmodo also allows a teacher to adjust the date on which an assignment or quiz will post to a class group so if students begin moving more quickly or slowly, you can adjust. Because my class is only one marking period, I am able to reuse assignments and quizzes created for previous marking periods since these are all stored within my Edmodo account.

When a student completes a quiz, it is automatically graded and added to the Edmodo grade book. Assignments can be graded within the program, and teachers can comment on student work and allow students to resubmit assignments. The teacher has the option of changing or adjusting a grade in the grade book. Edmodo assignments for my class have included Word documents, PowerPoint presentations, Paint pictures, digital graphic organizers, Voki avatars, and short-answer responses. Students are encouraged to help one another solve technology-related problems and to respond to one another's work on the class home page.

The culminating project for my technology classes is to take what they have learned and, working with a group, create a movie about cyber-bullying. I have found that, following self-paced, independent work, my students have become excellent at evaluating their own progress, and their group projects have improved. I now circle the room while a community of learners finds ways to improve work, collaborate, and accomplish goals. I believe Edmodo has had a positive impact on my students.

The teacher can also create polls to collect student responses and check for understanding, progress, feedback, or opinions. Some teachers have used the polling feature to practice evaluating essays according to a rubric. Students participated by choosing a score of 1, 2, 3, or 4 for the sample paper. Edmodo instantly graphs the responses, and this graph appears in the home feed. The class can then discuss the results, majority and outliers.

Teachers may also share parent access codes with parents so that they may track their child's progress. Parent accounts only have access to viewing their own student's work.

Other classroom uses include changing your name to a character or historical figure and addressing the class as that character, historical figure, scientist, or mathematician. These "visiting guests" can inspire students to think deeper into a subject. Within a class group, teachers can create small groups for book talks, or group projects.

Ever wish your students would watch the State of the Union address? Ask them to tune in and sign in to Edmodo. This "live" blog allows the teacher to answer questions and discuss speech points live during the broadcast.

Edmodo offers Communities as a great way to connect with other professionals and ask and answer questions about education, technology, and many other areas. Teachers can create their own group within Edmodo to use as a schoolwide, grade-level, or subject-area professional learning community. Teachers can use this group to share resources, worksheets, and activities.

Edmodo is a great way to connect classrooms within the same school, district, state, country, or around the world. As a technology coach, I love helping other teachers take advantage of this amazingly helpful tool. Two of my favorite projects involved making connections across states and across our district. I helped a sixth grade math class here in New Jersey connect to another in Illinois. Students here created vacations for their Illinois partner in Atlantic City. The Illinois students created vacations for our students in Chicago. Both classes joined a group on Edmodo, and within it students discussed their interests, shared favorites, and published their projects in the form of vacation videos. Students were excited to arrive at math class and log in to see if their cross-country partner had answered or asked a question.

The other project connected a first grade class at one school in the district to a sixth grade language arts class at the middle school. The first graders wrote stories and sent them to the sixth graders through Edmodo. The sixth graders then took their partners' stories and "blew them up." Using what they were learning about descriptive writing, they added detail to the story before recording it and sending it back to their partner. The first graders were then able to watch and listen to a new story based on their originals.

Figure 11.4 | Edmodo login page

## *How* Do You Get Started with Edmodo?

There are many ways Edmodo can spark excitement in the classroom and allow for collaboration and differentiation. But, the best part is that is it so easy to get started. Simply visit www.edmodo.com and create a free account. To begin using all of the available features, create your first group and go!

The Edmodo Teacher Manual (support.edmodo.com) offers the following instructions to help teachers sign up and create a group.

### How to Sign Up as a Teacher

You can start using Edmodo in your classroom in no time at all! Follow these three simple steps to create a Teacher Account:

1.  Navigate to www.edmodo.com and select the "I'm a Teacher" button to create your free account.

2.  Fill out the registration form and select the "Sign Up" button to complete the signup process.

3.  Check your email for a confirmation to view the next steps for setting up your Edmodo account.

### How to Create a Group

For a teacher, organization based on classes, subjects, or periods is key! Groups make it easy for the teacher to distribute notes, assignments, and quizzes, and provide a way for students to communicate and collaborate. You can make a separate group for each class or period. There is no limit to the number of groups you can create, and there is no limit to the number of groups a student can join.

## *Where* Can You Find More Information About Edmodo?

Edmodo homepage: www.edmodo.com

Edmodo offers a fabulous Help Center under your account. Any questions you may have are answered here in a simple and straightforward manner with pictures. If you are interested in finding out more, go to www.edmodo.com and create a free account, then join my training group with the Group code: rkppkj.

# Evernote

Steven Anderson
Instructional Technologist, Stokes County Schools, Danbury, North Carolina

## *What* Is Evernote?

Evernote is an online organizational tool that allows you to clip text, images, audio, and PDF files from the web and save them to one location. The information can be shared across several platforms and devices.

## *Why* Is Evernote a Useful Tool?

When students are assigned any type of research in school, the first place they go is the internet. And why wouldn't they? Students have access to vast amounts of information, from the archives of the Smithsonian to the research notes of people working on the pyramids in Egypt.

One problem is that students often have a hard time organizing information. For example, I assigned a research project on the elements of the periodic table. Students visited the computer lab, and by the end of the hour they had used up three packs of paper and an ink cartridge in the printer. Students printed entire web pages so that they could have the notes to compile later. I learned that to save on the amount of paper we were using, they needed to cut and paste into a document. That worked, but they couldn't save recordings of interviews or other audio resources.

Evernote makes organizing notes and information for research easy. After a simple and free registration process, students can save text, pictures, audio, and PDF files from the web. The program is available for several platforms, including PC, Mac, iPhone/iPod touch, Blackberry, and Palm Pre.

Students can download the software, use the web version of the program, or just use the bookmarklet to save information. (A bookmarklet is a shortcut you add to your bookmarks or favorites toolbar in your internet browser.) When you are on a page you want to save, simply click the Evernote bookmarklet, enter the name of the page, determine some tags, and add any other notes. Once it is saved, you will have the same access to the information as if you had used the other methods.

Once information is clipped from the web and saved, students can go in and review it, either online or offline. They can remove information they don't need with a simple edit, combine clips, and even start to write their research papers or reports online or offline.

One of the best features is that highlighted and clipped text keeps all the links intact and clickable inside the program, so it is easy to continue researching. Another great feature is that when students clip items from a web page, the address is also clipped, so the reference information is there for students to use to cite their sources.

## *When* Do You Use Evernote?

I have seen Evernote used in several different types of classrooms. One high school teacher uses it with her American history students to organize a year-long project highlighting major topics in American history. Within the class's Evernote notebook, they have a page for each topic that is part of their project. As they conduct their research, they organize pictures, text, quotes, audio, and other information for topics such as the American Revolution, the presidency, the Civil War, the growth of trade, immigration, the role of America on the world stage, and others. Then, at the end of the year, they have 15 to 20 pages, all organized, annotated, and clickable, to demonstrate their understanding of the progression of American history.

In an elementary classroom, the teacher uses Evernote to teach her students the right and wrong ways to conduct research and how to organize their thoughts. The program acts as their digital "brain," where they can think, write, organize, and learn, as she puts it. For example, in a unit on weather, students choose a type of cloud. They then use their Evernote notebook to gather, clip, and organize images and text from the web.

Using exercises just like this throughout the year, a teacher is able to easily teach what is good information and what is not, and students can easily delete pieces of unnecessary information in their Evernote notebooks. The teacher can also teach research organization skills, because students can move information around in their notebooks to make it more cohesive. Finally, the students learn about proper citation of sources, because as they snip information from the web, the address of the information is also saved. The exercise turns into an excellent teaching tool for citing sources.

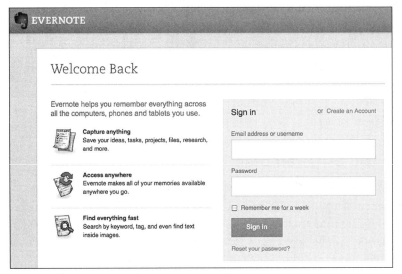

**Figure 11.5** | Evernote registration screen

## *How* Do You Get Started with Evernote?

Getting started with Evernote is as easy as visiting www.evernote.com and signing up for a free account. Students will need to provide a username, password, and email address. The free account gives you 40 MB of space to save per month. A premium account ($5/month, $45/year) gives you 500 MB a month.

According to Evernote, the free space provides approximately 20,000 text notes, or 400 mobile snapshots, 270 web clips, 40 audio notes, or 11 high-resolution photos per month.

## *Where* Can You Find More Information About Evernote?

Evernote video library: Tutorials, demos, tips and tricks:
http://evernote.com/video

Expand Your Brain with Evernote (Adam Parish, Lifehacker.com):
http://lifehacker.com/5041631/expand-your-brain-with-evernote

7 Ways to Use Evernote (Joel Falconer, Stepcase Lifehack):
www.lifehack.org/articles/technology/7-ways-to-use-evernote.html

# Lino

Renee Owens
Eighth grade communication arts teacher and department coordinator,
Hershey Middle School/Derry Township, Hershey, Pennsylvania

## *What* Is Lino?

Lino (http://linoit.com) is a free service that allows users to create online sticky notes. Sticky notes are posted to a web-based canvas; notes can be used to post words, photos, links, and video. Users can create an unlimited number of canvases and have a variety of sharing options available: share the link of the canvas or of a particular sticky note.

## *Why* Is Lino a Useful Tool?

Lino is a useful tool in the classroom and as a personal tool. In my classroom, it helps build participation, engages students in discussion, allows for collaboration and sharing, and serves as a tool I can use for checking for understanding.

**Building participation.** Like blogging, "posting notes" on Lino provides a way for students to share ideas in a nonthreatening way. The teacher and other students can respond to their posts, and students can respond to feedback or questions. In addition to being a place where students can share ideas, pose questions, and so forth, it is a place where a community of learners can be developed. Over time, students develop confidence (as their ideas are shared, appreciated and addressed) and begin to participate more in class. Teachers can moderate the posts, so they can guide students who may need help with their responses and prevent inappropriate material from being shared. Even in the best-managed classroom, the teacher cannot control how a student reacts to another student's questions or ideas—which is why students who are not confident in their responses may not participate. Lino will help build that confidence and trust, as well help to develop respectful behavior in how students respond to classmates.

**Engaging students in discussion.** Engagement requires interest, relevance, and meaningful content, so the teacher has a huge responsibility in choosing the type of discussion or task students are asked to complete. Lino can assist in engaging students because it encourages participation and allows for all students to participate at once. It assists the teacher in developing behavioral engagement. Likewise, the canvases of discussion help to build a community of learners—students feel part of developing meaning and understanding, so Lino provides opportunity for emotional engagement. Furthermore, it provides several options for response—text, links, image, and video—which provides an opportunity for choice in method of response for students; this helps in developing cognitive engagement. Unlike some similar sticky note services, Lino allows users to alter the size and color of fonts—an added feature that makes it enjoyable for students to use.

**Allowing collaborating and sharing.** Each canvas allows a classroom of students to post to the same canvas. Beyond the teacher posing a question or task on a canvas and requiring students to respond, a student could create a new canvas and share it with a small group. Students could use the canvas to have a discussion about a book they are reading (book club) or use it as a place to share their discussion ideas so other group members are prepared for live discussion. Students could use Lino to brainstorm on collaborative projects then outline tasks necessary to complete those projects. The tasks can be assigned due dates on each sticky note. Students could post resources to help with their group work. Note: Attaching files to Lino stickies allows you and your students to post PDFs or other documents that may not be available online.

**Checking for understanding.** Because users are notified when someone posts on their canvas, teachers can provide immediate (or timely) feedback. Because users have the ability to edit the sticky note, teachers (and students if desired) can provide specific feedback on the note. Lino is a great closure or "ticket out the door" alternative. After working with the librarian on research, the teacher could ask students to list a link that they thought was helpful, explain why, and ask them to post the link. This allows the teacher to see if students are being successful and if they understood the purpose of the lesson. It will also allow students who are struggling to find sources they can check. In addition to being used as the "ticket out the door," a Lino canvas is something that you can set up ahead of time or quickly use during a class to pose a check-for-understanding question or task.

As a personal tool, Lino lets users create to-do lists, organize photos, or plan for a trip. Users can assign due dates and email stickies to delegate tasks.

Lino is a tool that is easy to use and share. Canvases can be embedded or shared via the URL. In addition, multiple users can collaborate on the same project/canvas.

You can access Lino on your desktop, laptop, tablet or cell phone—via the website or by downloading the app.

## *When* Do You Use Lino?

I use Lino in my communication arts (English) eighth grade classes, and I use it in the professional development sessions I present.

As a result of using the sticky notes in Lino, students learn about other students' perspectives and ideas. In addition, they can receive and give feedback from/to their peers. It is a great tool for me, as the teacher, to check in on students' thinking and understanding. I also use it to help students build discussions; it has been an aid in helping students understand what a good discussion requires before they begin their book clubs.

I use Lino as a "bell ringer" (beginning of class to have students get started right away), during class as a check for understanding or for discussion, as a station activity (students rotate work stations), as a ticket out the door or closure task, and sometimes for a homework task.

Following are examples of canvases created in Lino.

**Responding to Literature Circles/Book Club** (http://linoit.com/users/rowens/ canvases/Responding%20to%20the%20Text%20%28Adam%29). Students read a variety of books that dealt with law/disorder/crime/punishment, and I ask them to post comments, pose questions, or respond to others in regard to the crime or punishment in their books: Did they think the punishment was fair? Was the punishment effective? How did the punishment affect the main character (and/or others) in the text? These opinion statements became the basis of discussion and the formation of claims. Students then found and used specific text evidence to support their claims and discussion counterclaims.

**Professional Development Canvases** (http://linoit.com/users/rowens/canvases/ The%20Benefit%20of%20Flipping). Based on a presentation I did with another teacher, we asked participants to share a benefit or the benefits they see in flipping their instruction.

**Ideas for bell ringers and closure tasks** (http://linoit.com/users/rowens/canvases/ Transitions). Based on a presentation I did on APL strategies, I had teachers post ideas for bell ringers and closure tasks.

**How are teachers using Lino** (http://linoit.com/users/rowens/canvases/ Using%20Lino%20It%20in%20the%20Classroom). This canvas shows how a number of teachers (different grade levels and disciplines) used Lino.

## *How* Do You Get Started with Lino?

1. Go to http://linoit.com.

2. Sign up. Users can sign up with Twitter, Facebook, or Google, or they can create a username and password and then use an email address to join. After signing up, users will log in with username and password.

3. Take a look at the main page. A number of sticky notes posted there provide useful information.

4. Under My Canvases, select Create New Canvas.

5. Create a note. Select a sticky color from the menu in the upper right-hand corner. Use the easy-to-use editing tools that appear when the sticky is chosen. Use the icons at the bottom of each sticky note to edit, share, or "peel off" (delete) the note.

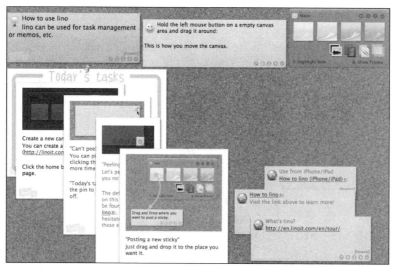

**Figure 11.6** | Lino main page

## *Where* Can You Find More Information About Lino?

The Techy Teacher Librarian "Lino-it for Collaboration" blog post:
http://madamewells.blogspot.com/2012/07/lino-for-collaboration.html

Free Technology for Teachers "Lino It—Collaborative, Multimedia Sticky Notes" blog post: www.freetech4teachers.com/2010/05/lino-it-online-collaborative-multimedia.html#.UoUqHI26tGE

Michael Gorman's 21st Century Educational Technology and Learning, "Part 1—Digital Collaboration Series: Linoit" blog post: http://21centuryedtech.wordpress.com/2011/08/14/part-1-digital-collaboration-series-linoit-no-student-log-in-plus-50-integration-ideas/

# Manga High

Linda Gutierrez
Sixth grade math teacher, Heights Middle School, Farmington, New Mexico

## *What* Is Manga High?

Manga High is a math game site (www.mangahigh.com). It has many high-interest, complex math games, plus quizzes or challenges aligned to Common Core standards for second grade through most high school math classes. It is gaming based, and the students can earn badges. There are also leader boards and competitions against other schools. It is a free site, although some extra features are available for a small fee.

## *Why* Is Manga High a Useful Tool?

Manga High is a useful tool because of the level of engagement that students have with it. They love the immediate feedback, the games, and especially the competition. It is teacher friendly and gives incredible analytics of your students' performance. It encourages the students to learn and moves them into deeper levels as they progress through the games and challenges. For a small fee, you can upgrade to the A+ Quest package, and then you can easily differentiate the challenges for each student. The site will also recommend challenges to the students, or they can set their own from any grade level.

## *When* Do You Use Manga High?

I use Manga High two to three times a week in my sixth grade math class. The students also use it often at home. It has replaced the math workbook in my classroom, because it is much more fun for the kids, gives them immediate feedback, and gives me accurate and up-to-the-minute data about my students.

The students learn many things with Manga High. Most importantly, they learn math. Because of the immediate feedback, students can self-monitor their learning and start to correct mistakes they are making. There is a self-teach mode for each challenge, as well as hints along the way and solutions at the end of each challenge. Once the students begin to show mastery of the basic concept being presented, they get a bronze medal and then are presented with more and more complex problems. Most problems are in a word problem format, so it encourages reading in the content area as well.

The games on the site are better than those on most other sites I've tried. They are challenging for kids and adults. The students will spend hours trying to master them and will learn interesting tricks to share with one another. If you don't use it for anything else, you have to check out these games!

What I've found is that the site really levels the playing field for students. Some of our most reluctant learners are often in the top of the class on the site, because it is based on effort and persistence, not just math knowledge. The students love the complex games and will work even harder during the Fai-to competitions that we have where we go head-to-head against another school from around the world. It has taught the kids a little geography as well, as we map our competitors' schools.

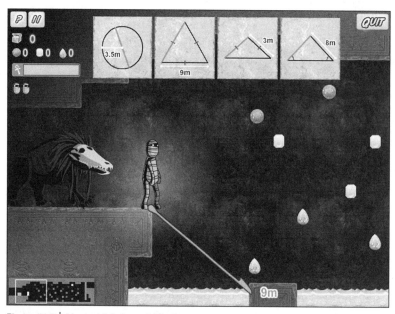

**Figure 11.7** | Manga High Pyramid Panic game
(www.mangahigh.com/en_us/games/pyramidpanic)

## *How* Do You Get Started with Manga High?

It is very easy to sign up for Manga High. Once signed up, you can easily add your own students, or you can email your roster to the customer service people and they will do it for you. Your students will need your school's specific link and their username and password to get started. Once in, you can start assigning games and challenges, or you can just let your students explore the site on their own.

I would highly recommend the A+ Quest option. It is reasonably priced and can be purchased either by the students' families or by a school district. It is not essential to using the site, but it makes your job as a teacher much easier and turns the site into more of a remedial site that is easy to differentiate for each learner's needs.

Manga High provides instructions for setting up an account for your school (http://start.mangahigh.com/setting-up-your-school-2). Once one teacher from your school has been registered, additional teachers can be added to the account (http://start.mangahigh.com/adding-more-teachers). The website also provides instructions for adding your classes (http://start.mangahigh.com/adding-your-classes).

## *Where* Can You Find More Information About Manga High?

Manga High homepage: www.mangahigh.com

There is a question mark on the dashboard once you're in the site. When you click on it, it gives lots of valuable information about the site as well as contact information to find out more. I've used the site consistently for the past two years, and I've always had good customer service when I've contacted them. They serve a lot of schools all over the world, so sometimes their response time is a bit longer, but I've always had a response within 24 hours. They also have a Twitter account and a Facebook page.

# Moodle

Miguel Guhlin
Instructional Technology Services, San Antonio ISD, San Antonio, Texas

## *What* Is Moodle?

Moodle is a course management system, providing educators with the benefits of a website but with many more learning activities that can be built in for students. Teachers can easily arrange instructional materials and activities as well as facilitate discussions online.

Moodle allows teachers to create a safe online learning center for themselves and their students to work in. It allows them to post class materials and extend learning beyond the classroom walls. For many, Moodle is a one-stop shopping solution that can include blogs, wikis, podcasts, quizzes, and survey questionnaires that print incredible graphs. Moodle also allows teachers to post grades and create online forums, with attachments.

## *Why* Is Moodle a Useful Tool?

Moodle is invaluable for students because it provides them with a safe, virtual environment that enables them to engage with content and with each other as they learn. Teachers find it indispensable because it extends their physical classroom into an online virtual space. Moodle has a variety of features, including discussion forums; a built-in grade book; and ways to post learning activities, hand in assignments via the internet, and embed interactive activities such as crossword puzzles and quizzes created by others.

Moodle is also customizable, and educators can add new modules and themes. I've listed a few examples of what you can do.

### Share Questionnaires with Students, Parents, and Anyone on the Internet

Moodle's questionnaire module enables you to quickly design a survey, share it with others, and then graph the data with horizontal, multicolored bar charts.

You can download the raw data into Excel or other spreadsheet programs for further number crunching, which is great for students to work with.

### Create Task-Based Activities

Using Half Baked Software's Hot Potatoes tool (which is free and available for Windows and Macintosh), teachers can quickly and easily design crossword puzzles, multiple-choice quizzes, text-entry quizzes, jumbled-word exercises, fill-in-the-blank exercises, and matching exercises. These activities are automatically scored in Moodle—saving the teacher the effort—and grades are put into the grade book.

### Podcast with Moodle

Students can record their audio and share it as a podcast by adding a podcast module to Moodle. In my school district, our Bilingual/ESL Department is using iPods to facilitate second language learning using podcasts on iPods or MP3 players. Teachers load content from sources such as United Streaming and other third-party vendors, and students create their own content using the Audio Recorder Module in Moodle (there are other modules, too). Using the podcast module in Moodle, both students and teachers can post their podcasts and subscribe to others in iTunes or via RSS readers (e.g., Bloglines).

## *When* Do You Use Moodle?

The most widespread use of Moodle in our district began with conducting literature circles online. When we think of literature circles, we think of kids sitting in a circle reading books and sharing their thoughts on them based on the role they are assigned. Discussing books helps students build connections, sets a purpose for reading beyond the intrinsic motivation we all prize, and motivates them. It also helps them read, observe, question, discuss, answer questions, and write about what they are reading. It's a fantastic activity, rich with opportunities for reflective learning. Students can post online book talks to persuade other group members to choose their book for literature circles, vote on book selections, and use the Moodle discussion forums to discuss their book, upload images, and more. Several thousand students are involved in using online literature circles as a result of Moodle.

Writing teachers want to provide students with immediate feedback. However, using traditional notebooks can be a bit of a deterrent, because there are too many for teachers to carry around. Using Moodle, students can submit their writing via the Assignment Module in Moodle. Writing teachers are able to score the writing samples as well as provide feedback without printing out the writing. This makes providing feedback for many student writers much easier than before and without using precious resources such as paper and ink, which are limited in my district.

Finally, Moodle is catching on as a tool to facilitate online professional learning for district staff. More than 300 educators have participated in online professional learning that has been facilitated 100% online via Moodle. You can see examples of courses online at http://intouch.saisd.net/plc.

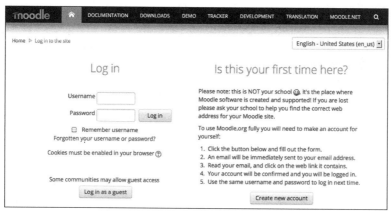

Figure 11.8 | Moodle login page

## *How* Do You Get Started with Moodle?

To get started with Moodle, you can work with your school district or organization to set up a web server and install Apache, PHP, and MySQL on it. These tools create the environment that Moodle needs, because it is part web page, part database. You can get everything to start with online at http://moodle.org.

## *Where* Can You Find More Information about Moodle?

For basic tips and tricks for Moodle, visit Moodle Habitudes. You will find a wealth of resources online at http://mguhlin.wikispaces.com/ MoodleHabitudes.

There are videos and ways to use Moodle in schools, as well as help on how to set it up online, at http://docs.moodle.org/22/en/Moodle_video_tutorials. You can also a view video discussion of how to use Moodle in schools online at www.youtube.com/watch?v=XjLukDNtf3k.

Furthermore, join the live conversation available via Twitter using the #moodle hashtag (search on Moodle via http://search.twitter.com) to find what people are sharing about Moodle use.

# Museum Box

Chad Evans
Learning facilitator of 21st-century literacies and middle school social studies teacher,
Quakertown Community School District, Quakertown, Pennsylvania

## *What* Is Museum Box?

Museum Box is a web-based tool that allows students to create a gallery of digital artifacts. Each "box" has a number of cubes that expand to six editable sides. Each side can have text, images, audio, and video inserted to give a full description of the item, person, place, or response.

## *Why* Is Museum Box a Useful Tool?

The tool affords students an opportunity to organize and categorize information around people, places, and things. The viewers of each box can view the sides of each of the cubes to have a better understanding of each artifact as well as look for similarities and differences between the cubes.

## *When* Do You Use Museum Box?

I asked my eighth grade social studies students to explore the causes, events, and results of the American Revolutionary War by selecting physical artifacts that it would be essential to include in a virtual museum of the American Revolution. The students identified the artifacts and selected images. Then, on various sides of each cube, they described the physical characteristics of the artifact, stated why the artifact should be included in the museum, interpreted the role of the artifact in the overall cause or outcome of the war, and finally included any additional videos or images to help a new learner better understand the impact of that artifact.

General examples of museum boxes can be found here: http://creator.museumbox.e2bn.org/gallery

## *How* Do You Get Started with Museum Box?

To use Museum Box, you will need to register your school and create an individual teacher account. The service recently switched to a paid version, which amounts to around $100 per year per school. Once the school is registered and the teacher account set up, you will be able to create additional teacher accounts and set up student user accounts, either one at a time or by uploading a spreadsheet (.csv) file. Although there is a fee and some back-end management, Museum Box is a web-based tool that would easily integrate across content areas and is very student friendly. Once students log in with their individual accounts, they create a one-, two-, or three-level box with eight cubes in each box. When selected, each cube expands to show the six sides that can be edited. Text, videos, audio, images, and other files are easily added to the cube, based on familiar web editing icons.

Museum Box provides the following instructions on registration and creating student accounts (http://museumbox.e2bn.org/teachers/view.php?id=74):

### Registering as a new school

If your school is not already registered you should register here: http://gas.services.e2bn.org/registration?appID=museumBox

Your details will be checked by an E2BN administrator, this may involve phoning your school so please make sure you provide your school's contact details. We will try to complete this process as quickly as possible but it does rely on your school details being correct. (Please allow a few days for this process to complete). You will receive an email notifying you when your account has been activated.

*Do not give your password to students, it allows them teacher access to moderate and publish student work!*

### To create student user accounts:

Watch the video at http://museumbox.e2bn.org/teachers/view.php?id=76 or follow the instructions below.

Go to: http://gas.services.e2bn.org or click the link to the Teachers Administration page.

Click the Students tab and then click Add students.

## *Where* Can You Find
## More Information About Museum Box?

To learn more about Museum Box, please go to the Museum Box website found here: http://museumbox.e2bn.org

Also, for a solid YouTube explanation and how-to from eduTecher, click here: www.youtube.com/watch?v=U6fDRktWIGg

**Figure 11.9** | Museum Box homepage

# Netvibes

Jeff Utecht
Elementary technology and learning coordinator, International School,
Bangkok, Thailand

## *What* Is Netvibes?

Netvibes is a content aggregator site. It pulls information from a variety of sources on the web and displays them on a single site for viewing. Think about having all your favorite sites in one place, on one page. That is Netvibes.

## *Why* Is Netvibes a Useful Tool?

Imagine if you could pull all the web resources you use in your class to one place. Imagine if you could give students one URL that had all the websites, blogs, newspapers, and images that you wanted them to use for a research project. Imagine if you could read the content of 200 sites on one page.

Netvibes has many uses in the classroom, from following student blogs, to creating sites for students, to using as a resources hub. Netvibes allows you to create your own site for free and without ads.

## *When* Do You Use Netvibes?

We're using Netvibes at our school as a way to keep track of student blogs and link students to other blogging classrooms around the world. Going to our site (www.netvibes.com/isbg5) will show how fifth grade teachers and students are developing a one-stop shop for all their blogging and connecting needs. Tabs on the site represent teachers at the school who have their students blogging. From here the teacher can track, read, and quickly respond to students who are writing on their blogs.

Teachers also allow class time for students to read each other's blogs. By using Netvibes, the students have access not only to other classmates' blogs, but also to bloggers in other rooms around the world. They can read, respond, and browse in a safe environment, set up by teachers, using educationally appropriate links teachers have approved and put there.

If students have individual Netvibes pages, teachers can "Share a Tab" of information with a student by simply entering their email address into the share-tab box. The tab and all the content on that tab will then be copied over to the student's Netvibes site. For example, a teacher could create a tab of content related to a science topic; find RSS feeds, news articles, links, games, and so forth; and add them all to their science tab. Once they have gathered the content they want, they then enter the student's email address, and all that information is transferred to the student's account.

Netvibes has many widgets that students add to their own personal page to help keep them organized at school. For example, some use a simple to-do list to remind them of due dates and class assignments, a calendar to allow them to keep their own schedule of events in their lives, and a digital notepad to jot down quick notes to themselves. Students can even sign up for a service such as box.net, which lets them upload files and store them on the web as a way to manage their own documents.

The power of Netvibes is in the individualization of each account. Allowing students to customize their own learning environment is a powerful way to start teaching the power of the web.

## *How* Do You Get Started with Netvibes?

Getting started with Netvibes is simple and straightforward. Head to www.netvibes.com and click Sign In in the upper right-hand corner of the site. Once you follow the sign-up process, your personal page will be created for you. Now the only thing you have to do is add content by clicking on the big green Add button in the upper left-hand corner. Once there, explore the possibilities and widgets that Netvibes has to offer.

When you've explored a bit, make a public site with the Activate My Public Page option under the Dashboard menu.

From there you can create and name your public site, turning any or all of your tabs public for the world to see. You can make some of your tabs public while keeping other tabs private, so don't think it's an all-or-nothing deal. You can have the best of both worlds!

**Figure 11.10** | Netvibes start page

## *Where* Can You Find More Information about Netvibes?

The best place to get more information about Netvibes is on their FAQ page. From there you can quickly learn all you need to know to get started using this powerful site with your students and school. Go to http://faq.netvibes.com.

# Padlet

Bob Sprankle
Technology Integrator, Wells-Ogunquit Community School District, Wells, Maine

## *What* Is Padlet?

Padlet is a "drag and drop-dead" easy way to publish work with very little effort. If you know how to "drag and drop," or type, then using it will literally takes seconds to create a dynamic and collaborative webpage.

## *Why* Is Padlet a Useful Tool?

It used to take me **hours** to set up a webpage to publish student work. Now, with Padlet, the students take care of creating the page, by simply dragging their work onto the webpage you've set up for them. Students are even able to share files that others can download (pictures, MP3s, video, documents, etc.). There are numerous ways to approach the maintenance of who can publish and what can be published. I have found that the easiest way is to set up a page with an easy-to-remember name, set a password for only the teacher, and then moderate postings when I have time.

Padlet will even automatically send you an email update when you have new postings to approve. A teacher also has the option of creating a private and hidden wall that can only be seen by her students or the parents of the students. Students could even create their own walls and have digital portfolios with little effort. Padlet is cloud based and works great on mobile devices as well as desktop computers. Padlet offers a variety of themes to set as the background (you could even upload your own). This is useful in helping students identify the correct wall if you are using multiple walls.

Padlet is free!

## *When* Do You Use Padlet?

Padlet would work with any grade level. At present, I am using multiple pages with each grade level I teach for students to display their work. When a student drags a file to the wall, or even just double clicks, he or she is able to write a title or a name, which stands out in a red, bold font. Below that field, students are able to write more in a smaller, black font (with formatting options such as bold, italic, centered).

Also at this time, I have created a Padlet wall for the entire community to post to. The wall has started to evolve into a place where students are writing compliments to each other and leaving me (their teacher) messages.

No posting will show up for others viewing the page until I have **approved** the post. In my elementary school, I have yet to have anyone outside of the school post to the wall, and there has not been a single inappropriate post. Students have expressed their "love" for the wall and are invested in keeping it focused on positive and creative entries. Through using Padlet, students are working on collaboration and communication skills.

Padlet has two layout options: "Freeform" and "Stream." I personally like the Freeform, as it mirrors a bulletin board and students can easily write responses to other posts and drag them to the area that is best. The Stream view puts everything in a column. This is extremely helpful when I want to see if there are any new and yet-to-be-approved postings. This would also be very helpful if teachers use the wall as an assessment tool. Freeform would be difficult in that situation because it would be almost impossible to see who has handed in work (again, it would resemble a bulletin board with people posting all over it in a **freeform** way). I like to set all my pages to Freeform. I am able to change the view to Stream to check postings, then immediately set it back to its previous Freeform state.

And, don't worry about running out of space on the page. Padlet just keeps "growing" (or **extending** down) with each new posting.

Another great thing about Padlet is that when you want to empty a page, you can just delete it, but you **don't lose that page**. In other words, if you called your page "http://padlet.com/WORK," then you would be able to start a new page with that exact name after you've deleted the original. Many sites don't allow this (once a name has been used, you're usually told that the same name is no longer available).

Here is a link to our schoolwide Padlet Wall: http://padlet.com/wall/weskids.

Don't be surprised if you get there and it's different. It just means that we've created something new.

When I teach how to use the wall, it is an excellent opportunity to teach good digital citizenship or netiquette. With the students, we generate qualities of what makes a "good" post, as compared to a "bad" post.

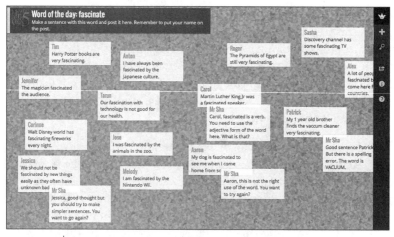

Figure 11.11 | Sample Padlet page with student posts

## *How* Do You Get Started with Padlet?

To get started, it's as simple as going to http://padlet.com and signing up with an email. When you create walls, you will have access to the settings where you can turn on moderation for posts, and set the level of privacy that you want. This is also where you can set the background and layout choices, as well as turning on email notices telling you that you have new entries to approve (Padlet sends you only one a day, so you won't be overwhelmed with emails).

Padlet's instructions are very straightforward:

Click "Build a wall" button.

Start posting: Double click or drag a file anywhere to post.

Modify wall: Add title, description; change background or privacy. [Click Modify Wall button]

## *Where* Can You Find More Information About Padlet?

Padlet homepage: http://padlet.com

For more information, check out the support page that Padlet offers: http://padlet.com/features

# Pinterest

Amy Migliore
Visual Arts Coordinator and High School Art Teacher, Quakertown Community School District, Quakertown, Pennsylvania

## *What* Is Pinterest?

Although the developers may define the tool as a visual bookmarking site, its power goes far beyond the aesthetic appeal of visually organizing resources and collections. While some may use it to window-shop for their dream weddings, travel destinations, and favorite food recipes, Pinterest has so much potential in the academic realm for both teachers and students. There is the enticing draw of being able to visually access ideas and objects while sharing them with others and documenting their own development. This is a huge educational asset for learners and one of the reasons why I believe Pinterest has been so successful.

## *Why* Is Pinterest a Useful Tool?

Art and design students are always in need of visual resources and inspiration. Pinterest allows students to search from any online technological device and store their discoveries virtually by themselves or in collaboration with others. Not only does this tool serve as a web-based "mood board" and resource library for the individual creative student, it also allows groups of learners to work together asynchronously. Pinterest is designed to invite comments, descriptors, and visual discoveries. Participants are given a connective space in which to share visual resources, and from it an ongoing portfolio of information and learning can take shape!

This tool can help to make 21st-century collaboration and its documentation an equitable and achievable goal for all discoverers. For instance, students are able to "pin" their sketches, pictures, and videos from their phones, iPads, and other digital devices to their boards to share with their group partners and teacher. This makes it possible for students to work through the investigation and documentation process for projects from home or other times and places beyond the classroom. This has made it possible for me as a teacher to see what resources have been gathered and what steps a student has taken toward the end goal. Not only can the inspirational resources show the forethought and steps of a student's intended goal, but boards can be used to document and share end results and reflections, too.

## *When* Do You Use Pinterest?

I teach visual art and design to senior high and college students, and Pinterest provides a platform for accountability and student-directed learning. Rather than looking through only Google Images or magazines to find visual ideas, students who use Pinterest have been able to work on this easily at home and then store it to the "cloud" of the Pinterest site. This makes it a convenient and easy process to access their resources on the school's computer lab or their own personal digital devices, without the hassles of forgetting to bring magazine pages or a flash drive of images copied from their home computer. This also makes it very convenient for doing group projects—students can write their name and small captions under the images they find or submit, so it is easy for the teacher to track which student was responsible for contributing the information.

The students and I both benefit from the ability to follow people's boards because the search tool is broken up into Pins, Boards, and Pinners. Therefore, if you find someone who has similar interests or boards dedicated to a chosen subject matter, you get the opportunity to have rich collaboration with strangers in a safe and immediate manner—otherwise known in teaching as "sharing willingly and stealing shamelessly." The shameless part comes into play because the great quality Pinterest has is that you can follow an image back to its source and attribute credit to the original posting, which teaches all users to respect the very current and important idea of attribution.

## *How* Do You Get Started with Pinterest?

Go to www.pinterest.com.

Select to sign up with either your email address or Facebook account.

To sign up with email, enter your name, email address, and create a username and password.

To sign up with Facebook, login into your Facebook account, and Pinterest will ask permission to access your public profile, friend list, email address, birthday, personal description, and likes.

Pinterest provides instructions to add, edit, or delete a board. You can also add and edit boards from the iPad, iPhone, and Android apps.

## *Where* Can You Find More Information About Pinterest?

From the home page (www.pinterest.com), you can watch brief visual definitions about Pinterest and follow the official blog (www.blog.pinterest.com), which features the trending topics of the larger Pinterest community. However, it seems most people are invited by a friend and then end up connecting with others who have similar interests. Chances are, someone you know is pinning!

Pinterest Basics: http://about.pinterest.com/basics

3 Ways to Pin with Friends:
http://blog.pinterest.com/post/54515626128/3-ways-to-pin-with-friends

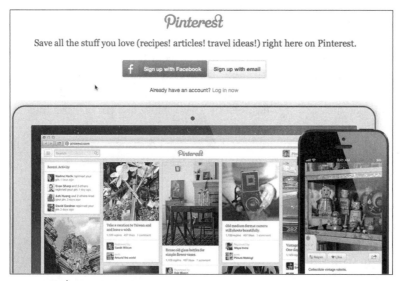

Figure 11.12 | Pinterest home page

# Planboard

Andrew Bieronski
Teacher, Huron Heights Secondary School, Waterloo Region District School Board, Kitchener, Ontario, Canada

## *What* Is Planboard?

Planboard allows for web-based lesson planning for educators, but that description does it a disservice. In a nutshell, Planboard allows educators to do their lesson planning online with a variety of helpful features not found elsewhere. You can embed video, add images, and hyperlink to external websites. Lessons can be shared with a link or embedded in a separate website. Through Planboard's Discover feature, you can search lessons other educators have chosen to share. This is only the tip of the iceberg for the variety of features that Planboard offers.

## *Why* Is Planboard a Useful Tool?

Planboard has completely transformed the way I look at lesson planning, as it has both simplified my life and made my lessons much more dynamic. It allows an educator to have access to lesson plans from any device that has an internet connection. Within it, you can upload files and store them in the cloud attached to specific lessons, quickly and easily add curriculum expectations you are covering to individual lessons, embed video and other multimedia within lessons, share lessons through a link with students/parents, and either publish your lessons online to share with the world or search Planboard's database of lessons other teachers have shared.

## *When* Do You Use Planboard?

Using Planboard with my class allows me to share my lessons more publicly and gear them specifically toward my students. I can include learning goals and success criteria to share with my students at the start of a lesson, while including files to share or multimedia to view right from the lesson itself.

I am able to easily share lessons with students who are absent through a quick email or by simply posting a link to the lesson that can be viewed online without an account. I use Planboard a number of times throughout each day.

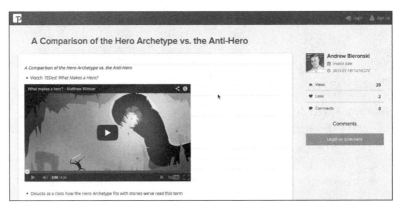

Figure 11.13 | Planboard lesson example
(http://planboard.it/5502cbc751b2802a5e5bc1b0d417404)

This page shows some uses of Planboard: www.planboardapp.com/features.

## *How* Do You Get Started with Planboard?

It's incredibly easy to get started with Planboard. Follow the basic setup that the website takes you through, and start planning dynamic lessons! The user interface is very intuitive.

Go to www.planboardapp.com and create an account. You can use an email address or your Facebook or Google+ login to do so. (If you use an email address to sign up, Planboard will send you a confirmation email to get started.)

Click the link to confirm the email from Planboard, and then you'll be redirected back to their site to set up your Planboard account. This takes four easy steps: schedule, preview, semester, and password. A tutorial video for these steps can be found here: http://support.planboardapp.com/hc/en-us/articles/200146774.

### *Where* Can You Find More Information About Planboard?

Planboard home page: www.planboardapp.com

Planboard Blog: http://blog.planboardapp.com

Andrew's presentation on what Planboard is and how it can be used: http://goo.gl/T1d1u

# Present.me

Mike Hasley
Secondary Social Studies Specialist, Henrico County Public Schools, Henrico, Virginia

## *What* Is Present.me?

Present.me is an online presentation tool that teachers and students can use in the classroom. With this tool, teachers can upgrade lectures created in PowerPoint or Keynote. Teachers simply upload their old or new presentation, and then record a video narration to accompany each slide. Students can also use this tool to create a product to share with other students.

There are paid and free versions. The free version allows for 15-minute presentations and 10 recordings per month. However, once a presentation is uploaded, it can be viewed at any time and for an unlimited number of views. This should be enough for most teachers.

## *Why* Is Present.me a Useful Tool?

Lately, the flipped classroom concept has been written about and imple-mented in many schools. Whether you flip a class, unit, or lesson, this would be a great tool to present lecture material. The students see you and see your presentation at the same time. If you are teaching an online or blended class, this is also a tool that would personalize a lecture.

Even if you're not flipping the classroom or teaching online, keeping your recorded lectures is helpful for students who were absent or need to see lectures more than once. Students in an Advanced Placement class can teach parts of a unit to each other, to be viewed at home, so you can have more time in class for other hands-on projects.

This tool allows a teacher to be more flexible with classroom instruction. Recording the session requires a little work up front, but you can always use the lecture the next year or next block. Imagine how much more class time you can have if your students watch the lecture at home!

## *When* Do You Use Present.me?

This is a very flexible tool. Students can use it. Any teacher can use it for any grade level. Building principals should use it.

I actually began using this tool with my department chairs. I wanted my meetings to be about instruction, not what I call "one-way information." So, I created PowerPoint presentations, added narration using Present.me, then assigned the videos as "homework" for our department meetings. The department chairs watched the information on their own time (I'd send this to them a week before the face-to-face meeting) and answer any comments left on the presentation. By the time we met, the minutia was settled and we could get down to sharing instructional strategies. It saved time, allowed them to review the online meeting if necessary, and modeled the flipped classroom.

I would suggest that building principals do this before faculty meetings. Record the "one-way information" (e.g., when paperwork is due, explaining the bell schedule) and leave the face-to-face meetings for discussions on good instruction. That way, other teachers can lead the meeting.

I have seen teachers use this as well with their students—to introduce topics, and as a review. Again, many teachers in my county have attempted to flip their classroom. This tool is simple and easy to use for this purpose. With this, students not only learn the material at their own pace (they can stop the video to take notes and not miss important information), but they can review the material at any time. When students create a Present.me, they learn public speaking skills.

Furthermore, teachers can use Present.me to grade presentations. For example, students can create a PowerPoint presentation, and then the teacher can upload the presentation and record their comments for the student.

Better yet, it can be shared. For example, a team of social studies teachers could split up a unit, each recording one lecture on Present.me for all students. The teacher does one lecture once, instead of five lectures multiple times—a huge timesaver!

**Figure 11.14** | Present.me for education home page
(http://present.me/content/for-education/)

This Present.me shows my first use with department chairs:
http://present.me/view/21891-2012-august-meeting-part-one

This shows a history presentation:
http://present.me/view/7819-world-war-ii-part-3

## *How* Do You Get Started with Present.me?

To create a Present.me account:

1. Go to http://present.me and click on Sign Up.

2. On the next screen, select the type of account that you wish to create. You can choose from several different options.

3. Choose a signup option: Facebook, Google+, or email address.

4. Fill in the form with the required information and click on the Create My Account button.

5. After a few minutes you will receive an email from Present.me to confirm your email address and subscription.

Watch a short video on how to make your first Present.me:
http://present.me/view/9911

## *Where* Can You Find More Information About Present.me?

Present.me homepage: http://present.me

Present.me for Education: http://present.me/content/for-education/

Tutorials and How-to's: http://support.present.me/categories/20043211

Present.me User Guide (downloadable PDF):
http://support.present.me/entries/23665613

# Skype

Kevin Jarrett
Technology Facilitator, Northfield Community School, Northfield, New Jersey

## *What* Is Skype?

Skype (www.skype.com) is a free program that turns your computer into a worldwide videoconferencing system featuring text (instant messaging) capabilities, file transfers, and even the ability to call land-line telephones.

## *Why* Is Skype a Useful Tool?

Skype is a powerful, easy-to-use software application that can effortlessly connect classrooms and communities around the world. Its combination of voice, video, and instant messaging (IM) technologies enables classroom teachers such as Cheryl Lykowski (http://globalexplorers.wikispaces.com), who teaches fifth grade in Bedford Public Schools (http://bedford.k12.mi.us) in Bedford, Michigan, to create rich, cross-curricular interactions with students around the globe. She and her students have been connected with a school in Colombia. They have collaborated on lessons, shared information about each other's culture and school practices, created podcasts, and conducted multiple projects.

From its inception in 2003, Skype has rapidly grown to become one of the world's most popular internet applications. Today, hundreds of millions of people worldwide have Skype accounts. On any given day, many millions of them are online and communicating with each other.

New features are added with each version. For example, classrooms can now collaborate in real time with other classrooms. Students can make calls using audio only, video with audio, or text (instant messaging). They can send files of any kind directly over the Skype connection in real time. Students can send text messages while another user is offline, and that person will get them once he or she signs in again. Skype also supports voice mail, but there is an extra cost.

Users can share their screens, even between different platforms, to illustrate ideas, work collaboratively, or demonstrate software. No special software is required other than the Skype connection. Skype is available in many languages, which opens up a wide range of curricular possibilities for students to communicate and learn.

## *When* Do You Use Skype?

We are starting to use Skype more and more in our district. For example, last year we Skyped with a Guatemalan immigrant who came to the United States 12 years ago and who is now a network engineer and administrator for a very large school system in Alabama. Third grade students working on a unit about immigration interviewed him about his experience coming to this country. They asked him about his impressions of the United States and about living here, building his career, and starting and owning his own business. Students found it to be an extremely powerful and memorable experience.

This year, classrooms in our elementary school will be collaborating with schools in New York, South Carolina, Georgia, and New Zealand. One third grade class will conduct a "read-aloud" collaboration and compare and contrast cultural interpretations of the texts. A fourth grade class will be developing "Study Buddies," and they will initially assist each other with math and science subjects at various times during the day. Multiple classrooms are planning to Skype with authors of books they read in class. All of these activities are free!

## *How* Do You Get Started with Skype?

Skype is a free download, so start with the download (www.skype.com/download). During the installation process, the software will guide you through setting up your account (called a Skype ID). Afterward, a wizard will help you test your microphone, speakers, and webcam (if installed) by making a test call to the Skype Call Testing Service. The instructions are visual and simple to follow.

**Figure 11.15** | Skype's start-up screen

*Caution:* Educators in districts with restrictive firewalls or other controls on internet-based programs or the installation of software on local machines should consult with people in their district responsible for information technology before trying to use Skype. Firewall and client computer configuration changes may be necessary for Skype to work properly in such environments.

## *Where* Can You Find More Information about Skype?

Once an educator has a Skype account, the next step is to find other Skype-using educators to collaborate with. One such directory is available at http://skypeinschools.pbworks.com/Directory/.

Another great place to locate possible collaboration partners is Lucy Gray's Global Education Conference Network (www.globaleducationconference.com).

Usually, once educators make connections to others using Skype, ideas for projects, lessons, and collaborations flow freely. For those who need a head start, this blog post presents many great suggestions: http://blogs.skype.com/2013/08/30/celebrating-top-ways-to-use-skype-in-the-classroom/

# SoundCloud

Serge Danielson-Francois
Librarian at Divine Child High School, Archdiocese of Detroit, Dearborn, Michigan

## *What* Is SoundCloud?

SoundCloud (http://soundcloud.com) is an audio recording app that stores file streams to the cloud. Stored files may be edited and shared via Facebook, Twitter, Pinterest, StumbleUpon, Tumblr, Blogger, WordPress, MySpace, or traditional email. The companion website allows subscribers to manage multiple streams and follow users with similar interests.

## *Why* Is SoundCloud a Useful Tool?

SoundCloud is a social sound platform where anyone can create sounds and share them with others. Recording and uploading sounds to SoundCloud lets students share them privately with classmates or publicly to blogs, sites, and social networks. You can access files anywhere using iOS and Android apps as well as other creation and sharing apps built on the SoundCloud platform.

## *When* Do You Use SoundCloud?

I teach Journalism I, II, and III, and my student journalists use the app to capture, archive and share audio interviews for their feature stories. In addition to leveraging the tool for field reporting, students currently use the SoundCloud website to follow different news podcasts and plan to use it to research new and emerging artists for music reviews.

We cover a number of science journalism stories in both my Journalism class and the Scientific Literacy class that I co-teach over the summer. SoundCloud podcasts are more engaging for our high school students than the print stories available online (no matter how many hyperlinks are embedded). It is particularly effective in the classroom because we meet in a computer lab, and students bring their headphones and listen to the podcast while they are completing other daily tasks. Our typical 50-minute classroom session begins with students reviewing the day's tasks, taking the NYT Current Events quiz (http://learning.blogs.nytimes.com/category/current-events/), skimming peer-reviewed research articles in Science Direct (www.sciencedirect.com) on a particular theme (our spring 2013 themes were environmental impacts of NAFTA, chronic traumatic encephalopathy, CAFE standards and auto emissions, e-waste, and learning accommodations in the classroom), and blogging in either Blogger or Tumblr about their angle on the story. They complete these tasks while listening to SoundCloud podcasts, and I rotate around the room to check on their progress and discuss their story ideas.

SoundCloud is also used in other ways at the school.

Adam, a senior, is a Dylan enthusiast and has started a series analyzing classic performances. He writes the script, provides the narration, and splices in the music excerpts for his podcast (he also plays guitar on the intro and outro of the second podcast). He posts these podcasts on the school's student news site. Two of his podcasts can be found here:

http://dcfaithinaction.org/please-excuse/2013/06/20/gaslight-recording/

http://dcfaithinaction.org/please-excuse/2013/07/02/
review-of-bob-dylan-1963-carnegie-hall/

He was inspired to start this series because of an NPR piece on the anniversary of Dylan's tribute to Medgar Evers (www.npr.org/2013/06/12/190743651/bob-dylans-tribute-to-medgar-evers-took-on-the-big-picture).

Students analyze and discuss podcasts from the Guardian Science Weekly podcast. A good example of the podcasts students listen to is this one on dark matter (http://soundcloud.com/guardianscienceweekly/science-weekly-podcast-the-20).

In addition, foreign language teachers use SoundCloud to record listening comprehension exercises and to review and grade student oral language proficiency samples. Hear a German listening comprehension example at soundcloud.com/libraryatalexandria/german-listening-comprehension (http://snd.sc/11EvT5s).

Figure 11.16 | Guardian Science Weekly podcast page

## *How* Do You Get Started with SoundCloud?

The first step is to create a SoundCloud account online at http://soundcloud.com. You can sign up with either your email or Facebook or Google accounts. Once you have signed up, download the iTunes or Google Play app onto your mobile device. This app integrates nicely with device-native microphones.

SoundCloud provides information about how to record and upload a sound from the computer (http://help.soundcloud.com/customer/portal/articles/1207834).

## *Where* Can You Find
## More Information About SoundCloud?

SoundCloud home page: http://soundcloud.com

Help/101s: http://help.soundcloud.com/customer/portal/topics/43094-101s/articles

CNET review: http://news.cnet.com/8301-17939_109-9974332-2.html

MacLife review: www.maclife.com/article/reviews/soundcloud_review

Appholic description and screenshots: www.appholic.cc/music/soundcloud2

"Your Stream on the Cloud" page (Note: you must be logged in to see this page): http://soundcloud.com/you/tracks

"SoundCloud Dashboard" (Note: you must be logged in to see this page): http://soundcloud.com/stream

# Sqworl

Elizabeth Kahn
Library Media Specialist at Patrick F. Taylor Science and Technology Academy,
Avondale, Louisiana

## *What* Is Sqworl?

Sqworl (http://sqworl.com) is a curation tool that students and teachers can use to organize, save, and share web links. Multiple sqworls, called groups, can be created by each user, and each collection that the user creates has a unique URL for easy sharing. The downside to Sqworl is the ads, which can be eliminated for a nominal fee.

## *Why* Is Sqworl a Useful Tool?

The web is huge, and it is crucial that we help students learn how to manage the web through curation. This may mean the teacher does the curating and gives the students a list of sites to use for an assignment, or it may mean that the students collect and save their own sites that they need for a class or assignment. By learning how to use curation tools to organize and manage web resources, the students will have gained a 21st-century skill that they can use throughout their school years and beyond.

Sqworl is very versatile and can be used with a variety of age groups. It has a simple interface, so there is a very short learning curve. I have curated sites for students to use for a particular class assignment, and also used this tool for students to curate their own sites for a particular project.

## *When* Do You Use Sqworl?

I worked with a sixth grade class on their Louisiana History project about the World War II–era Higgins boats. The objective was for students to understand how a curation tool could assist them in organizing their research as well as offer an easy way to save information from the web.

I first explained to the students what curation meant, and then I showed them several curation sites that might work for them. The teacher and the students all thought Sqworl would work best for what they wanted to do.

The teacher then created a Sqworl group with links to history sites, pictures, videos, articles from the Gale Virtual Reference Library (to which the school subscribes), and several history museums (http://sqworl.com/3bsrub). Because the topic was related to our locale, it was difficult for the students to find quality information. The teacher vetted all sites for accuracy.

The next part of this project was the creation of a book featuring a chapter on each topic. I thought that this was a great idea, but when I saw the final project, I was blown away. Each chapter listed tips for each topic and gave links to some of the great websites that the students found, as well as QR codes so the reader could get to the links easily on a smartphone. Then one of the students acquainted me with a site that sells self-published ebooks. Their teacher was familiar with the site, so she encouraged her students to upload their book to this site. It took some work to format it correctly, but the students uploaded their work and made their book available for purchase. What a great idea!

This project involved several 21st-century skills:

**Critical thinking.** Students designed the project, decided topics of interest, decided what sites to feature, and decided how to present what they learned to others.

**Creativity.** Students chose a product and designed the product to make it user friendly.

**Collaboration.** Students worked closely together to complete the project and collaborated with their teacher and librarian.

**Communication.** Students made a formal PowerPoint presentation at the end of the semester to a group of their peers and teachers. They put together a written document, curated sites that could be shared, and put the book up for sale in electronic format.

Sqworl has been used in other ways at our school.

- A teacher created a group to document all the online reviews that were written by students and were published in a national journal's online newsletter (http://sqworl.com/thwdxz).

- Students created a group for all the images that they wanted to use in a book trailer that they were going to create.

- Students created a set of groups for a special project. They wanted to put together an online resource for high school seniors to give them resources on how to take care of themselves once they go away to college. The groups included laundry tips, eating healthy, and ways to be fiscally responsible. Sqworl was a great organizing tool for this project, and the students can continue to edit and share this resource now that they have graduated from high school.

## *How* Do You Get Started with Sqworl?

I was searching for a curation tool that would be more visual rather than a list of sites in a text format. I wanted to use Pinterest, but this site is blocked at my school. I showed the students several possible tools, but they liked Sqworl. Once I used it with one class, then I tried it with several others.

This is an extremely easy program to use. Here are the steps to get started with Sqworl:

1. Go to the website: http://sqworl.com.

2. Register by creating a username and password.

3. Log in to the site with your username.

4. Begin by creating a group. A group is the set of web links that you want to put together.

5. Give a name to the group and write a brief description (the description cannot be edited later, but the title can).

6. Once you create a group, Sqworl will give you a unique URL that you can use to share the group.

7. Insert the URL to your first link site and type a very brief description (this description can be edited later).

8. Once you add your first URL, there will be a box allowing you to continue adding sites. Sites can easily be deleted.

9. When you reopen the Sqworl later, you will need to open the group you want to edit by clicking the box. Then at the bottom next to the title of the group is an edit button that is very small. Click the edit button to open and edit to add or delete web sites.

10. When you click your username, all of your groups will be available for you to view. Just click the title to open or the edit button to add sites.

11. You can save your groups or delete as needed.

## *Where* Can You Find More Information About Sqworl?

Sqworl home page: http://sqworl.com

You can view a screencast of how to use Sqworl here: http://vimeo.com/2952029

Other curation tools that may be useful for students and teachers: www.diigo.com/list/taylorlibrarian/curation-tools

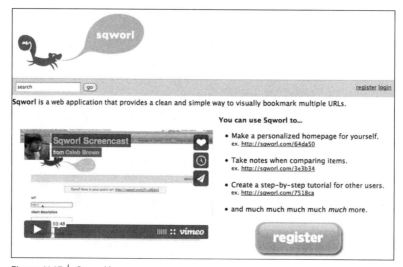

**Figure 11.17** | Sqworl homepage

# VoiceThread

Bob Sprankle
Technology Integrator, Wells-Ogunquit Community School District, Wells, Maine

## *What* Is VoiceThread?

VoiceThread (http://voicethread.com) is an online tool that takes media presentations to a new level by allowing for conversation. Users can create a VoiceThread with voice, video, text, or images and invite others to add to the presentation with voice, video, or text. It is an incredibly simple tool, easy to set up and get going in a matter of minutes.

## *Why* Is VoiceThread a Useful Tool?

VoiceThread is a tool that allows student (and teacher) work to be transformed into a conversation with an authentic global audience. Student work used to be shared in the hallway on a bulletin board, where others in the building could only view the work. VoiceThread allows anyone in the world not only to view the work, but to also interact with the creator by leaving reflections, comments, questions, or kudos. Rather than limiting students with feedback from only one teacher in the classroom, many other educators and students can be invited into dialogue around the work. Feedback can be typed, recorded by voice or video, uploaded as audio, or even recorded by phone. Commenters can even "draw" on the slides in order to illustrate a point.

## *When* Do You Use VoiceThread?

I've used VoiceThread with students in a variety of ways. One of the most powerful uses is for assessment purposes. For example, I've had my second graders use VoiceThread to report what they have learned about using another piece of software, Google Earth. Because students can "speak" their reflections, I get more in-depth thoughts from most students at this level than I would with a written or typed response.

One of my favorite uses of VoiceThread was when students gave feedback to a software company that asked us to beta test a new product. Rather than the CEO of the company hearing only a summary of ideas from me, the teacher, he was able to listen to each and every student. The students were thrilled and empowered that they were able to speak directly to the CEO and help shape the evolution of the product.

This year I plan to use VoiceThread with third graders to create electronic portfolios. The students will post all of the work they do in the computer lab within their own VoiceThreads. Their teachers, parents, and other family members will be the only ones allowed to view the VoiceThreads and will be able to record comments, questions, and kudos.

I've used VoiceThread as a home-school connection tool to explain to parents what is offered at our website and give them information about the technology curriculum. I've also used VoiceThread with other educators to provide tutorials, or as a forum for discussions of practice and pedagogy.

**Figure 11.18** |   The VoiceThread start page

## *How* Do You Get Started with VoiceThread?

VoiceThread offers free and paid educator subscription options. Head to http://voicethread.com to sign up, and then dig into the excellent tutorials that VoiceThread offers at http://voicethread.com/support.

## *Where* Can You Find
## More Information About VoiceThread?

VoiceThread includes a plethora of information with the above-mentioned tutorials and on the company's help page found at http://voicethread.com/support/faq. They also display exemplary educational uses of VoiceThread on their Library page (http://voicethread.com/about/library). They keep you up-to-date on their blog (http://blog.voicethread.com), where they announce new features such as their acquisition of more than 700,000 New York Public Library images and the learning modules that accompany them. The blog also provides further tutorials and documentation of the effects of VoiceThread on learning.

# Voki

Christine Southard
Special Education Teacher, Herricks UFSD, New Hyde Park, New York

## *What* Is Voki?

Voki (www.voki.com) is a free online service and Web 2.0 tool that allows you to create personalized speaking avatars. These avatars can then be embedded in any online space that accepts HTML, such as a website, blog, or wiki.

## *Why* Is Voki a Useful Tool?

Voki is a great motivational tool to use with students because of its creative nature and visual appeal. From a teacher's perspective, a Voki is an ideal tool for educators to use with younger students to improve their literacy skills.

Before working in the program, students must research the characters, people, or topics, or all three, that they intend to speak about using their avatar. Students can then write and edit scripts based on their research. Scripts can be centered on writing lessons that focus on the author's purpose, and they can also be used as opportunities for editing. Rereading scripts before recording gives students the opportunity to improve their fluency.

## *When* Do You Use Voki?

Voki is a useful tool because you can have students create speaking avatars for just about any subject. Students can portray themselves as a Voki and reflect their opinion or knowledge on a particular topic. Students can also create Vokis to role-play a variety of fiction and nonfiction characters. Language teachers can have students create Vokis to practice their language skills. The options are limitless.

I have seen a few teachers use a Voki avatar embedded in their website or blog to introduce themselves to students at the beginning of the year. Teachers have also used Vokis to introduce students to a new lesson or unit and have embedded the avatar in a school website or wiki.

In our fifth grade class, we log in the students under our Voki account while they are in school. Then the students go through a number of prompts to create the look of their Voki. They have a variety of characters to choose from, including animals, real and fictitious people, and some odd and interesting characters. Students can also choose a background setting from Voki or upload their own. This is a great opportunity to discuss the importance of setting. Students can then add their own voice to the Voki by using the phone (with teacher supervision), a microphone, or the text-to-speech option within Voki, or by uploading an audio file.

In our classroom, we usually allow our students to choose to use a Voki as a response to an activity. For example, in a unit on time zones, a number of children chose to use Vokis to describe what they were doing at various Greenwich Mean Times (GMT). They wrote their scripts and then pasted their text and chose a speaker within Voki. We embedded their final products in our timezoneexperiences wiki. Here are some examples from our wiki:

(Girl) Student Example:
http://timezoneexperiences.wikispaces.com/Zero+O%27Clock

(Girl) Student Example:
http://timezoneexperiences.wikispaces.com/Fifteen+O%27Clock

(Boy) Student Example:
http://timezoneexperiences.wikispaces.com/Three+O%27Clock

Because Voki is a presentation tool, students are more actively involved in the learning processes of writing before using the application. Whatever the topic students are going to speak about, they must research, brainstorm, organize, write, and edit a script that fulfills the needs of the assignment. Before recording their Voki, students must practice their fluency skills by rereading their script and tailoring their tone of voice to the topic and intended audience. However, there is a text-to-speech option within the Voki application that will speak for you.

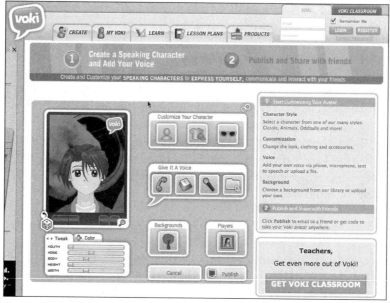

**Figure 11.19** | Voki create screen

## *How* Do You Get Started with Voki?

Go to Voki.com and create a login for yourself. Choose and customize your avatar, pick a background setting, and then give your Voki a voice. Embed the final product in your website or blog.

## *Where* Can You Find More Information About Voki?

Voki home page: www.voki.com

Voki offers a classroom management system (Voki Classroom) that allows students to do classwork and homework with Voki: www.voki.com/products. php#vokiClassroom

# Wordle

Samantha Morra
Glenfield School Technology Coordinator, Montclair Public Schools,
Montclair, New Jersey

## *What* Is Wordle?

Wordle creates word clouds from text. These clouds, or visual representations of text, give prominence to words that appear more frequently in the text.

## *Why* Is Wordle a Useful Tool?

Wordle is much more than just about creating pretty pictures with words. It is a great visualization tool that can become a catalyst for discussion and insight. It is about understanding and discovering patterns in text and generating conversations among students and teachers.

## *When* Do You Use Wordle?

When I first discovered Wordle, I decided to share it with my middle school students. We were discussing the power of words and images, and it seemed like a perfect fit.

We went to the federal government's Our Documents website (www. ourdocuments.gov), which has the text of all the documents that are important in U.S. history. We selected the text of the Declaration of Independence. Then we went to Wordle (www.wordle.net) and created a word cloud with it. Students could see instantly which words were most important.

Next, I gave students the assignment to choose another one of the "100 Milestone Documents" on the Our Documents site and analyze the word clouds they produced. Students enjoyed this exercise and learned more about the power of words.

The conversations they had about the assignment were amazing. One student chose the Gettysburg Address. He said he chose to make the colors gray because it was about war, and it was sad. Another student chose Andrew Jackson's "Message to Congress On Indian Removal." As she read it over, she commented that the words *whites* and *civilized* were together and the words *Indians* and *savage* were together. This sparked a discussion about racism and the creation of our country. I could not get my students to leave when the bell rang. I knew this was one site I wanted to share with other teachers.

In addition to teaching, I conduct staff development workshops for teachers in my district. We usually create a word cloud with the Declaration of Independence or a piece of literature. It never ceases to amaze me how Wordle just clicks (pardon the pun) with so many teachers, no matter what their level of technology. Out of all the tools I cover, teachers start using Wordle first after they leave my workshop.

One of the social studies teachers in my school always asks her students to create an interesting cover for their reports. She likes to encourage creativity, but some students complained that they could not draw and hated that part of the assignment. Her technology skills were not that strong, but she heard about Wordle. She gave them the option of copying and pasting their reports into Wordle, making adjustments for layout and color, and using that as the cover. Many of her students chose that option. One student put her report into Wordle and saw that "also" was the largest word. She showed it to her teacher and said, "I guess I use 'also' too much." The teacher made a lesson out of it, and now the students are much more aware of the word choices they make. This teacher now uses Wordle with all of her students, and it has become a word variety self-assessment tool.

## *How* Do You Get Started with Wordle?

You go to the Wordle site at www.wordle.net. There is no login or membership. You can just copy any text from a Word file, the web, or any other source, and make it into a word cloud by pasting it into the box. As you press the create button, there is a magical moment where unwieldy text is transformed into an image on the screen. The larger words can help the viewer identify the main ideas from the text quickly and easily. You can also enhance your word clouds by changing the font, layout, and colors.

Figure 11.20 | Wordle image from the U.S. Declaration of Independence

## *Where* Can You Find More Information About Wordle?

You can find Wordle at www.wordle.net.

I also find the Wordle group on Diigo a valuable source for information: http://groups.diigo.com/groups/wordle. It is a great way to collaborate with other educators about the use of Wordle. It is also a great place to find examples, tips, and innovative ways to use Wordle in education.

# 12

# 200 Tools to Get Started

This book has examined the ways educators are using Web 2.0 tools for instructional practices and professional development. This chapter presents a collection of these tools, many of which are discussed earlier in the book, so readers can find tools they need quickly and easily. It's also a way to see the range of tools available for classrooms today.

We recognize two important things: First, tools will come and go, and web addresses will change. We apologize for that in advance. Second, we know that each of you is a creative, adventurous educator; thus, we encourage you to use these tools in a way that is meaningful for you and your students. There are no Web 2.0 tool police! Be creative, have fun, and maximize the instructional value.

# Tool Categories

We hope you will find this list useful. Because there are almost 200 tools listed here, we organized them into the following 24 categories:

Annotation and Note Taking

Audio and Podcast Tools

Blogs

Calendars

Collaborative Writing Tools

Communication and Online Discussion Tools

Content Management Systems and Learning Spaces

Educator and Student Communities

Idea or Mind Mapping

Infographics

Online Whiteboards

Maps

Microblogging and Microblog Readers

Photo Editing and Photo Sharing

Presentation and Video-Editing Tools

Publishing and Drawing Tools

# Tools

## Annotation and Note Taking

**Diigo** (www.diigo.com). Diigo allows you to bookmark links to archive, attach highlights and stickies to webpages, and share annotation through Twitter, Facebook, and Google Buzz. This program can be accessed through your computer, iPhone, iPad, and Android and is operated via Google Chrome.

**Evernote** (http://evernote.com). Evernote allows you to write a note or capture something from a web page and save it so that it is indexed and searchable by keywords, titles, and tags.

**Gumnotes** (www.gumnotes.com/home). With Gumnotes, you can annotate websites and saved documents. You can also use this program to annotate emails, contacts, and appointments; set up reminders; and even share your notes with others.

**Lino** (http://en.linoit.com). Lino allows you to create online sticky notes which can be posted to a web-based canvas. Within the notes you can include text, photos, links, and videos.

**NotePub** (www.notepub.com). NotePub is an online notepad and a great way to manage and share information. It allows you and your students to take notes and include images, files, links, and tags. You can make your students' notes public, private, or shared with a group by setting permissions for each note.

**Notezz** (http://notezz.com). Notezz is a note-taking tool for students and teachers. It can be used to take and save notes online with just a click of the mouse.

**SoundCloud** (http://soundcloud.com). SoundCloud is an audio recording app that enables you to store files in the cloud. You can share what you store on Facebook, Twitter, StumbleUpon, Tumblr, Blogger, WordPress, MySpace, and email. You can also search other audio files contained within the site and follow users with similar tastes.

**Springpad** (http://springpad.com/about). Springpad is very similar to Evernote. This application allows you to quickly and easily save anything you want to remember and develop personalized notes.

**Workflowy** (http://workflowy.com). Workflowy is a tool that enables you to organize to-do-lists, collaborate on team projects, take notes, develop research papers, and more. This can be a great tool for your students to use in the classroom to help them organize class assignments and keep up to date with tasks they need to finish.

## Audio and Podcast Tools

**A.T.TIPScast** (http://attipscast.com). Assistive Technology: Tools in Public Schools is an award-winning podcast that uses technology to help students meet their educational goals. The site regularly posts new podcasts addressing a wide range of educational topics.

**Audacity** (http://audacity.sourceforge.net). Audacity is free, open-source software that you download to record and edit sounds.

**Audiopal** (www.audiopal.com). Audiopal lets you record your voice or use built-in voices and incorporate the audio into a web page, blog, or social networking site.

**BBC podcasts** (www.bbc.co.uk/podcasts/genre/childrens). This site contains a number of educated related podcasts that you could use to enhance your classes.

**Bookwink** (www.bookwink.com). Bookwink provides video book talks (three minutes each) about new books for children in Grades 3 through 8.

**Chirbit** (www.chirbit.com). Chirbit allows you to record, upload, listen to, and share sound; create micropodcasts and short audio clips; and incorporate these into websites such as Twitter and Facebook.

**Digital Podcast** (Educational) (www.digitalpodcast.com/categories/20-education-podcasts). Digital Podcast (Educational) is a collection of topics that range from lessons in languages, relaxation, and history alive, to lessons in filmmaking. It allows you to add your own podcasts, tag them, and share them with the world.

**Fetch!** (http://pbskids.org/fetch/show/podcasts.html). PBS offers a wide variety of free children's podcasts. The site also includes information for parents and teachers.

**GarageBand** (www.apple.com/ilife/garageband). GarageBand is the popular Mac application that you can use to create music, record voice, and share your creations with others.

**Inkless Tales Podcasts for Kids** (http://inklesstales.wordpress.com). This site provides retelling of familiar and ethnically diverse stories.

**iSpeech** (www.ispeech.org). iSpeech is a text-to-speech converter that transforms your blog into a talking blog so that people can listen to the text on the page.

**iTunes** (www.itunes.com). With iTunes you can download music, video, and podcasts to your PC, iPad, or iPod. There is a Kids & Family category for children's podcasts (http://itunes.apple.com/us/genre/podcasts-kids-family/id1305?mt=2).

**Odiogo** (www.odiogo.com). Odiogo allows you to mobilize your media through transforming text content into audio formats. You can download your audio creations directly to your PC, iPod/MP3 player and mobile phone.

**Podbean** (www.podbean.com). Podbean allows you to create podcasts in three easy steps and upload, publish, manage, and promote your podcasts. It also allows you to store and manage podcast subscriptions.

**Podcast Alley** (www.podcastalley.com). Podcast Alley is another great place for you to search for podcasts. The site publishes the Top 10 podcasts list, which is voted by the users of the site.

**PodcastDirectory.com** (www.podcastdirectory.com). Podcast Directory allows you to download over 6 million podcast episodes and is now one of the largest podcast directories in the world.

**Podcasts for Educators, Schools, and Colleges** (http://recap.ltd.uk/podcasting/ subjects.php). This site offers curricular podcasts already categorized by subject area.

**Podomatic** (www.podomatic.com). Podomatic allows you to create, find, and share podcasts, customize a podcast page, get audience data, share video and photos, and be part of a podcast community.

**Poetry Podcasts** (www.learnoutloud.com/Podcast-Directory/Literature/Poetry). The podcasts in this directory can bring poetry to you and your students.

**Read the Words** (www.readthewords.com). Read the Words allows you to convert text to speech, including words you type in, uploaded files, and web pages, and embed the results in email or a web page.

**Reading Rockets** (www.readingrockets.org/podcasts/classroom). Reading Rockets is a tool where you can use pod- and vodcasts to help your students learn to read.

**Storynory** (www.storynory.com). Storynory offers podcasts of familiar stories (Jack and the Beanstalk or Little Red Riding Hood) as well as less familiar ones. Happily, these stories come with full English text so that beginning readers or English language learners (ELLs) can see the words as they are spoken.

**TED Talks on Education** (www.ted.com/topics/education). TED Talks is a nonprofit devoted to Ideas Worth Spreading. It started in 1984 as a conference bringing together people from three worlds: Technology, Entertainment, and

Design. Since then its scope has become even broader and includes the award-winning TED Talks video site, which tags some of its videos specifically for education.

**Vocaroo** (http://vocaroo.com). Vocaroo allows you to record your voice and send voice messages. You can install a widget on your website or blog to allow visitors to record and play back their own voices.

**Voki** (www.voki.com). Voki allows you to create personalized speaking avatars and use them on your blog, on your profile, and in your email messages.

**Yodio** (http://yodio.com). Yodio provides an audio player to embed on websites so that you can create and listen to sound along with your photos or presentations, as well as share narratives such as an audio postcard or narrated photo album or storybook.

# Blogs

**BlogEasy** (www.blogeasy.com). BlogEasy offers free blog hosting, free web page publishing, and a syndication service that allows you to quickly share information, such as breaking news, reviews, blogs, journals, weblogs, diaries, and photos.

**Blogger** (www.blogger.com). Google's Blogger provides a platform for blogs so that students can share their thoughts in writing, photos, and videos. They can post from the web or mobile phone and can personalize their blogs with themes, gadgets, and more.

**CheckThis** (www.checkthis.com). CheckThis calls itself a community of story-tellers. It is not technically a blog because the pages are not linked and each has a distinct URL, but it is an easy way for your students to publish and share content in writing and multimedia.

**Class Blogmeister** (www.classblogmeister.com). Class Blogmeister is a blogging engine or online publishing tool that was developed specifically for classroom use so that students can publish assignment-based writing. Teachers set up and maintain accounts and are responsible for them.

**CoverItLive** (www.coveritlive.com). CoverItLive allows you to turn live blogging into an online event by streaming live onto your web pages or blog so that others can hear from you in real time. You can add pictures and videos.

**Edublogs** (www.edublogs.org). Edublogs allows you to create and manage student blogs which can include useful features for podcasting and displaying videos, photos, and more. Getting started with Edublogs is easy as the site provides step-by-step instructions and video tutorials.

**ePals** (www.epals.com). ePals is a K–12 online community with school-safe email and blog tools for students to connect, collaborate, and learn. It features a global community of connected classrooms and collaborative learning projects.

**Gaggle** (www.gaggle.net). Gaggle provides email, blogs, chat rooms, message boards, and digital lockers for students.

**Glogster EDU** (http://edu.glogster.com/what-is-glogster-edu). Glogster EDU has become popular in recent years and is now the leading global educational blog creation platform. Glogster allows you and your students to create Glogs, which are online multimedia posters that include text, photos, videos, graphics, sounds, drawings, data attachments, and much more.

**Kidblog** (http://kidblog.org/home). More than 3 million K–12 students now use Kidblog, and the site has become trusted by teachers around the world. Kidblog was designed specifically for K–12 teachers to assist individual students to create their own blogs so that they can practice participating in the online educational environment.

**LiveJournal** (www.livejournal.com). LiveJournal provides the tools to express yourself, share, and connect with others online. You can use LiveJournal as a private journal, a blog, a discussion forum, or a social network.

**OhLife** (www.ohlife.com). OhLife is a great blogging option for older students. The site requires an email address because it generates a message that prompts students to write. Your students reply with their thoughts, which become journals.

**Storify** (www.storify.com). Storify is a platform for combining original writing with stories from the web or social media aggregation tools. Students search for a topic and drag the content they want into the story pane.

**Tumblr** (www.tumblr.com). Tumblr is a popular microblogging platform and social networking website. You can create your own blog and follow others.

**21Classes** (www.21classes.com). 21Classes allows you to create, host, and manage a virtual classroom or blog to communicate with your students and encourage student writing and communication. Students can upload text and photos, or insert videos into their blog posts.

**TypePad** (www.typepad.com). TypePad provides a platform for control over what, when, and how you publish content to your blog. You can customize the look and feel of your blog design, publish different types of media, and manage comments.

**Weebly** (www.weebly.com). Weebly allows you to create a classroom website and blog with a drag-and-drop interface, as well as host a domain, at no cost. Teachers can manage their students' accounts, accept homework assignments online, and keep parents up to date.

**WordPress** (www.wordpress.com). WordPress.com is a state-of-the-art, open-source publishing platform that requires you to have a hosting account, a database, FTP, and other features, which many schools and districts do have. WordPress adds the missing features so that you can set up blogs with a choice of design, 3 GB of file storage, integrated statistics, a spam blocker, and versions in more than 50 languages.

## Calendars

**Assign-A-Day** (http://assignaday.4teachers.org). Assign-A-Day is a free tool designed to enhance your and your students' communication and organizational skills through an online teacher-managed calendar. You can create a calendar for each of your classes and add assignments for students to view. Students can also view their teachers' calendars to see assignments for classes they might have missed and stay generally up-to-date with in-class happenings.

**Google Calendar** (www.google.com/calendar/render). Google Calendar allows you to synchronize your Google accounts, keep track of important dates, and set up reminders.

**Shortcal** (www.shortcal.com). With Shortcal, you can create calendars for a set number of days and receive email reminders directly to your personal email. Shortcal is especially effective for short-term planning and time-oriented goal setting.

**30 Boxes** (www.30boxes.com). Simple and with a quick learning curve and sharing that is easily arranged, 30 Boxes might be the calendar of choice for your students. With this tool, you can also include an RSS subscription to monitor items of interest or items you wish your students to hear or read.

**Weekis** (http://weekis.com). Weekis is a free online weekly planner that allows you to easily organize your daily affairs in a simple and easy to use online platform.

## Collaborative Writing Tools

**BoomWriter** (http://boomwriter.com). BoomWriter is a free and easy-to-use collaborative writing tool that enables your students to interact to create original stories. BoomWriter is equivalent to an online game of literary Telephone.

**Buzzword** (www.adobe.com/uk/acom/buzzword). Adobe's Buzzword is a new online word processor that you can use to collaborate with others. Students can write, edit, and comment on documents; add images; and share with others. Teachers can control access levels and versions, track edits by contributor, and keep track of changes.

**Draft** (http://draftin.com). Draft is a simple writing editor for your students to post their work and has collaborative tools that lets them invite peers to edit and comment.

**EtherPad** (http://etherpad.org). EtherPad is a web-based word processor that allows people to work together in real time, edit the same document simultaneously, and see changes instantly reflected on everyone's screen.

**Google Apps for Education** (www.google.com/enterprise/apps/education). Google Apps for Education is a free suite of hosted communication and collaboration tools designed for schools and universities. It includes email, messaging, calendars, word processing, spreadsheet, forms, and presentation software.

**Google Drive** (http://drive.google.com). Operated by Google, this tool allows you to create and edit documents online while collaborating with others in real time.

**Hackpad** (http://hackpad.com). Hackpad is a tool that was developed to help you work collaboratively in note taking and can be used to help your students develop paper outlines.

**HyLighter** (www.hylighter.com). HyLighter provides a collaboration plugin for collective thinking and editing as contributors interact. Instead of actually changing the original document, as in a wiki or online editor, or redlining, as in Track Changes, it points to the locations in the document where reviewers have made comments or recommended changes.

**iRows** (www.irows.com). This is another option for spreadsheets that can be stored online and collaboratively constructed. This tool does allow the creation of charts and saves in a variety of formats.

**MixedInk** (www.mixedink.com). MixedInk takes an approach to collaborative writing in which people weave their best ideas together. An organizing group runs each topic and invites others to join. It was designed for short texts that get attention, such as an op-ed, mission statement, or open letter.

**My Simple Surface** (www.mysimplesurface.com). My Simple Surface works on the principle of writing surfaces. Your students create as many surfaces as they need and link them to one another and can manage large projects with linked surfaces.

**PrimaryPad** (http://primarypad.com). PrimaryPad is an online word processor designed for classrooms so that you and your students can work together on documents in real time.

**Scribd** (www.scribd.com). Scribd is the place where you can publish, discover, and discuss original writings and documents. People can share their writing or find others' works. It is a platform for readers, authors, publishers, and others seeking to express themselves, share ideas, and exchange information.

**Scribblar** (www.scribblar.com). Scribblar is a simple and effective online collaboration tool. It provides you with a multiuser whiteboard, live audio, image collaboration, text chat tools, and more.

**Smartsheet** (www.smartsheet.com). Smartsheet allows you to work alone or in groups to plan a project, assign tasks, collaborate with others, coordinate activities, manage workflow, set reminders, and collect, organize, and track data.

**TextFlow** (http://textflow.com). TextFlow is a collaborative tool that allows several users to work concurrently, all on their own versions of the same document.

**Titanpad** (http://titanpad.com). Titanpad allows you to work on the same document simultaneously with others.

**Wizehive** (www.wizehive.com). Wizehive allows your students to share files, manage projects, track their activity, and collaborate with others. It provides a secure and private collaborative workspace that includes several tools that students use on a single platform.

**Wunderkit** (www.wunderkit.com). Wunderkit is a free, online collaborative workspace that provides your students with an open space to work together on projects.

**Zoho Docs** (www.zoho.com/docs/). Zoho Docs provides sharing and collaboration. Post your documents online and share them with those in the group for collaboration in real time. You can upload documents from the desktop, Google Drive, or anywhere on the web and download and save them to your computer.

## Communication and Online Discussion Tools

**Chatzy** (www.chatzy.com). Chatzy provides a chat service that allows its users to create chat rooms, send out invitations to people they know, and communicate privately in these chat rooms. It is often used as a backchannel Dweeber.

**Dweeber** (http://dweeber.com). Dweeber was designed to help students work on their homework and build a community of peers for side conversations during presentations.

**FlashMeeting** (http://flashmeeting.e2bn.net). FlashMeeting is an online meeting application that allows a dispersed group of people to meet from anywhere in the world with an internet connection. Someone books a meeting and informs participants, who can then click on the link to enter the meeting at an arranged time.

**Google Hangouts** (www.google.com/+/learnmore/hangouts). Google Hangouts is Google's version of instant messaging. With Google Hangouts, you can text, voice, and even video chat with your Gmail contacts.

**iSpeech** (www.ispeech.org). iSpeech is a text-to-speech application that allows you to easily convert text content (Word, Excel, PowerPoint, PDF, blogs, RSS feeds, etc.) into audio. It is easy to use and has wide applications.

**MentorMob** (www.mentormob.com). MentorMob is a place where teachers can curate the web into learning playlists and then share them with their students via a link or embedding into a site. See more at: www.guide2digitallearning. com/tools_technologies/top_sites_summer_sampling#sthash.mbHVYeJC.dpuf

**Mikogo** (www.mikogo.com). Mikogo is a cross-platform desktop sharing tool, ideal for web conferencing, online meetings, or remote support.

**Neat Chat** (www.neatchat.com). Neat Chat allows your students to have an online conversation with a group or team.

**Scribblar** (http://scribblar.com). Scribblar is an online collaboration tool to use for training and tutoring, working with images, brainstorming, and demonstrating. It includes a real-time multiuser whiteboard, image upload and download, text chat, and live audio.

**SnapYap** (www.snapyap.com). SnapYap is a video communication tool that allows you to participate in live video calls, record video messages, and send and receive video emails with just a webcam and an internet connection. Users can launch video calls in their web browsers.

**Stinto** (http://stinto.net). Stinto lets your students create a chat and invite others to join in.

**Thinkbinder** (http://thinkbinder.com/index.php/unsupported). Thinkbinder is a platform that your students can use to create study groups.

**Yackall** (http://yackall.com). Yackall provides a way to communicate with a group while on the go. It provides a means to have a continuous long-running conversation no matter when it is or where the participants are located.

**Yuuguu** (www.yuuguu.com). Yuuguu offers cross-network instant messaging, instant screen sharing, real-time collaboration, web conferencing, and remote support.

## Content Management Systems and Learning Spaces

**Blackboard Engage** (formerly School Fusion) (www.blackboard.com/platforms/engage/overview.aspx). Blackboard Engage is a tool that helps districts build fully customized websites that can include content management, online calendars, classroom websites, and personal space.

**Drupal** (http://drupal.org). Drupal is a free, open-source software package that allows you to publish, manage, and organize a wide variety of content on a website. You can use it for a school or community web portal, discussion site, social networking site, personal website or blog, and more.

**Haiku** (www.haikulearning.com). Haiku is a learning management system that allows you to organize, manage, and deliver course content, assignments, and assessments. You can securely conduct discussions, exchange messages, take attendance, and collect and grade homework.

**Moodle** (http://moodle.org). Moodle is a course or learning management system. Educators can use this free web application to create effective online learning sites with dynamic content. To work, it needs to be installed on a web server.

**Planboard** (www.planboardapp.com). Planboard enables you to do your lesson planning online. It is great site for streamlining lesson plans, finding resources, and even collaborating with others.

**Symbaloo** (www.symbaloo.com). Symbaloo is a neat and easy-to-use tool that lets you organize your favorite links onto a single start page for quick access. Symbaloo displays your links in a grid and tile format. To access your links, just click the tile of the site you wish to visit.

## Educator and Student Communities

**Badoo** (http://badoo.com). Badoo is a worldwide socializing site that supports members meeting new people and friends in and around their local areas. It includes the interactions and activities of most social networks, but it focuses on expanding social circles locally. One of Badoo's strengths is the control users have over the exposure of their profiles; it also has instant messaging and uploads of photos and videos.

**Bebo** (www.bebo.com). Bebo is a popular social networking site that connects you to individuals and information globally. It combines community, self-expression, and entertainment in a way that allows you to share, with selected others in your network, digital content that you create yourself or that you admire.

**Blackboard** (www.blackboard.com). Blackboard has become an immensely popular format for online learning. You can post lessons, PowerPoints, and syllabi; chat with your students; and import class-related readings, videos, and links. Within Blackboard, you can also email with your students and hold online class sessions.

**Classroom 2.0** (www.classroom20.com). Classroom 2.0 is a social network for those interested in Web 2.0 and collaborative technologies in education. The site, built on a Ning, hosts discussions, and educators can find and connect with colleagues.

**Curriki** (www.curriki.org). Curriki is a community of educators, learners, and experts who create free, open-source instructional materials for a repository that will benefit teachers and students.

**Digiteen** (http://digiteen.ning.com). Digiteen is a place for teens to communicate in a Ning that focuses on what it means to be a digital teenager today.

**Edmodo** (www.edmodo.com). Edmodo has recently become very popular among tech-savvy educators. This educationally oriented social networking tool provides you with a safe and easy way to connect and collaborate with your students and other educators. With Edmodo, you can share content, access homework and grades, post school notices, and collaborate with other teachers.

**English Companion** (http://englishcompanion.ning.com/group/teachingwith technology/forum/topics/introducing-ning-to-students). English Companion is an English education Ning set up to foster the use of Nings in classroom curriculum and to help you begin the journey of integrating these tools into the classroom.

**Engrade** (www.engrade.com). Engrade is an online classroom community with a free set of web-based tools that allows you to manage classes online and provide parents and students with 24/7 real-time class information that's private and secure. It includes an assignment calendar, online messaging, grade book, attendance book, and progress reports.

**Facebook** (www.facebook.com) and MySpace (http://myspace.com). Facebook and MySpace are websites that connect people through personal expression, content, and culture. With a global community of millions of users, they provide forums for personal profiles, photos, videos, messaging, games, and music. Individuals find old friends, establish new friendships, and interact at multiple levels.

**FieldFindr** (http://fieldfindr.wikispaces.com). FieldFindr works to help global volunteers with teachers and their students. You can create posts if you are looking for volunteers or people who have expert knowledge to enrich your classes' study of immigration, peace studies, playgrounds, and the Holocaust.

**Flat Connections** (www.flatconnections.com). Flat Connections was designed to transform learning through global collaboration. You find projects from class-rooms around the world and your students can post ideas of connections they would like to start.

**Friendster** (www.friendster.com). Friendster is a global online social network with more than 110 million members worldwide. It is focused on helping people stay in touch with friends and discover new people and things that are important to them. Friendster prides itself in delivering an easy-to-use, friendly, and interactive environment where users can connect easily with anyone around the world.

**Greenovation** (www.greenovationnation.com). Greenovation was designed to "energize education and inspire action." You can go to Greenovation and engage your students or the entire school in a project designed around environmental action.

**Hi5** (http://hi5.com). Hi5 is a global social entertainment network designed primarily for youth. It is available in more than 50 languages. It is a highly interactive social experience and ranks as one of the fastest growing youth sites, particularly for social media.

**LinkedIn** (www.linkedin.com). LinkedIn is a widely interconnected network of professionals (50 million!) from around the world. You can connect your network of trusted colleagues to others' networks in a safe environment and set up collaborations, consultations, and interactions. LinkedIn represents 170 industries and 200 countries.

**Museum Podcasts abound:** Many museums offer podcasts to prepare classrooms or families for a visit. For example, the Smithsonian Museum (www.si.edu/Connect/Podcasts); Museum of Science, Boston (www.mos.org/museum-online); and the Metropolitan Museum of Art (www.metmuseum.org/en/metmedia/audo).

**Ning** (www.ning.com). Ning provides a social platform that allows people to join and create Ning Networks. Creators control the layout and have a wide choice of features—videos, photos, chat, music, groups, events, and blogs—in addition to a latest-activity feature, member profile pages, friends, messaging, email notifications, RSS support, and third-party applications.

**Project Peace** (http://projectpeace.ning.com). Project Peace is a social community designed to teach English through students' singing, promoting peace. You can join the network and have your students create videos, podcasts, and other projects to post online along with others from around the globe.

**Rolling on the River** (http://rollingontheriver.ning.com). This website is centered on the study of rivers and other bodies of water. It is "a resource for global collaboration" where you can "share information, find global partners, and learn more about rivers, lakes, and oceans through participation and collaboration."

**WizIQ** (www.wiziq.com). WizIQ is an online teacher community for learning and collaboration. Students and teachers can find, share, download, and upload PowerPoint presentations on educational subjects and topics. Teachers can teach and learn live in WizIQ's virtual classroom.

## Idea or Mind Mapping

**Bubbl.us** (http://bubbl.us). Bubbl.us is a web application that lets you brainstorm online. Students can create colorful mind maps, share and work in teams, embed a mind map in a blog or website, email and print a mind map, or save it as an image.

**Debategraph** (www.debategraph.org). Debategraph is a wiki debate visualization tool that lets you present the strongest case on any debate that matters to you, openly engage the opposing arguments, create and reshape debates, make new points, rate and filter the arguments, monitor the evolution of debates via RSS feeds, and share and reuse the debates online and offline.

**Gliffy** (www.gliffy.com). Gliffy is online diagram software used to create professional-quality flowcharts, diagrams, floor plans, technical drawings, and more. The online diagram editor makes it easy to create diagrams, drawings, and mind maps.

**Mayomi** (www.mayomi.com). This free flash-based mind-mapping tool is a great way to help your students prepare to write a report or organize their information.

**Mind42** (www.mind42.com). Mind42 is a browser-based, online mind-mapping tool that allows you to manage and keep track of ideas alone, in teams of two, or in a large group. Students can brainstorm and collaborate and then immediately get an updated view of all the collected ideas.

**MindMeister** (www.mindmeister.com). MindMeister provides web-based mind mapping with real-time collaboration to allow global brainstorming sessions. Students can create, manage, and share mind maps online. They can access them anytime, from anywhere. They can work on the same mind map simultaneously and see each other's changes as they happen.

**Mindomo** (www.mindomo.com). Mindomo is a visual tool that lets you organize your ideas and work and gain insights into the relationships between various parts of a problem to formulate a solution. Teachers can plan and track projects, manage tasks and priorities, and define goals and objectives as students learn visually.

**Netvibes** (www.netvibes.com/en). Netvibes lets you create a dashboard for all of your apps, pictures, and tweets. This tool is a reader for real-time articles and also allows you to sync what you choose to place on your Netvibes desktop on your mobile and tablet devices.

**Webspiration** (www.mywebspiration.com). Webspiration allows you to combine the power of visual thinking and outlining to enhance thinking, learning, and collaboration. Students can use Webspiration to map out ideas, organize with outlines, and collaborate online with teams or colleagues.

## Infographics

**Easelly** (www.easel.ly). Easel.ly is a web-based tool that you can use to create infographics. The tool allows you to easily organize your data and create interesting graphic presentations and visualizations.

**Infogr.am** (http://infogr.am). Infogr.am is a web-based infographic tool that allows you to illustrate your data visually with more 30 different types of charts and graphs.

**NerdGraph** (www.nerdgraph.com). NerdGraph is an infographic tool that you and your students can use to create posterlike representations that include visual data representations and text.

**Piktochart** (http://piktochart.com). Piktochart is another great infographic tool that allows you to quickly and easily create professional-looking visual representations of your data.

## Online Whiteboards

**CoSketch** (http://cosketch.com). CoSketch is a multiuser online whiteboard that provides you with the ability to visualize and share your ideas as images quickly. Anything you paint will show up in real time for all other users in the room. You can save a sketch as an image for embedding on forums, blogs, and so forth.

**Draw It Live** (www.drawitlive.com). Draw It Live is a free application that allows you to draw and create with others in real time.

**RealtimeBoard** (http://realtimeboard.com). RealtimeBoard provides you with an online collaborative whiteboard where you can upload images, draw, add text, post notes, and comment. You can also save what you have created and even chat with others while you work.

**Scriblink** (http://scriblink.com). Scriblink is a free digital whiteboard (with no registration) that users can share to collaborate online in real time. Features include privacy, dynamic tools, and file options such as printing, saving, and emailing work, uploading images, and in-screen chat or voice-over-IP conferencing.

**Twiddla** (www.twiddla.com).Twiddla is an online playground where your students can mark up web pages, graphics, and photos or brainstorm.

## Maps

**GEarthHacks** (www.gearthhacks.com). GEarthHacks works in concert with Google Earth and allows you to overlay downloaded files and use them with Google Earth.

**Google Earth** (www.google.com/earth). Google Earth lets you "fly" anywhere on Earth (and beyond) to view satellite imagery, maps, terrain, and 3D buildings, from mountain peaks to the canyons of the ocean. You can even tour the solar system and distant galaxies. You can explore rich geographical content, save your toured places, and share with others.

**Google Maps** (www.google.com/maps). Google Maps allows you to enter addresses to locate places geographically and get directions from one place to another.

**Google Sky** (www.google.com/sky). Google Sky provides a way to browse and explore the universe. You can find the positions of the planets and constellations and even watch the birth of distant galaxies as seen by the Hubble Space Telescope. Google Maps has teamed up with astronomers at some of the largest observatories in the world to provide these views of the sky.

**Quikmaps** (www.quikmaps.com). Quikmaps is a free mashup service. It enables you to draw directly onto a Google Map. You can view it online, on your website, in Google Earth, or on your GPS. You can scribble on it, do line tracing, add text labels, and save a map to your desktop.

## Microblogging and Microblog Readers

**Plurk** (www.plurk.com). Plurk is a microblogging site that allows you to chronicle and share information, ideas, thoughts, and activities and then communicate them to others using Plurk.

**Socialoomph** (www.socialoomph.com). Socialoomph is a tool that enables you to engage in free and paid productivity enhancement services for your social media sites.

**TodaysMeet** (www.todaysmeet.com). TodaysMeet is a microblogging website that allows you to create a chat room or backchannel where your students can post messages with 140 or fewer characters.

**TweetDeck** (www.tweetdeck.com). TweetDeck provides a personal browser for staying in touch with what's happening online by connecting you with your contacts across Twitter, Facebook, and more.

**Twitter** (http://twitter.com). Twitter is a microblogging site that provides a real-time, short messaging service (SMS) that works over multiple networks and devices. You can use it to follow the sources most relevant to you and access information online or via SMS as it happens—from breaking world news to updates from friends.

**Twitter4Teachers wiki** (http://twitter4teachers.pbworks.com). With Twitter4Teachers, you can add people whom others find interesting and create an online community of people who share such things as subject area to create a personal learning network.

**Twitterrific** (http://iconfactory.com/software/twitterrific). Twitterrific is a Mac application that lets you read and publish posts or tweets to the Twitter website.

**TwtPoll** (www.twtpoll.com). TwtPoll lets you create custom polls in advance and link to content. Your poll generates a URL that students can access. The result is data you can use. There's a minimal charge for TwtPoll.

**Twuffer** (http://twuffer.com). Twuffer is a great tool if you have a Twitter account as it allows you to organize lists of future tweets, and even schedule when they are tweeted.

## Photo Editing and Photo Sharing

**BeFunky** (www.befunky.com). BeFunky is an online photo editor that provides digital effects tools to turn photos into special-effects digital artwork. You can save images to a private or public space.

**Cartoon Pho.to** (http://cartoon.pho.to). Cartoon.Pho.to transforms photos into cartoons with the click of the mouse. This application also allows you to alter the appearances of your uploaded photos in a fun way.

**Dumpr** (www.dumpr.net/sketch.php). Dumpr allows you to create a digital photo pencil sketch from an uploaded picture. You can even draw and modify the image in creative ways.

**Flickr** (www.flickr.com). Flickr is a free online photo management and photo sharing application. You can upload an image, edit it, organize your photo collections, share the images with others, and create cards, photo books, and other items.

**Fotoflexer** (http://fotoflexer.com). Fotoflexer is an online image editor that allows you to create interesting effects and provides the tools to retouch and enhance images.

**Instagram** (http://instagram.com). Instagram is a photography app that allows you to take photos with a mobile device, edit and save them on the device, and then upload to the cloud.

**Photobucket** (http://photobucket.com). Photobucket is a video site that provides free web-based versions of Adobe's video remix and editing tools.

**Photoshop** (Online) (www.photoshop.com). Adobe provides Photoshop.com, an online image editor that has many of the same tools as their commercial software so that you can edit images professionally.

**Photo Story** (http://microsoft-photo-story.en.softonic.com). Microsoft's free downloadable software allows you to create a presentation from digital photos, with narration, effects, transitions, and music.

**Photosynth** (http://photosynth.net). Photosynth allows you to take a collection of photos of places or objects. It analyzes them for similarities and displays them in a reconstructed 3D space.

**Picasa** (http://picasa.google.com). Picasa is Google's free photo-editing software that you can use to edit and enhance images, share them with others, and organize them into albums on your computer using the desktop application. Picasa is available for PC and Mac and requires downloading.

**Pinterest** (http://pinterest.com). Pinterest is a photo-sharing website that allows you to "pin" photos to your own "pinboard" and organize them by theme. You can also view others people's pinboards and share them with others through email and social media.

**Pixlr** (www.pixlr.com). Pixlr is a free online photo editor that allows you to make quick fixes to your images using a wide range of editing tools.

**Webspiration** (www.mywebspiration.com). Webspiration allows you and your students to create, organize, and share ideas visually.

## Presentation and Video-Editing Tools

**Animoto** (http://animoto.com/education). Animoto provides an assortment of tools for you and your students to create videos with images, video clips, and music. You can sync music and images for high production values and then share the video in several ways.

**Empressr** (www.empressr.com). Empressr is a free online storytelling tool that allows you to create, manage, and share rich-media presentations online. Upload your video, images, and audio to get started creating slideshows.

**Flipsnack** (www.flipsnack.com). Flipsnack allows your students to take a document in any format that is converted to a PDF and create a flipbook to display a virtual presentation.

**Jing** (www.techsmith.com/jing). Jing is screen capture software that allows you to share a snapshot of a project, collaborate on it, narrate it, or add comments. You can select a window or region, and Jing will record up to five minutes of video of everything that appears in that area. Point to things with your mouse, scroll, flip through photos, click around in a website or application, and Jing captures it. Teachers and students can create tutorials.

**Movie Maker** (http://download.live.com/moviemaker) and Windows Live Movie Maker (http://explore.live.com/windows-live-movie-maker). Movie Maker is downloadable video-creating and video-editing software that is a part of Microsoft's Windows Live.

**Museum Box** (http://museumbox.e2bn.org). Museum Box provides the tools for you to build up an argument or description of an event, person, or historical period by placing items in a virtual box. You can display anything from a text file to a movie. You can also view the museum boxes submitted by other people and comment on the contents.

**PhotoPeach** (http://photopeach.com/education/premium). This is a great site for creating digital slideshows and presentations. You can create interesting slideshows quickly and insert music, captions, and comments to enhance the viewing experience.

**PhotoShow** (www.photoshow.com). You can create photo shows and stories online and view them at this site or post them to others. You add pictures and videos you want to include in your show, view an automatically generated slideshow, customize it, and then share it.

**Present.me** (http://present.me). Present.me is an online presentation tool that you and your students can use in and outside of the classroom. You can update your PowerPoint presentations and even add visual narrations to your slides.

**Prezi** (http://prezi.com). Prezi's free online presentation tool allows you to create public-only presentations online that you can show either online or offline. You can create groups; import images, videos, and other media files; share and collaborate; edit; download the results; and embed them in blogs and on websites.

**Sketchcast** (http://web20fortheclassroom.wikispaces.com/Sketchcast). Sketchcast allows you to communicate online by recording a sketch and including your voice. You can embed the sketch in your blog or website for people to play back, and you can also point people to your sketchcast channel (or let them subscribe to your sketchcast RSS feed).

**Sliderocket** (www.sliderocket.com). The free version of Sliderocket is an online presentation maker that includes authoring tools, uploading of PowerPoint slides, an asset library, printing, publishing, and online support.

**Slideshare** (www.slideshare.net). Slideshare provides an online tool for sharing presentations. You can upload your PowerPoint presentations, Word documents, and Adobe PDF Portfolios and share them publicly or privately. You can add audio to make a webinar or embed slideshows in your blog or website.

**ThinkFree Show** (www.thinkfree.com). This Java-based presentation tool feels similar to PowerPoint. You can create presentations and then show them or save them to view in PowerPoint.

**VCASMO** (http://vcasmo.com). VCASMO provides a multimedia presentation solution for creating a photo-video slideshow, presentation, training, seminar, conference, meeting, or live event. Features include a variety of file formats, the synchronization of music, a simple editor, the option to save privately or publicly, and more.

**VIDDIX** (www.viddix.com). VIDDIX provides a video platform that allows users to add all kinds of web content to their video timeline. You can interact with your audience and choose from two types of players: overlay and dual screen.

**Vimeo** (www.vimeo.com). Vimeo is similar to YouTube. With this site you can publish and share your own video creations with the world.

**VoiceThread** (http://voicethread.com). VoiceThread is a tool for having conversations about media. Teachers can organize student discussions about various types of media, such as images, video, and presentations. Students can navigate around an image and add comments, create digital stories, and collaborate and share stories with others.

**World of Teaching** (www.worldofteaching.com). This web page contains a variety of PowerPoint presentations concerning the topics of biology, chemistry, math, English, history, physics, geography, and Spanish. This site is a great presentation resource for both you and your students.

**Zentation** (www.zentation.com). Zentation provides you with video and slides to create online presentations that simulate a live experience to use for webinars, webcasts, training, and virtual events. You can synchronize your YouTube video and PowerPoint slides and get a simple outline for viewers. Viewers can use a comment section to blog about your presentation.

**Zoho Docs** (www.zoho.com/docs). Zoho Docs provides an online tool for making presentations that includes pre-built themes, clip art, and shapes, but also allows for document sharing and management. It has features such as drag-and-drop that make it an easy application to use. You can access it from anywhere, share and collaborate, present remotely, and embed the presentation in your blog or website.

## Publishing and Drawing Tools

**Calameo** (http://en.calameo.com). Calameo allows you to upload documents in all major formats and convert them into digital publications. You can share your published work on the site or embed it in a website or blog.

**Comicbrush** (www.comicbrush.com). Comicbrush provides a simple way to create, publish, and share a comic. Their stock artwork includes a collection of comic backgrounds, characters, and props that you can mix with your own photos. You can add speech balloons, text, your own artwork, and more, and then publish your comic to the web.

**Comic Creator** (www.readwritethink.org/files/resources/interactives/comic). Comic Creator provides tools for students to compose their own comic strips for a variety of contexts (pre-writing, pre- and post-reading activities, response to literature, and so on). Students can choose backgrounds, characters, and props, and compose dialogue.

**Formatpixel** (www.formatpixel.com). Formatpixel allows you to create an online magazine, fanzine, brochure, catalog, portfolio, and more. You can design projects, lay out text, upload images, add interactivity, and customize the appearance by moving, inserting, or deleting pages to create multipage presentations.

**GoAnimate** (http://goanimate.com). GoAnimate enables you to create computer-animated stories, satires, and sentiments that can be shared online. The site offers features to customize animations, and you can include items from GoAnimate's library of ready-made characters, backgrounds, props, sound effects, and music.

**Issuu** (http://issuu.com). Issuu provides a digital publishing platform for stories, books, reports, and other documents. You can create a digital edition of any writing by uploading your work to produce an online publication that simulates the look of a professional magazine.

**Kerpoof** (www.kerpoof.com). Kerpoof provides tools for students to create artwork; make animated movies; tell a story; make printed cards, T-shirts, and mugs; and view the stories and movies of others. It includes instructions for making a picture using Picture Maker and a movie using Animation Studio.

**LetterPop** (www.letterpop.com). LetterPop provides tools to create newsletters, presentations, invitations, picture collages, and more. You can browse templates and drag-and-drop the one you want, type in ideas, upload pictures, and save your work.

**MakeBeliefsComix** (www.makebeliefscomix.com). MakeBeliefsComix provides the tools to create comic strips. It promotes creativity, tests new ideas, and provides ways to communicate through art and writing by offering a choice of characters with different moods for which users can write words and thoughts.

**OpenZine** (www.openzine.com). OpenZine provides a social publishing platform with browser-based tools to create work and display it as well as to share, control, and manage ideas. You create a cover and images online; add shapes, text, and effects; and gather your information to create the zine by mixing and matching content from multiple sources (with approval). However, be wary of some adult content.

**Padlet** (http://padlet.com). Padlet, formally known as Wallwisher, is a very easy way for you and your students to practice publishing websites. With Padlet, your students can create their own unique pages just by dragging their work to a webpage you created for them.

**Pikistrips** (sponsored by Comeeko) (http://pikistrips.com). Pikistrips allows you to create comic strips, upload photos, add bubble comments, and then make them available to others. You can also create items (T-shirts, for example) that can be purchased, if you choose.

**Pixton** (http://pixton.com). Pixton is a remixable, animated comic website on which schools can create private, customizable, classroom sites as well as develop print-based materials. Students can create, share, and remix comics around content topics and also focus on grammar and spelling.

**Plotbot** (www.plotbot.com). Plotbot offers collaborative screenwriting software for educators or students to develop their own plays.

**Stripcreator** (www.stripcreator.com). Stripcreator is a website that allows you to create and save your own comic strips. You can print, export, and share these comics, or you can keep them private.

**Stripgenerator** (http://stripgenerator.com). Stripgenerator allows you to create individual comic strips or a comic strip blog to explain, explore, or expand on your comic strip. You can save strips and make them public, or you can keep them private for specific groups of individuals.

**Tikatok** (www.tikatok.com). Tikatok is an online publishing environment for children. They can start with a blank book or use one of many "story starters." After including drawings, decorations, and designing all aspects of the book, they can then save it. For a small fee, they can create a hardcover or paperback book.

**Toondoo** (www.toondoo.com). Toondoo provides you with tools to create your own comic strips and then publish, share, and discuss them.

**Tux Paint** (www.tuxpaint.org). Tux Paint is a free drawing program for children aged 3 to 12 (PK–6). It has an easy-to-use interface and includes sound effects (which can be disabled) and an online cartoon mascot who guides children as they use the program. It is also available in several languages. Students can print drawings or turn off this feature.

## Portals and Social Bookmarking

**Delicious** (http://delicious.com). Delicious is a social bookmarking site that allows you to tag, save, manage, and share web pages from a server that stores such information. You can share tags with the general community or with an approved group of individuals. These resources are available from any computer. You can also access others' favorite tagged recommendations.

**Diigo** (www.diigo.com). Diigo is a resource to annotate, archive, organize, and share web resources; build a personal learning network by sharing those resources; and create a collaborative group for developing knowledge, assignments, or activities. These can be public or private.

**Jog the Web** (www.jogtheweb.com). Jog the Web is a bookmarking and tracking site. It allows teachers to organize and lead students through topic-related web pages for safe, guided exploration. Educators can create "tracks" of content or explore other educators' already-created sets of websites.

**Netvibes** (www.netvibes.com). Netvibes provides a free web service that you can use to bring together media sources and online services as a start page online or personal portal. You can include blogs, news, weather, videos, photos, social networks, email, and more. Everything is automatically updated every time you visit your page.

**Only2Clicks** (www.only2clicks.com). Only2Clicks is a tool that enables users to organize their bookmarks in efficient ways. Users can add their new favorite links into categories for easy access.

**Pearltrees** (www.pearltrees.com). Pearltrees is a unique visual collaborative tool that allows you to organize, collect, and share your favorite places on the web. You can share links, photos, and notes with others online and organize them in your own customized pearltree. Each link or photo you add to the tree is referred to as a pearl.

**Sqworl** (http://sqworl.com). Sqworl is a tool that allows you to bookmark multiple URLs within a single URL. You can share your multiple bookmark pages with others.

**StumbleUpon** (www.stumbleupon.com). StumbleUpon is a web-sharing site that enables you to preselect a group of keywords or specific friends and see only the sites that are highly rated and match your choices. You can also rate sites you see, and others will have the option of viewing those. It is considered community-based surfing and can be organized for students as well.

**Themeefy** (www.themeefy.com/index). Themeefy was developed with participatory creation in mind. This tool can help you organize and work efficiently with the complexities and sheer size of the social web. You can also use this tool to publish lessons, teach online, and collaborate with your peers.

## Quiz and Activities Generators

**Amazing Space** (http://amazing-space.stsci.edu). This site was created by the Space Telescope Science Institute, which is responsible for the scientific operation of the Hubble Space Telescope. Amazing Space provides you with a variety of interactive web-based space lessons and related activities.

**Apps for Children with Special Needs** (http://a4cwsn.com). Apps for Children with Special Needs is a site created to assist the families and caregivers of children with special needs, and also the educators and therapists who support them.

**Archimy** (www.archimy.com). This tool allows you to draw graphs of all kinds with a wide array of functions. Math and statistics teachers could use this tool to help their students learn how to display results in graphical form. The program must be downloaded, but it is free.

**Cells Alive** (www.cellsalive.com). Cells Alive was developed for students in elementary through high school. It is a great interactive website for educators who wish to teach their students about the function and purpose of cells in dynamic ways.

**EcoKids** (www.ecokids.ca/pub/games_activities/index.cfm). EcoKids is an interactive environmental online tool for children, families, and educators.

EcoKids provides up-to-date information about the environment through interactive, fun, educational games and activities.

**Exploratorium** (www.exploratorium.edu). The Exploratorium in San Francisco was one of the first science museums to build a site on the World Wide Web. The site now contains more than 15,000 web pages exploring hundreds of different topics.

**Flash Card Creator** (www.aplusmath.com/Flashcards/Flashcard_Creator.html). This site and tool from Aplus Math allows for the easy creation of online and printable math flash cards.

**Geometry Lab** (http://geometrylab.org) Geometry Lab is an online lab for physics, chemistry, and biology where you can perform thousands of new experiments with real diagrams. The software is available free from the site.

**Google Art Project** (www.googleartproject.com). With Google Art Project, you can explore 17 museums from around the world and zoom in on artwork for close-up views. You can also create your own art collection and share your collection with others.

**Journey North—A Global Study of Wildlife and Seasonal Migration** (www.learner. org/jnorth). Journey North was created to engage students in the study of global migration and seasonal change. You can study how season change affects the migration patterns of animals and make field notes while you interactively journey through a rich and engaging online environment.

**Manga High** (www.mangahigh.com). Manga High is a math game website that includes complex math games, quizzes, and challenges. Your school and class can complete the quizzes and even compete with other schools!

**Math.com** (www.math.com/students/puzzles/puzzleapps.html). This tool has a great number of math puzzles and games. Many of them can be used with an interactive whiteboard.

**MyStudiyo** (www.mystudiyo.com). MyStudiyo allows you to create quizzes, surveys, and homework challenges and add them to your website or blog. Multiple-choice formats are now available, but other formats are being developed.

**Neuroscience for Kids** (http://faculty.washington.edu/chudler/neurok.html). This site was designed to help your students learn more about the nervous system. It includes links with information on the brain, spinal cord, neurons, the senses, and other related topics.

**Quia** (www.quia.com). Quia provides you and your students with the abilities to create, share, and use online learning activities available in a searchable format. Activities include games, quizzes, surveys, and other types of learning materials.

**Quizlet** (http://quizlet.com). Quizlet allows you to create online flash cards or find flash cards others have created. Students receive immediate feedback on their performance, and they can use the same flash cards repeatedly.

**Wordle** (www.wordle.net). Wordle is a tool for generating "word clouds" from text that you provide. The clouds—word images—give greater prominence to words that appear more frequently in the source text. You can print them out or save them to the Wordle gallery to share.

## RSS

**Bloglines** (www.bloglines.com). Bloglines provides one location for searching, subscribing, and sharing aggregates of your personal web preferences. The service is available in many languages and brings your selected news and information to you on any computer.

**Feedly** (http://feedly.com) Feedly allows you to blend your favorite selections of news, information, and more into a single reader that is available to you on a mobile device or a computer. You can also follow specific thinkers, blogs, or journals.. Educators or students can subscribe to national or international news, keep current on specific topics, and have access to multiple resources.

## Timelines

**Dipity** (www.dipity.com). Dipity allows you to create a timeline on a particular event, track current events, or use others' timelines. Students must be 13 or older. Current events are routinely tracked as well. You can view timelines graphically, as a list, or in a map format.

**Timetoast** (www.timetoast.com). Timetoast is an online interactive timeline creation tool with which you can design your own or search for others' timelines on many topics. You can publish these timelines on Twitter or other social networking sites.

**XTimeline** (www.xtimeline.com). XTimeline is a web-based system for creating timelines and customizing them with pictures, videos, and more. A large database of timelines is available to use or customize for students.

## Videoconferencing

**FaceTime** (www.apple.com/ios/facetime). FaceTime was developed by Mac and is an easy, user-friendly video-chat platform. You operate this tool through your iPhones, iPad, and Mac computers.

**Skype** (www.skype.com). Skype is a free, downloadable tool that allows you to make free phone calls (with or without video) from your computer to another Skype user. You use your internet connection to turn your computer into an internet phone.

**Ustream** (www.ustream.tv). Ustream is a live, interactive video broadcast platform that allows anyone with an internet connection and a camera to engage an audience by creating a broadcast channel. It is considered a one-to-many site but also allows viewer-to-viewer interaction. It provides a backchannel to interact with talk shows, sports events, or political events, as well as music performances.

## Video Sharing

**BrainPOP** (www.brainpop.com). BrainPOP provides you and your students with more than 1,000 short educationally oriented animated movies for students in grades K–12. This tool also provides your students with opportunities to view supplemental information and take quizzes.

**Khan Academy** (www.khanacademy.org). Khan Academy provides you and your students with more than 4,300 educational and instructional videos that address a vast range of academic subjects.

**Next Vista** (www.nextvista.org). Next Vista for Learning is a free, online library of short teacher- and student-made videos for learning. Teachers and students are invited to view or create videos on serious topics for others to use. Teachers can create discussions around the topics to guide student learning.

**SchoolTube** (www.schooltube.com). SchoolTube is designed as a safe media-sharing website that approves all materials prior to posting. Tags help educators search for appropriate videos and allow creators to assist others with the use of their materials.

**TeacherTube** (www.teachertube.com). TeacherTube is an online repository for videos by and for teachers. These videos are appropriate for classrooms and can also be used to assist parents in supporting their children's learning.

**YouTube** (www.youtube.com). YouTube is a video-sharing website where you can upload and share videos as well as watch others' videos. Some schools and districts use security software to allow access to the educational aspects of this public forum.

## Virtual Worlds

**Atlantis Remixed** (http://atlantisremixed.org). In Atlantis Remixed, your students work to change the doomed future of the mythical city of Atlantis by conducting environmental study, interviewing members of the community, studying other cultures, and developing action plans.

**Club Penguin** (www.clubpenguin.com). Club Penguin is a virtual world for children; it is dedicated to creativity and safety. Participants create a penguin avatar and wander around this virtual world. They enjoy collaborative and individual games and filtered chats. With a subscription, participants gain access to other specialized activities. This site works to foster global citizenship and community service.

**Jibe** (http://reactiongrid.com/what.aspx). Jibe is a MUVE platform that was created by ReactionGrid. Within Jibe, you can create, publish, and monitor your own virtual world.

**Mission US** (www.mission-us.org). Mission US, which was developed for elementary students studying social studies, is a free multimedia project that engages your students in U.S. history through interactive gaming.

**River City Project** (http://rivercity.activeworlds.com). The River City Project was designed to represent a virtual 19th-century American town, but the town happens to be plagued by disease. In the simulation, your students work in teams, study the materials presented, and then develop a hypothesis regarding the cause of the disease. They also have the ability to read documents, examine photographs, visit the hospital, and interview River City citizens.

**Second Life** (http://secondlife.com). Second Life is an online, 3D, virtual environment that can be used for education, professional development, social networking, and more. Many institutions have "islands" in Second Life where you can join others, create a virtual community, and even take courses.

**Webkinz** (www.webkinz.com). Webkinz is an online social environment for owners of Webkinz pets. These are plush animals that come with a unique secret code. With it, you enter Webkinz World, where you can care for your virtual pet, answer trivia questions, earn KinzCash, and play learning and other games.

## Wikis

**PBworks** (http://pbworks.com/education). PBworks offers a web publishing and wiki site for educators to collaborate and share their content. A Basic Edition is free and allows public or controlled access to your class or collaborative wiki.

**What Is a Wiki** (and How to Use One for Your Projects) (www.oreillynet.com/pub/a/network/2006/07/07/what-is-a-wiki.html). This site is a great resource for you to use. It explains how teachers can use wikis in their classrooms.

**WikiEducator** (www.wikieducator.org). WikiEducator is a collaborative community to plan educational projects around the world, develop free content for teachers and students, and create open education resources for all to share.

**Wikispaces** (www.wikispaces.com). Wikispaces is a wiki and publishing site in which you can embed documents, images, and audio and video files. The creator of each wiki controls access, and educational information is extensive.

## Other Tools

**Educade** (www.educade.org). Educade is a free site that provides information about web tools for educators to review. It has hundreds of apps, games, and maker kits that are aligned with standards to use in classrooms.

**eFax** (www.efax.com). For when you find yourself with email but no fax machine or you wish to make something available to others. This program allows you to receive the fax through a temporarily assigned phone number. You can receive for free, but there is a small price for sending.

**Google in Education** (www.google.com/edu/teachers). Google reportedly supports teachers in their efforts to empower students and expand the frontiers of human knowledge. This is a great site for you to check out.

**Google News** (http://news.google.com). Google news allows you to create a news-oriented homepage where you can receive news updates directly to your Google account.

**Google Play** (http://play.google.com/store). Google Play allows you to browse and download music, magazines, books, movies, television programs, and applications that are published through Google.

**Google Sites** (http://sites.google.com). This is Google's web-creation tool and is a very easy place to learn how to develop your own webpage.

**Google Translate** (http://translate.google.com/?hl=en#). Google Translate is a great free translation service that produces instant translations between 58 different languages. You can use the tool to translate words, sentences, and web pages between any combinations of the 58 different languages.

**Graphite** (www.graphite.org). Graphite is a free online guide to digital learning products compiled by Common Sense Media. Graphite is a nonprofit organization that reviews and rates digital products, including apps, games, websites, and digital curricula, for K–12. This is a great resource you should check out.

**Instapaper** (www.instapaper.com). Instapaper is handy when you want to read something (a web page or other document) but are unable to do it at the time you come across the material. Once you have registered, you will just click a "read later" button to be able to access it from your computer, a phone, or offline.

**JotNot Scanner** (http://itunes.apple.com/us/app/jotnot-scanner/id310789464?mt=8). This app allows you to turn your smartphone camera into a portable scanner.

**LibraryThing** (http://librarything.com). LibraryThing is an online book club. You can catalog your books, make comments about what you read, and look for recommendations from other people with similar literary tastes.

**Scratch** (http://scratch.mit.edu). Scratch is a programming language designed for students age 8 and up so that they can develop stories, games, music, and more. The goal is to teach students digital-age learning skills. Educational resources and strategies are also available to assist in using this tool.

**TinyURL** (http://tinyurl.com). TinyURL allows you to create short URLs that stand for long ones. They make it easier to share websites with others, and the URLs never expire.

# References

## A

Amendola, E. (2011, September 3). Many U.S. schools adding iPads, trimming textbooks. Retrieved from http://usatoday30.usatoday.com/news/education/story/2011-09-03/Many-US-schools-adding-iPads-trimming-textbooks/50251238/1

Anderson, S. (2011). Back to school with social media [Digital learning blog]. Retrieved from www.guide2digitallearning.com/blog_steven_anderson/back_school_social_media

Anderson, S. (2013a, May 30). So … you wanna use blogs in the classroom [Blog post]. Retrieved from www.guide2digitallearning.com/blog_steven_anderson/soyou_wanna_use_blogs_classroom

Anderson, S. (2013b, March 1). Formative assessments are easier than you think [Digital learning blog]. Retrieved from www.guide2digitallearning.com/blog_steven_anderson/formative_assessments_are_easier_you_think

Anderson, S. (2013c, January 21). It's all about the hashtag [Digital learning blog]. Retrieved from www.guide2digitallearning.com/tools_technologies/it's_all_about_hashtag

Atkinson, T. (2008). Second Life for educators: Inside Linden Lab. *TechTrends*, 52(2), 18–21.

## B

Barab, S., Thomas, M., Dodge, T., Carteaux, R., & Tuzun, H. (2005). Making learning fun: Quest Atlantis, a game without guns. *Educational Technology Research and Development*, 53(1), 86–107.

Barack, L. (2009). Green libraries grow in SL. *School Library Journal*, 55(1), 12–13.

Barnes, B. (2009, July 16). An animated film is created through Internet consensus. *The New York Times*. Retrieved from www.nytimes.com/2009/07/16/movies/16mass.html?_r=1&ref=arts

Bergmann, J., & Sams, A. (2008–2009). Remixing chemistry class: Two Colorado teachers make vodcasts of their lectures to free up class time for hands-on activities. *Learning & Leading with Technology, 36*(4), 22–27.

Bergmann, J., & Sams, A. (2012). *Flip your classroom: Reach every student in every class, every day.* Eugene, OR: International Society for Technology in Education.

Bolliger, D. U., & Supanakorn, S. (2011). Learning styles and student perceptions of the use of interactive online tutorials. *British Journal of Educational Technology, 42*(3), 470–481.

Botterbusch, H. R., & Talab, R. S. (2009). Ethical issues in Second Life. *TechTrends, 53*(1), 9–12.

Burns, M. (2013, May 19). Edit student work on iPads. Retrieved from www.techlearning.com/Default.aspx?tabid=67&entryid=5844

Burgess, M. L., & Caverly, D. C. (2009). Tech talk: Second Life and developmental education. *Journal of Developmental Education, 32*(3), 42–43.

Byrne, B. (2013a, May 1). Teacher technology bucket list: Hurry, you have until September to complete it [Digital learning blog]. Retrieved from www.guide2digitallearning.com/blog_brian_byrne/teacher_technology_bucket_list_hurry_you_have_until_september_complete_it

Byrne, B. (2013b). Help has arrived and it's free. Retrieved from www.guide2digitallearning.com/blog_brian_byrne/help_has_arrived_and_it%E2%80%99s_free_0

## C

Center for Digital Education. (2013, April 15). *Technology strides by U.S. school districts—top 10 districts honored.* Retrieved from www.centerdigitaled.com/awards/digital-districts/Technology-Strides-by-US-School-Districts-Top-10-Districts-Honored.html

Chatzopoulos, N. (2013). iPads in the classroom: the right questions you should ask. Retrieved from www.edudemic.com/2013/05/ipads-in-the-classroom-the-right-questions-you-should-ask/

Crook, C. (2008). Web 2.0 technologies for learning: The current landscape—opportunities, challenges and tensions. (Research report from Becta, Coventry, England.) Retrieved from http://partners.becta.org.uk/upload-dir/downloads/page_documents/research/web2_technologies_learning.pdf

Collins, C. (2008). Looking to the future: Higher education in the metaverse. *Educause Review, 43*(5), 52–63.

Common Core State Standards. (2013a). Common Core State Standards initiative. Retrieved from www.corestandards.org

Common Core State Standards. (2013b). Retrieved from www.corestandards.org/ELA-Literacy/CCRA/SL/1

Creative Commons. (2013). Homepage. Retrieved from http://creativecommons.org

Curious, S. (2009, January 11). Listening and learning: Mark Smilowitz's classroom teaching podcasts. [Blog post]. Retrieved from http://siobhancurious.wordpress.com/2009/01/11/listening-and-learning-mark-smilowitzs-classroom-teaching-podcasts/

Czarnecki, K. (2008). Virtual environments and K–12 education: A tour of the possibilities, Part I. *Multimedia & Internet Schools,* 15(4), 14–18.

Czarnecki, K., & Gullett, M. (2007). Meet the new you. *School Library Journal,* 53(1), 35–39.

## D

Dalrymple, J. (2012, February 17). iPad improves kindergartners' literacy scores. *Loop Magazine.* Retrieved from www.loopinsight.com/2012/02/17/ipad-improves-kindergartners-literacy-scores

Dalton, B., & Proctor, P. (2008). The changing landscape of text and comprehension in the age of new literacies. In J. Coiro, M. Knobel, C. Lankshear, & D. Leu, (Eds.), *Handbook of research on new literacies* (pp. 287–324). New York, NY: Lawrence Erlbaum Associates.

ddeubel. (2007, August 30). Re: Social networking [Blog comment]. Retrieved from www.classroom20.com/forum/topics/649749:Topic:45491

Dede, C., Dieterle, E., Clarke, J., Ketelhut, D. J., & Nelson, B. (2007). Media based learning styles. In M. M. Moore, W. Anderson, & W. G. Anderson (Eds.), *Handbook of distance education* (2nd ed., pp. 339–352). New York, NY: Routledge.

Dodge, T., Barab, S., & Stuckey, B. (2008). Children's sense of self: Learning and meaning in the digital age. *Journal of Interactive Learning Research,* 19(2), 225–249.

## E

Eberly Center for Teaching Excellence and Educational Innovation. (2013). Collaboration tools [Website]. Retrieved from www.cmu.edu/teaching/technology/collaborationtools.html#communication

Edutopia. (2013). K–5 iPad apps according to Bloom's taxonomy. Retrieved from www.edutopia.org/ipad-apps-elementary-blooms-taxomony-diane-darrow

Evans, C. (2013). Collaboration is not a time, it's a mindset [Digital learning blog]. Retrieved from www.guide2digitallearning.com/blog_chad_evans/collaboration_not_time_it039s_mindset

## F

Ferdig, R. (2007). Examining social software in teacher education. *Journal of Technology and Teacher Education,* 15(1), 5–11.

Forde, J. (2012, November 27). Twitter and STEM: Perfect together [Digital learning blog]. Retrieved from www.guide2digitallearning.com/blog_jim_forde/twitter_and_stem_perfect_together

Forde, J. (2013). Got video? Great video resources for your class [Digital learning blog]. Retrieved from www.guide2digitallearning.com/blog_jim_forde/got_video_great_video_resources_your_class

Friedman, T. L. (2007). *The World Is Flat* (Rev. ed.). New York, NY: Farrar, Straus and Giroux.

Friedman, T. L. (2013). It's a 401(k) world [Opinion Page]. Retrieved from www.nytimes.com

## G

Gliksman, S. (2013). 10 steps to a successful school iPad program. Retrieved from www.teachthought.com/ipad-2/10-steps-to-a-successful-school-ipad-program

Green, H., & Hannon, C. (2007). Their space: Education for a digital generation [Pamphlet]. Retrieved from www.demos.co.uk/publications/theirspace

Gutierrez, L. (2013a). Flipping classrooms on a 21st century network [Webinar]. Retrieved from www.techlearning.com/sections/upcoming-webinars/41197#flippingclassrooms

Gutierrez, L. (2013b, August 26). Student centered in a 21st century classroom [Digital learning blog]. Retrieved from www.guide2digitallearning.com/teaching_learning/student_centered_21st_century_classroom html?ref=opinion

## H

Hahnstadt, J. (2013, May 21). Gym class can go high-tech too [Guest blogger]. Retrieved from www.techlearning.com/default.aspx?tabid=67&entryid=5851

Hartley, M. D., Ludlow, B. L., & Duff, M. C. (2013). Using Second Life to teach collaboration skills to preservice and inservice special educators. In K. Nettleton, & L. Lennex (eds), *Cases on 3D technology: Application and integration in education* (pp. 336–358). Hershey, PA: IGI Global.

Harris H., & Park S. (2008). Educational uses of podcasting. *British Journal of Educational Technology,* 39(3), 548–551.

Hechinger, J. (2009, June 12). Data-driven schools see rising scores. *The Wall Street Journal*. Retrieved from http://online.wsj.com/home-page

Headden, S. (2013). The promise of personalized learning. *EducationNext, 13*(4), n.p. Retrieved from http://educationnext.org/the-promise-of-personalized-learning

Hickey, D. T., Ingram-Goble, A. A., & Jameson, E. M. (2009). Designing assessments and assessing designs in virtual educational environments. *Journal of Science Education and Technology, 18*(2), 187–208.

Hoosen, S. (2012). *Governments' open educational resources (OER) policies*. Vancouver, BC: Commonwealth of Learning.

Hudson, K., & Degast-Kennedy, K. (2009). Canadian border simulation at Loyalist College. *Journal of Virtual Worlds Research, 2*(1), 3–11.

Huff, L. (2008). Using wikis as electronic portfolios [Blog post]. Retrieved from www.guide2digitallearning.com/technology_curriculum_integration/using_wikis_electronic_portfolios

## I

Inman, C., Wright, V. H., & Hartman, J. A. (2010). Use of Second Life in K–12 and higher education: A review of research. *Journal of Interactive Online Learning, 9*(1), 44–63.

International Data Corporation. (2013a, May 30). Tablet shipments into the U.S. education sector expanded by 103% in 2012 with greater adoption yet to come, according to IDC [Press release]. Retrieved from http://online.wsj.com/article/PR-CO-20130530-907237.html

International Data Corporation. (2013b, May 28). Forecasts worldwide tablet shipments to surpass portable PC shipments in 2013, total PC shipments in 2015 [Press release]. Retrieved from www.idc.com/getdoc.jsp?containerId=prUS24129713

## J

Jakes, D. (2005, December 1). Making a case for digital storytelling. Retrieved from www.techlearning.com/article/4958

Johnson, L., Adams Becker, S., Cummins, M., Estrada, V., Freeman, A., & Ludgate, H. (2013). *NMC Horizon Report: 2013 K–12 Edition*. Austin, TX: New Media Consortium.

## K

Kahn, E. (2013a, March 2). Do you know instagrok.com? [Blog post]. Retrieved from www.talesfromaloudlibrarian.com/2013/03/do-you-know-instagrokcom.html

Kahn, E. (2013b). Great example of 21st century learning part 2 [Blog post]. Retrieved from www.talesfromaloudlibrarian.com/2012/12/great-example-of-21st-century-learning_30.html

Kay, R. H. (2012). Exploring the use of video podcasts in education: A comprehensive review of the literature. *Computers in Human Behavior, 28*(3), 820–831.

Ketelhut, D. J. (2007). The impact of student self-efficacy on scientific inquiry skills: An exploratory investigation of River City, a multi-user virtual environment. *Journal of Science Education and Technology, 16*(1), 99–111.

Kelton, A. J. (2008). Virtual worlds? Outlook good. *Educause Review, 43*(8), 15–22.

Khan Academy. (2013). Our mission. Retrieved from www.khanacademy.org/about

Kharbach, M. (2013). The best 8 tablets for teachers. *Educational Technology and Mobile Learning.* Retrieved from www.educatorstechnology.com/2013/01/the-best-8-tablets-for-teachers.html

Knittle, B. (2008). *An introduction to Second Life for educators.* Retrieved from www.bethknittle.net/IntroToSLforEd.pdf

Kucher, K. (2012). SD unified rolls out iPads in a big way. Retrieved from www.utsandiego.com/news/2012/Apr/29/sd-unified-rolls-out-ipads-in-a-big-way

# L

Lai, E. (2012, August 30). Chart: Top 100 iPad rollouts by enterprises & schools (updated Oct. 16, 2012). Retrieved from www.zdnet.com/blog/sap/chart-top-100-ipad-rollouts-by-enterprises-and-schools-updated-oct-16-2012/1274

Larkin, P. (2013, January 21). From the principal's office: Ignore the iPads! Looking back at year one of 1:1 with iPads, Part Seven. Retrieved from www.techlearning.com/Default.aspx?tabid=67&entryid=5292

Lave, J., & Wenger, E. (1991). *Situated learning. Legitimate peripheral participation.* Cambridge, England: Cambridge University Press.

Leese, M. (2009). Out of class—out of mind? The use of a virtual learning environment to encourage student engagement in out of class activities. *British Journal of Educational Technology, 40*(1), 70–77.

Levin, B. B., & Schrum, L. (2012). *Leading technology-rich schools: Award-winning models for success.* New York, NY: Teachers College Press.

Liao, C. L. (2008). Avatars, Second Life, and new media art: The challenge of contemporary art education. *Art Education, 61*(2), 87–91.

Lim, C. P., Nonis, D., & Hedberg, J. (2006). Gaming in a 3D multiuser virtual environment: Engaging students in science lessons. *British Journal of Educational Technology, 37*(2), 211–231.

# M

Madden, M., Lenhart, A., Cortesi, S., Gasser, U., Duggan, M., & Smith, A. (2013). *Teens, social media, and privacy. Pew Internet & American Life Project Report.* Washington, DC: Pew Research Center.

Magnifico, A. M. (2010). Writing for whom? Cognition, motivation, and a writer's audience. *Educational Psychologist, 45*(3), 167–184.

Meadows, M. S. (2008). I, *Avatar: the culture and consequences of having a second life.* Berkeley, CA: New Riders.

Miller, R. (2013). Flipped learning [Digital learning blog]. Retrieved from www.guide2digitallearning.com/blog_robert_miller/flipped_learning

Mr.Balch. (2009, May 24). Re: Calling All Teachers!!! [Blog comment]. Retrieved from www.google.com/support/forum/p/sites/thread?tid=1b9ad8f1959c2f4d&hl=en

Mrs. Yollis' Classroom Blog. (2012a, August 19). Second and third graders learning and sharing together [Blog post]. Retrieved from http://yollisclassblog.blogspot.com/2012/08/rewards-of-teaching-young-students-to.html

Mrs. Yollis' Classroom Blog. (2012b, August 19). Rewards of teaching young students to blog [Blog post]. Retrieved from http://yollisclassblog.blogspot.com/2012/08/rewards-of-teaching-young-students-to.html

Murray, T. (2013, April 24). Utilizing twitter chats for professional development [Digital learning blog]. Retrieved from www.guide2digitallearning.com/blog_tom_murray/utilizing_twitter_chats_professional_development

# N

National School Boards Association. (2007). Creating & connecting: Research and guidelines on online social and educational networking. Alexandria, VA: Author. Retrieved from www.nsba.org/SecondaryMenu/TLN/CreatingandConnecting.aspx

Nielsen, L. (2009). Eight ways to use school wikis [Web page]. Retrieved from www.techlearning.com/curriculum/0035/eight-ways-to-use-school-wikis/46216

# O

Orech, J. (2009). Why I tweet [Digital learning blog]. Retrieved from www.guide2digitallearning.com/blog_jon_orech/why_i_tweet

Owen, M., Grant, L., Sayers, S., & Facer, K. (2006). Social software and learning. (Report from Futurelab, Bristol, England.) Retrieved from www.futurelab.org.uk/resources/documents/opening_education/Social_Software_report.pdf

## P

Partnership for 21st Century Skills. (2004). *P21 framework definitions.* Retrieved April 28, 2010, from www.ocmboces.org/tfiles/folder1041/P21_Framework_Definitions.pdf

Phillips, V., & Hughes, R. L. (2012). Teacher collaboration: The essential Common-Core ingredient. *Education Week, 32*(13), 32–35.

Project Tomorrow. (2013a). From chalkboards to tablets: The digital conversion of the K–12 classroom [Report]. Retrieved from www.tomorrow.org/speakup/pdfs/SU12EducatorsandParents.pdf

Project Tomorrow. (2013b). From chalkboards to tablets: The digital conversion of the K–12 classroom [Report Summary]. Retrieved from www.tomorrow.org/speakup/SU12_DigitalConversion_EducatorsReport.html

Project Tomorrow. (2013c). From chalkboards to tablets: The emergence of the K–12 digital learner. Retrieved from www.tomorrow.org/speakup/pdfs/SU12-Students.pdf

## R

Roscorla, T. (2011, February 9). *The impact of the iPad on K–12 schools.* Center for Digital Education. Retrieved from www.centerdigitaled.com/classtech/Impact-iPad-K12-Schools.html

Rupp, A., Choi, Y., Gushta, M., Mislevy, R., Thies, M. C., Bagley, E., Nash, P., Hatfield, D., Svarovsky, G., Shaffer D. W. (2009). *Modeling learning progressions in epistemic games with epistemic network analysis: Principles for data analysis and generation.* (Paper presented June 25, 2009, at the Learning Progressions in Science conference (LeaPS), Iowa City, Iowa). Retrieved from http://epistemicgames.org/eg/wp-content/uploads/leaps-learning-progressions-paper-rupp-et-al-2009-leaps-format1.pdf

Rushkoff, D. (2005). *Get back in the box: Innovation from the inside out.* New York, NY: HarperCollins.

## S

Sculley, J. (1987). *Odyssey: Pepsi to Apple: A journey of adventure, ideas, and the future.* New York, NY: HarperCollins.

Shechtman, N., DeBarger, A. H., Dornsife, C., Rosier, S., & Yarnell, L. (2013, February). *Promoting grit, tenacity, and perseverance: Critical factors for success in the 21st century* (U.S. Department of Education Office of Educational Technology Draft Report). Retrieved from Office Educational Technology website: www.ed.gov/edblogs/technology/files/2013/02/OET-Draft-Grit-Report-2-17-13.pdf

Schrum, L., & Levin, B. B. (2012). *Evidence-based strategies for leading 21st century schools.* Thousand Oaks, CA: Corwin Press.

Six degrees of separation. (2010). In Wikipedia. Retrieved April 15, 2010, from http://en.wikipedia.org/wiki/Six_degrees_of_separation

Surowiecki, J. (2004). *The wisdom of crowds: Why the many are smarter than the few and how collective wisdom shapes business, economies, societies, and nations.* New York, NY: Doubleday.

Swan, C. (2013, June 10). From being social: How social media can transform your school classrooms [Digital Learning Blog]. Retrieved from www.guide2digitallearning.com/professional_development/being_social_how_social_media_can_transform_your_school_classrooms

# T

Tapscott, D., & Williams, A. D. (2006). Wikinomics: *How mass collaboration changes everything.* New York, NY: Portfolio Group.

Trotter, A. (2009, January 7). Students Turn Their Cellphones On for Classroom Lessons. *Education Week.* Available from www.edweek.org

# U

Updated Breaking News. (2008, July 8). Google announces Lively. *Virtual Worlds News.* Retrieved from www.virtualworldsnews.com/2008/07/breaking-news-g.html

# V

Vanderbilt, T. (2009, June 8). Data center overload. *The New York Times.* Retrieved from www.nytimes.com

Voyager, D. (2013, April 2). Second Life statistics 2013 spring update [Blog post]. Retrieved from http://danielvoyager.wordpress.com/2013/04/02/second-life-statistics-2013-spring-update/

# W

Wagner, C. (2008). Learning experience with virtual worlds. *Journal of Information Systems Education, 19*(3), 263–266.

Waiksnis, M. (2009, August 10). What is Your Favorite? [Blog post]. Retrieved from http://edleaderweb.net/blog

Walker, L. (2009, March 29). Nine great reasons why teachers should use Twitter. [Blog post]. Retrieved from http://mrslwalker.com

Web 2.0. (2013). In Webopedia. Retrieved from www.webopedia.com/TERM/W/Web_2_point_0.html

Webb, J. (2013). The iPad as a tool for education—a case study. Naace Research Papers. Retrieved from www.naace.co.uk/publications/longfieldipadresearch

White House, Office of the Press Secretary. (2013). President Obama unveils connectED initiative to bring America's students into digital age [Press release]. Retrieved from www.whitehouse.gov/the-press-office/2013/06/06/president-obama-unveils-connected-initiative-bring-america-s-students-di

Wilson, I. (2013). Apps v programs for learning. Retrieved from www.ipadineducation.ianwilson.biz/iPad_in_Education/Apps_v_Programs.html

Wilson, L. (2013, May 20). Figuring out future ed tech needs [Digital learning blog]. Retrieved from www.guide2digitallearning.com/blog_leslie_wilson/figuring_out_future_ed_tech_needs

Windman, V. (2013). Get organized with free apps. Retrieved from www.techlearning.com/Default.aspx?tabid=67&entryid=5613

Wortham, J. (2009). Cellphones now used more for data than for calls. *The New York Times*. Retrieved from www.nytimes.com

# Y

Yollis, L., & Morris, K. (2012, July 2). ISTE 2012: Flattening classroom walls with blogging and global collaboration [Blog post]. Retrieved from http://theedublogger.com/2012/07/02/iste-2012-flattening-classroom-walls-with-blogging-and-global-collaboration/

Yollis, L. (2013). How to compose a quality comment [Video file]. Retrieved from http://vimeo.com/15695021

Young, S. (2013). Interview with Steve Young on SchoolCIO. Retrieved from www.schoolcio.com/cio-profiles/0111/steve-young/53509

# B

# ISTE Standards

## ISTE Standards for Students (ISTE Standards·S)

All K–12 students should be prepared to meet the following standards and performance indicators.

1. **Creativity and Innovation**

   Students demonstrate creative thinking, construct knowledge, and develop innovative products and processes using technology. Students:

   a. apply existing knowledge to generate new ideas, products, or processes

   b. create original works as a means of personal or group expression

   c. use models and simulations to explore complex systems and issues

   d. identify trends and forecast possibilities

2. **Communication and Collaboration**

   Students use digital media and environments to communicate and work collaboratively, including at a distance, to support individual learning and contribute to the learning of others. Students:

   a. interact, collaborate, and publish with peers, experts, or others employing a variety of digital environments and media

**b.** communicate information and ideas effectively to multiple audiences using a variety of media and formats

**c.** develop cultural understanding and global awareness by engaging with learners of other cultures

**d.** contribute to project teams to produce original works or solve problems

### 3. Research and Information Fluency

Students apply digital tools to gather, evaluate, and use information. Students:

**a.** plan strategies to guide inquiry

**b.** locate, organize, analyze, evaluate, synthesize, and ethically use information from a variety of sources and media

**c.** evaluate and select information sources and digital tools based on the appropriateness to specific tasks

**d.** process data and report results

### 4. Critical Thinking, Problem Solving, and Decision Making

Students use critical-thinking skills to plan and conduct research, manage projects, solve problems, and make informed decisions using appropriate digital tools and resources. Students:

**a.** identify and define authentic problems and significant questions for investigation

**b.** plan and manage activities to develop a solution or complete a project

**c.** collect and analyze data to identify solutions and make informed decisions

**d.** use multiple processes and diverse perspectives to explore alternative solutions

### 5. Digital Citizenship

Students understand human, cultural, and societal issues related to technology and practice legal and ethical behavior. Students:

   **a.** advocate and practice the safe, legal, and responsible use of information and technology

   **b.** exhibit a positive attitude toward using technology that supports collaboration, learning, and productivity

   **c.** demonstrate personal responsibility for lifelong learning

   **d.** exhibit leadership for digital citizenship

### 6. Technology Operations and Concepts

Students demonstrate a sound understanding of technology concepts, systems, and operations. Students:

   **a.** understand and use technology systems

   **b.** select and use applications effectively and productively

   **c.** troubleshoot systems and applications

   **d.** transfer current knowledge to the learning of new technologies

# ISTE Standards for Teachers (ISTE Standards·T)

All classroom teachers should be prepared to meet the following standards and performance indicators.

1. **Facilitate and Inspire Student Learning and Creativity**

   Teachers use their knowledge of subject matter, teaching and learning, and technology to facilitate experiences that advance student learning, creativity, and innovation in both face-to-face and virtual environments. Teachers:

   a. promote, support, and model creative and innovative thinking and inventiveness

   b. engage students in exploring real-world issues and solving authentic problems using digital tools and resources

   c. promote student reflection using collaborative tools to reveal and clarify students' conceptual understanding and thinking, planning, and creative processes

   d. model collaborative knowledge construction by engaging in learning with students, colleagues, and others in face-to-face and virtual environments

2. **Design and Develop Digital-Age Learning Experiences and Assessments**

   Teachers design, develop, and evaluate authentic learning experiences and assessments incorporating contemporary tools and resources to maximize content learning in context and to develop the knowledge, skills, and attitudes identified in the ISTE Standards for Students. Teachers:

   a. design or adapt relevant learning experiences that incorporate digital tools and resources to promote student learning and creativity

   b. develop technology-enriched learning environments that enable all students to pursue their individual curiosities and become active participants in setting their own educational goals, managing their own learning, and assessing their own progress

c.  customize and personalize learning activities to address students' diverse learning styles, working strategies, and abilities using digital tools and resources

d.  provide students with multiple and varied formative and summative assessments aligned with content and technology standards and use resulting data to inform learning and teaching

## 3. Model Digital-Age Work and Learning

Teachers exhibit knowledge, skills, and work processes representative of an innovative professional in a global and digital society. Teachers:

a.  demonstrate fluency in technology systems and the transfer of current knowledge to new technologies and situations

b.  collaborate with students, peers, parents, and community members using digital tools and resources to support student success and innovation

c.  communicate relevant information and ideas effectively to students, parents, and peers using a variety of digital-age media and formats

d.  model and facilitate effective use of current and emerging digital tools to locate, analyze, evaluate, and use information resources to support research and learning

## 4. Promote and Model Digital Citizenship and Responsibility

Teachers understand local and global societal issues and responsibilities in an evolving digital culture and exhibit legal and ethical behavior in their professional practices. Teachers:

a.  advocate, model, and teach safe, legal, and ethical use of digital information and technology, including respect for copyright, intellectual property, and the appropriate documentation of sources

    **b.** address the diverse needs of all learners by using learner-centered strategies and providing equitable access to appropriate digital tools and resources

    **c.** promote and model digital etiquette and responsible social interactions related to the use of technology and information

    **d.** develop and model cultural understanding and global awareness by engaging with colleagues and students of other cultures using digital-age communication and collaboration tools

5. **Engage in Professional Growth and Leadership**

Teachers continuously improve their professional practice, model lifelong learning, and exhibit leadership in their school and professional community by promoting and demonstrating the effective use of digital tools and resources. Teachers:

    **a.** participate in local and global learning communities to explore creative applications of technology to improve student learning

    **b.** exhibit leadership by demonstrating a vision of technology infusion, participating in shared decision making and community building, and developing the leadership and technology skills of others

    **c.** evaluate and reflect on current research and professional practice on a regular basis to make effective use of existing and emerging digital tools and resources in support of student learning

    **d.** contribute to the effectiveness, vitality, and self-renewal of the teaching profession and of their school and community

# ISTE Standards for Administrators (ISTE Standards·A)

All school administrators should be prepared to meet the following standards and performance indicators.

## 1. Visionary Leadership

Educational Administrators inspire and lead development and implementation of a shared vision for comprehensive integration of technology to promote excellence and support transformation throughout the organization.

### Educational Administrators:

**a.** inspire and facilitate among all stakeholders a shared vision of purposeful change that maximizes use of digital-age resources to meet and exceed learning goals, support effective instructional practice, and maximize performance of district and school leaders

**b.** engage in an ongoing process to develop, implement, and communicate technology-infused strategic plans aligned with a shared vision

**c.** advocate on local, state, and national levels for policies, programs, and funding to support implementation of a technology-infused vision and strategic plan

## 2. Digital-Age Learning Culture

Educational Administrators create, promote, and sustain a dynamic, digital-age learning culture that provides a rigorous, relevant, and engaging education for all students. Educational Administrators:

**a.** ensure instructional innovation focused on continuous improvement of digital-age learning

**b.** model and promote the frequent and effective use of technology for learning

c. provide learner-centered environments equipped with technology and learning resources to meet the individual, diverse needs of all learners

d. ensure effective practice in the study of technology and its infusion across the curriculum

e. promote and participate in local, national, and global learning communities that stimulate innovation, creativity, and digital-age collaboration

## 3. Excellence in Professional Practice

Educational Administrators promote an environment of professional learning and innovation that empowers educators to enhance student learning through the infusion of contemporary technologies and digital resources. Educational Administrators:

a. allocate time, resources, and access to ensure ongoing professional growth in technology fluency and integration

b. facilitate and participate in learning communities that stimulate, nurture, and support administrators, faculty, and staff in the study and use of technology

c. promote and model effective communication and collaboration among stakeholders using digital-age tools

d. stay abreast of educational research and emerging trends regarding effective use of technology and encourage evaluation of new technologies for their potential to improve student learning

## 4. Systemic Improvement

Educational Administrators provide digital-age leadership and management to continuously improve the organization through the effective use of information and technology resources. Educational Administrators:

a. lead purposeful change to maximize the achievement of learning goals through the appropriate use of technology and media-rich resources

    **b.** collaborate to establish metrics, collect and analyze data, interpret results, and share findings to improve staff performance and student learning

    **c.** recruit and retain highly competent personnel who use technology creatively and proficiently to advance academic and operational goals

    **d.** establish and leverage strategic partnerships to support systemic improvement

    **e.** establish and maintain a robust infrastructure for technology including integrated, interoperable technology systems to support management, operations, teaching, and learning

## 5. Digital Citizenship

Educational Administrators model and facilitate understanding of social, ethical, and legal issues and responsibilities related to an evolving digital culture. Educational Administrators:

    **a.** ensure equitable access to appropriate digital tools and resources to meet the needs of all learners

    **b.** promote, model, and establish policies for safe, legal, and ethical use of digital information and technology

    **c.** promote and model responsible social interactions related to the use of technology and information

    **d.** model and facilitate the development of a shared cultural understanding and involvement in global issues through the use of contemporary communication and collaboration tools

# ISTE Standards
# for Coaches (ISTE Standards·C)

All technology coaches should be prepared to meet the following standards and performance indicators.

### 1. Visionary Leadership

Technology Coaches inspire and participate in the development and implementation of a shared vision for the comprehensive integration of technology to promote excellence and support transformational change throughout the instructional environment. Technology Coaches:

  a. contribute to the development, communication, and implementation of a shared vision for the comprehensive use of technology to support a digital-age education for all students

  b. contribute to the planning, development, communication, implementation, and evaluation of technology-infused strategic plans at the district and school levels

  c. advocate for policies, procedures, programs, and funding strategies to support implementation of the shared vision represented in the school and district technology plans and guidelines

  d. implement strategies for initiating and sustaining technology innovations and manage the change process in schools and classrooms

### 2. Teaching, Learning, and Assessments

Technology Coaches assist teachers in using technology effectively for assessing student learning, differentiating instruction, and providing rigorous, relevant, and engaging learning experiences for all students. Technology Coaches:

  a. Coach teachers in and model design and implementation of technology enhanced learning experiences addressing content standards and student technology standards

**b.** Coach teachers in and model design and implementation of technology-enhanced learning experiences using a variety of research-based, learner-centered instructional strategies and assessment tools to address the diverse needs and interests of all students

**c.** Coach teachers in and model engagement of students in local and global interdisciplinary units in which technology helps students assume professional roles, research real-world problems, collaborate with others, and produce products that are meaningful and useful to a wide audience

**d.** Coach teachers in and model design and implementation of technology-enhanced learning experiences emphasizing creativity, higher-order thinking skills and processes, and mental habits of mind (e.g., critical thinking, metacognition, and self-regulation)

**e.** Coach teachers in and model design and implementation of technology-enhanced learning experiences using differentiation, including adjusting content, process, product, and learning environment based upon student readiness levels, learning styles, interests, and personal goals

**f.** Coach teachers in and model incorporation of research-based best practices in instructional design when planning technology-enhanced learning experiences

**g.** Coach teachers in and model effective use of technology tools and resources to continuously assess student learning and technology literacy by applying a rich variety of formative and summative assessments aligned with content and student technology standards

**h.** Coach teachers in and model effective use of technology tools and resources to systematically collect and analyze student achievement data, interpret results, and communicate findings to improve instructional practice and maximize student learning

### 3. Digital Age Learning Environments

Technology coaches create and support effective digital-age learning environments to maximize the learning of all students. Technology Coaches:

**a.** Model effective classroom management and collaborative learning strategies to maximize teacher and student use of digital tools and resources and access to technology-rich learning environments

**b.** Maintain and manage a variety of digital tools and resources for teacher and student use in technology-rich learning environments

**c.** Coach teachers in and model use of online and blended learning, digital content, and collaborative learning networks to support and extend student learning as well as expand opportunities and choices for online professional development for teachers and administrators

**d.** Select, evaluate, and facilitate the use of adaptive and assistive technologies to support student learning

**e.** Troubleshoot basic software, hardware, and connectivity problems common in digital learning environments

**f.** Collaborate with teachers and administrators to select and evaluate digital tools and resources that enhance teaching and learning and are compatible with the school technology infrastructure

**g.** Use digital communication and collaboration tools to communicate locally and globally with students, parents, peers, and the larger community

### 4. Professional Development and Program Evaluation

Technology coaches conduct needs assessments, develop technology-related professional learning programs, and evaluate the impact on instructional practice and student learning. Technology Coaches:

**a.** Conduct needs assessments to inform the content and delivery of technology-related professional learning programs that result in a positive impact on student learning

    **b.** Design, develop, and implement technology-rich professional learning programs that model principles of adult learning and promote digital-age best practices in teaching, learning, and assessment

    **c.** Evaluate results of professional learning programs to determine the effectiveness on deepening teacher content knowledge, improving teacher pedagogical skills, and/or increasing student learning

## 5. Digital Citizenship

Technology coaches model and promote digital citizenship. Technology Coaches:

    **a.** Model and promote strategies for achieving equitable access to digital tools and resources and technology-related best practices for all students and teachers

    **b.** Model and facilitate safe, healthy, legal, and ethical uses of digital information and technologies

    **c.** Model and promote diversity, cultural understanding, and global awareness by using digital-age communication and collaboration tools to interact locally and globally with students, peers, parents, and the larger community

## 6. Content Knowledge and Professional Growth

Technology coaches demonstrate professional knowledge, skills, and dispositions in content, pedagogical, and technological areas as well as adult learning and leadership and are continuously deepening their knowledge and expertise. Technology Coaches:

    **a.** Engage in continual learning to deepen content and pedagogical knowledge in technology integration and current and emerging technologies necessary to effectively implement the ISTE Standards·S and ISTE Standards·T

b. Engage in continuous learning to deepen professional knowledge, skills, and dispositions in organizational change and leadership, project management, and adult learning to improve professional practice

c. Regularly evaluate and reflect on their professional practice and dispositions to improve and strengthen their ability to effectively model and facilitate technology-enhanced learning experiences

# Index

## A

All About Letters Interactive Activities, 228
Amazing Space, 358
animation, 152–153
Animoto, 163, 165, 257–260, 351
annotation and note taking tools, 331–332
Apps for Children with Special Needs, 232, 358
Archimy, 358
Ask an Expert, 168–169
assessment, 249–250
Assign-A-Day, 337
@ symbol, 57
Atlantis Remixed, 180–181, 362
A.T.TIPScast, 332
Audacity, 332
Audiopal, 332

## B

backchannels, 55, 61, 200
Badoo, 343
Baltimore Learning Community Middle School
        Teachers in Action, 126
BBC podcasts, 333
Bebo, 343
BeFunky, 350
Beyond Penguins and Polar Bears, 88
Blackboard, 248, 343
Blackboard Engage, 342
blended learning, 160–161
BlogEasy, 335
Blogger, 335
Bloglines, 49, 360
blogs
    about, 26–28
    benefits of, 28–31
    classroom integration of, 32–34
    educational use examples, 36–46
    getting started with, 46–49
    journals versus, 32

professional development use, 34–35
resources, 49–50
rules for, 31–32
tools, specific, 335–337
writing process applied to, 32–33
Bloom's taxonomy, 231
Bookwink, 333
BoomWriter, 261–263, 338
BrainPop, 361
Bubbl.us, 157, 346
Buzzword, 338

## C

Calameo, 354
calendars, 337–338
Cartoon Pho.to, 350
casts. *See* podcasts and vodcasts
Catalyst Channel, 44–45
cell phones in the classroom, 83
Cells Alive, 358
Center for Teaching Quality, 86
challenges, 4–5, 15
change, 9–10, 253–254. *See also* future of
        education and the web
ChannelME, 199
Chatzy, 200, 340
CheckThis, 29, 335
Chirbit, 333
Class Blogmeister, 335
Classroom 2.0, 123, 343
Classroom Teaching podcast, 86
cloud computing and infrastructure, 13–14, 96,
        250–251
Club Penguin, 188–189, 362
Coach's Eye, 238–239
Coggle, 97
collaboration, 11, 33, 243–244, 338–340. *See also*
        wikis and other collaboration tools
Comic Creator, 354
Comicbrush, 354